IN SEARCH OF RUNNING REIN

The Amazing Fraud of the 1844 Derby

Tony Byles

Foreword by Tony Morris

APEX PUBLISHING LTD

Hardback first published in 2011 by
Apex Publishing Ltd
PO Box 7086, Clacton on Sea, Essex, CO15 5WN, England
www.apexpublishing.co.uk

British Library Cataloguing-in-Publication Data
A catalogue record for this book
is available from the British Library

ISBN HARDBACK: 1-906358-94-X   978-1-906358-94-5

Typeset in 10pt Baskerville Win95BT
Production Manager: Chris Cowlin
Cover Design: Siobhan Smith

Printed and bound in Great Britain by
Biddles Ltd., King's Lynn, Norfolk

Copyright:
Every attempt has been made to contact the relevant copyright holders,
Publishing Ltd would be grateful if the appropriate people contact us o
01255 428500 or mail@apexpublishing.co.uk

Contents

Preface

This book would never have been written had it not been for my daughter, Georgina. Her love of the horse had taken her to a job in the marketing department at Newmarket racecourse. It had little involvement with the horse, other than enabling her to go racing frequently at what I consider to be the best racecourse in the world.

Bereft of office space for redundant files, she had sought the possibility of storage in an outhouse at Westfield House. The outhouse was cluttered with boxes of files, folders, old books, letters, and even pictures. As she began organising space, her task was overcome by the fascination of scrutinising this Aladdin's Cave of old racing documents: racing calendars, stud books and racecards. But the jewel in the crown was none of these – it was a brown manila envelope.

Perusing the faded pages, she was overcome with a trembling excitement: they were letters and case notes relating to the 1844 Derby – the most infamous scandal in the annals of the Turf. It was an incredible find: there were letters from Lord George Bentinck, Colonel Peel, Earl Spencer, Lord Stradbroke and others. How could anyone with knowledge of the subject be so fortunate to stumble on such a find? Had she been unaware – which she may well have been had it not been one of her childhood stories – these documents could have been lost forever.

Her excitement at finding these most valuable documents was met, according to her, with the most surprising apathy. No one seemed to have the vaguest idea what she was talking about, despite vigorously drawing their attention to her copy of *Derby 200*. This was not surprising; few involved in the running of racing have, or would be expected to have, knowledge of its history. But this did not suppress her frustration.

These precious documents were handed over to Peter Amos at Jockey Club Estates, who, after I had expressed my interest, granted my access to them. The main document was not exactly related to the famous Trial, more so to witness statements as to how the Jockey Club could pursue those that had perjured themselves at the Trial. Even so, this document made fascinating reading, containing information that had certainly never been published before. There were references to other case notes – but where were they to be found? They certainly were not at Westfield House, despite Gina making a thorough search.

After a few calls to Weatherbys it appeared that my enquiries were coming to a dead end, but the helpful staff eventually put me in touch with an employee who was familiar with Running Rein: Adrian McGlynn. He invited me to their offices and produced letters and a fairly detailed 50-page document of case notes. These must have been those referred to in the notes that Gina had discovered at Westfield House.

I was now beginning to get excited – it was time to go in search of Running Rein.

I could not have imagined, when starting out, what a fascinating, and sometimes very moving, journey this would become. The quest took me over the length of the country: to the capital; to Newmarket and Epsom; to the almost unknown villages of Denton, and Norton in North Yorkshire; even to Poland, in an attempt to discover something of Zanoni – the name finally assumed by Maccabeus, who had impersonated the genuine Running Rein.

One of the most satisfying discoveries was the location of Dr Cobb's home, Sutton House, where the genuine Running Rein was bred.

Investigations with local authorities and archives were leading nowhere. There was a Sutton Grange but no Sutton House. Then a breakthrough came when I discovered an 'Old Map'. There was Sutton Grange – and, directly south of it, Sutton House.

The owner of the property was adamant that I had the wrong place: "This is Sutton Farm, not Sutton House." He was a rare product: an Irishman with not the vaguest interest in the horse. When I showed him the 'Old Map' he was convinced, although surprised, but he remained unimpressed with his property's connection with this remarkable incident in Turf history.

Many days were spent at the Newspaper Library at Colindale;

leaving at six in the morning, in order to get in a full day's work, and then the three-hour drive back. It was frustrating, poring over the difficult-to-read microfilm. *Bell's Life*, at times, was a nightmare. But it was very rewarding to come across an interesting letter here, a snippet of information there.

I have mentioned that the journey was very moving. For a lover of the thoroughbred racehorse this is probably not difficult to understand. Standing on the hallowed ground of Langton Wold, where John Scott was reputed to have said he would rather be hanged than feasted at Newmarket; in the stable at Sutton House, where Mab would have thrown her colt foal, by The Saddler, the genuine Running Rein; at the Old Lodge, in Malton, where Gladiator started his career as a stallion: the ghosts from the pages of our story go rolling by.

And it is for this reason that it has been such a privilege to write this book: a privilege to meet so many kind people, some of whom have become good friends and who have been prepared to give their time in its preparation, which has taken around eight years to complete. I am not a professional writer; had I been so, it would have taken a fraction of this time. On occasions I sat for a whole evening, sometimes several evenings, unable even to produce a single sentence. But, disadvantaged as I may have been, I was never deterred from completing the course.

The task is now complete. This, then, dear reader, to the best of my knowledge, is the complete story of the most amazing incident in the history of the greatest game on Earth.

Acknowledgements

Many kind people have helped me in the preparation of this book, and I owe them my grateful thanks. It is difficult to know where to start, but I suppose it should be with my daughter, Gina. I can still recall her excitement when she called to tell me of her find. Thanks, Gina, and for your veterinary knowledge of physic, teeth and bones. To Peter Amos, at Jockey Club Estates, who kindly gave me access to the case notes and letters, and the facilities to copy them, and his successor, William Gittus, who granted permission to use these notes. Likewise to Adrian McGlynn, at Weatherbys, who provided the bulk of the case notes dealing with the Trial, and again, facilities to copy them and also permission to use them and the extract from the *Racing Calendar*: 'Rule Relating to the Examination of the Age of Young Horses'.

Thanks also to Charles Wyville, a descendant of Sir Charles Ibbetson, who invited me to his home, Constable Burton Hall, and provided an essay on 'The Ibbetsons of Leeds and Denton'; and to Professor R.G. Wilson of the University of East Anglia for permission to make use of it. To the county archivists who answered my many questions, who are too numerous to mention individually, but I would single out Llinos Thomas, Allison Kenney and Hilary Davies at Westminster Archives, Bev Shew and Justine Pearson at Surrey History Centre, Jane Stafford at Bury St Edmunds Record Office, and Crispin Powell and Patricia Collins at Northamptonshire Archives. Thanks to you all.

A special thanks to Vic Maloney, who kindly showed me round Sutton House and allowed me to take photographs of this extraordinary building, which, as you will see, is mainly a barn, with the house tacked on the end. Thanks, Vic - this was a special day for me.

To Victor Tunkel of the Selden Society for explaining the legal jargon from the preliminary hearings at the Court of Common Pleas and Court of Exchequer. This was all very confusing to me. Thanks for improving my knowledge of nineteenth-century legalese.

In Search of Running Rein would not be complete without making some attempt to discover something of Zanoni's career as a stallion. Early on in my research I wrote to the Russian Jockey Club – twice, in fact, in case my letter had gone astray – but no reply. Then suddenly, out of the blue, about two years later, I received an e-mail from Dr Jacek Lojek, Head of the Horse Breeding Department, Faculty of Animal Science, at Warsaw Agricultural University, and a senior steward at the Polish Jockey Club. My letter had eventually filtered through to him.

Jacek invited me to Poland and provided pedigrees of Zanoni's offspring, from the Russian and Polish *Stud Books*. I spent a day at the Polish Jockey Club with Pawel Goclowski and Krzysztof Wolski, who desperately searched for information of their racing careers. Unfortunately, no Racing Calendars exist before 1863, and so their performances remain unknown. But thanks to you all for your enthusiasm, and at least providing the one result of possibly Zanoni's best son, in Russia – Manifik, who won an Emperor's Cup.

It was an honour to be assisted by Dr Mike Huggins, Emeritus Professor of Cultural History, at Cumbria University. Mike has written a number of books and academic papers on the social side of racing history and made a number of interesting contributions, in addition to giving his permission to use his essay: 'Lord Bentinck, the Jockey Club and Racing Morality in Mid-Nineteenth Century England: The 'Running Rein' Derby Revisited'.

A short time before I started on this quest, Lizz Ross, who runs the Bloodlines website, invited me to join her group. I have used the facilities of the Bloodlines database to generate the pedigrees in the Appendix, and I am grateful to Lizz for her agreement to this.

For anyone researching the thoroughbred racehorse there are few better places to start than Tim Cox's incredible library. Tim always seems to be on hand to answer questions or look up odd bits of information. It was Tim who suggested the theory as to why Goodman approached Thomas Ferguson for the hire of his horse, Goneaway, to impersonate Maccabeus. Thanks, Tim, for this gem and for all the other questions so graciously answered; and, of course, for reading the text.

Greg Way was helpful in providing a number of books and photocopies of extracts from books.

Lastly, and by no means least, a very special thanks to Tony Morris. Readers will know Tony as one of the foremost experts in the world of racing and breeding the thoroughbred. I contacted him at the beginning of my research and he kindly threw his exceptional library open to me; maybe not as vast as Tim's, but nevertheless housing many gems. Tony and I are traditionalists. We share a common love of the modern thoroughbred and an appreciation of the past that is, unfortunately, not shared by all racegoers. We have become good friends and have spent many an evening, on occasions into the early hours, discussing the past and present thoroughbred racehorse. I am also grateful to Tony for kindly agreeing to write the foreword.

Introductory Note:
The Value of Money

This amazing story is inevitably about the lure of money and the determination of those to accrue it by any means considered necessary - honestly in the case of some, by fraud and deception for others, both by the medium of betting. In the period following the Napoleonic Wars the obsession of gambling was ubiquitous; patricians at the centre of racing had amassed vast fortunes that, even by today's standards, were truly astonishing. When the inflation factor is applied – well, the sums become almost unimaginable. And they gambled their fortunes with a careless disregard for the consequences.

It is difficult to assess these values in today's terms, as our way of life has changed so much. Our world would be unrecognisable to our antecedents. The motor car, computers, mobile phones, etc., just serve to illustrate how money is spent differently as time moves on. The Office of National Statistics uses these modern items in their calculation of the retail price index, but for obvious reasons they are not included in earlier versions.

In addition, there are external factors, such as wars and civil unrest, that cause fluctuations in the value of currency. Bank of England records show that over the course of the First World War the pound lost just over half its value; and during the Second World War almost a quarter. During the 1973 oil crisis the pound lost 15 per cent, and during the winter of discontent, 12 per cent.

Overall, these irregular variations mean that comparisons of prices further back in time and over long periods are less accurate than comparisons over short periods in recent years.

As there is no single price index available for the period of this story, the Office of National Statistics uses a composite index produced by linking together prices from different published sources. As the Bank of England points out, the quality of the data deteriorates over time. But at least it gives you, dear reader, a rough idea of the scale of the money involved.

A few examples show that when Colonel Mellish lost £40,000 at the throw of a single dice, today this would represent around £2.5 million. Can you imagine a gambler today betting £40,000 on the throw of a dice – let alone £2.5 million? When Gladiator was sold to France in 1846 for £2,000, this would equate to about £175,000 today, which compares very favourably with some of the lots that pass through Tattersalls sale ring; and the bet said to be laid by Sam Rogers against his own ride, Ratan, of £2,000 to £10,000, in today's terms would be around £200,000 to win £1 million.

For those desiring to compare other values with today's prices there is an inflation calculator on the Bank of England website: http://www.bankofengland.co.uk/education/inflation/calculator/f lash/index.htm.

Foreword

IT was way back in my pre-teen years when I discovered racing, and while I liked to follow the form in my father's Daily Express and my aunt's Daily Mirror, it was not what The Scout or Newsboy was tipping that appealed to me. With pocket-money of half a crown a week, and sweets and comics to be bought, it was not realistic to think about the game as a medium for betting. No, what grabbed me most especially was the rich and colourful history of a sport whose origins pre-dated those of football and cricket, and the realisation that here was a pastime that had gripped imaginations for more than two centuries, that had been faithfully recorded throughout that time, and that offered me the opportunity to delve into a past so much more fascinating than Britain's loss of her colonies or the Napoleonic wars. The history I was taught in the classroom, about events whose cause and effects were so remote from my view of reality, could not begin to compare with the living history of horseracing, as exemplified by its continuity – including some contests that had been renewed annually from the time of George III down to the reign of Elizabeth II. It was natural for me to focus on the Derby, the race that through the generations since its inception in 1780 had been the one most coveted by every owner, breeder, trainer and jockey, and which still, in the middle of the twentieth century, held every enthusiast in thrall. I memorised the names of all the winners, and constantly sought more information about anything that appertained to the history of this great and fabled institution. Of all the Derby renewals I read about, one stood out as different from the rest. Yes, there were plenty of great winners and great contests to stir the imagination, but what happened in 1844 beat the lot as something apart – a landmark in the history of horseracing itself, with the first horse home disqualified, exposed as an impostor. I have waited over half a century for the full story of this scandalous and intriguing affair, and take my hat off to Tony Byles for the prodigious research he has undertaken in compiling this comprehensive account of a saga that shook the nation more than a century and a half ago, and is guaranteed to fascinate readers of the modern era.

Tony Morris

Best wishes
Tony Morris

www.apexpublishing.co.uk

1
Murky Practices and Dirty Tricks

As the sport of racing progressed, it was inevitable that it would eventually embrace the science of corruption. The nobility that had created the great game and nourished it in the early days was soon to be infiltrated by some pretty unsavoury individuals. Society was in a period gripped by a gambling fever, even involving pastimes of violence, such as rat-catching and the odious spectacle of cock-fighting, the results of which even the good Mr Cheny was disposed to record in his early racing calendars, and the turn of a card, or throw of a dice, could make you a very wealthy, or a very poor, man. Didn't Colonel Mellish lose £40,000 on the throw of a single dice.

The fascination for gambling was everywhere, not least on the Heath at Newmarket. The passion of the early breeders to race their horses with great wagers at stake could not, in the fullness of time, be divorced from gambling, fuelling the desire of the unprincipled to cheat and swindle the unwary. There was abundant scope for fraud. If cards could be marked and dice loaded, then it was certainly not beyond the bounds of possibility that a horse could be prevented from winning, or another could be ensured success. Bribery and corruption were rampant. Jockeys were the main targets, but there were various other avenues: stable lads, trainers, owners themselves, and even starters, who could set the field off with the chosen victim facing in the wrong direction.

Of course, racing had never been suspected of being the cleanest of pastimes. Probably the first aroma of chicanery – well, that's how the Newmarket crowd may have viewed it – that curled across the Heath, was the Escape affair. Escape was a son of the fantastic Highflyer, bred by the Prince of Wales and purchased by one Mr Franco, eventually finding his way back into the Royal household after beating the Prince's own Canto Baboo – no mean performer himself – in a match at Newmarket.

Within a couple of days of the first Newmarket October Meeting of 1791, Escape had twice thrashed the Duke of Bedford's Grey Diomed, over the Beacon Course. Therefore, at the second October Meeting two weeks later, there was no reason to suspect that he would not be successful in the two races he would enter: a two-mile race across the Ditch In Course on 20 October, and a four-mile affair over the Beacon Course the following day. He started as favourite for the first race, but finished last of the four runners. No doubt there were those who cursed their losses, hedged their bets for the following day and backed Lord Grosvenor's Skylark instead. Then they were very angry. Escape, this time an outsider in a field of six, had cantered in, reversing the previous day's form with Skylark. The cry of 'foul' echoed across the Heath. The accusations forced the Prince to turn his back on Newmarket, and old Sam Chifney, the most wonderful rider of his time, to articulate his innocence, and Escape's running, in his marvellous autobiography *Genius Genuine*, which in 1794, at the phenomenal price of £5 a copy (you would be lucky to pick up a first-edition copy today for less than £450), would have caused you to choke before you even had the opportunity to devour its contents.

The Escape affair was questionable. Today the discrepancy may have been adequately explained and accepted in the stewards' room. But, even if there had been a hint of treachery, it was nothing to the rampant scams, cheating, deceptions, substitutions and, yes, poisonings that were to plague racing in the years succeeding the Napoleonic Wars.

At the Newmarket First Spring Meeting of 1811, several horses died as a result of arsenic being administered to a drinking trough. The villainous poisoner, one Daniel Dawson, a well-known tout, was grassed-up by an accomplice, Cecil Bishop, who must have considered that the reward of £500 offered by the Jockey Club was a trifle more rewarding than poisoning racehorses. Dawson was tried at Cambridge Assizes. There was little doubt as to his guilt, but the judge directed that he should be discharged, on the grounds that he had been indicted as a principal, instead of an accessory before the fact, which in point of law could not be maintained. Unfortunately for Dawson, his apparent freedom was short-lived. He was detained on a further charge of poisoning horses three years earlier and was tried again, this time confessing that he had poisoned some twenty horses. On this occasion there were no legal uncertainties: he was duly sentenced to death and hanged.

The first case of any great notoriety concerning fraud by deception occurred between 1821 and 1825, involving – through no fault of his own, of course – a horse by the name of Tom Paine. In reality his true identity was that of a thoroughbred named Tybalt, by Thunderbolt out of Lord Grosvenor's famous Oaks-winning mare Meteora. Entered under a false pedigree, as by Prime Minister out of a mare by True Blue, his odyssean travels over the length and breadth of England enabled numerous rich pickings in races confined to half-breds, and earned him near celebrity status. Shortly after winning the Billesdon Coplow Stakes at Croxton Park in Leicestershire, recognised at the half-bred's Derby, the fraud was discovered. He was identified by his old master, Mr Valentine Kingston, and the stewards awarded the prize money to the owner of the second horse, Bogtrotter.

Although it seems that it was never investigated or proved, it is probable that the fraud was initiated by a certain Mr Field. Whether the horse's subsequent owners, Messrs Rowley and Watson, were knowing participants in the fraud is unknown; they did, however, unwittingly or not, certainly benefit from it. Even after the fraud was discovered he was still running under the name of Tom Paine, winning a race for his new owner, Mr Lewis, at Inverness. Under his true identity Tybalt had won a Royal Plate at Guildford in June 1821, only two months before the start of the trail of deception under his pseudonym.

There were some fairly discreditable episodes in both the Derby and the St Leger, and even the nobility were not averse to the odd fiddle. Was Lord Jersey beyond suspicion when Mameluke beat the favourite, Glenartney, by a couple of lengths in the 1827 Derby? There was certainly an element of cynicism amongst onlookers, who were firmly of the opinion that Glenartney was the better of his two and could have won if so desired. No declaration to win with Glenartney had been made by Lord Jersey. In fact, it was publicly declared that both Robinson and Edwards should run their own races. But Glenartney was 5 to 1, whereas Mameluke was 9 to 1, giving good reason to believe that the latter's victory was more suited to the pockets of Lord Jersey and his friends. There was no doubt that Mameluke, who was afterwards bought by John Gully for four thousand guineas, was a very good horse, but the fact that an offer of five thousand guineas for Glenartney was rejected would no doubt have fuelled suspicions that Glenartney's defeat was manipulated.

Mameluke may well not have won the Derby on merit, but his defeat in the St Leger of that year must rank as one of the most disgraceful episodes in the annals of that great race. It was Gully's aim to win with Mameluke. He had bought Mameluke on the understanding that confidentiality relating to his purchase was maintained for 24 hours so that he could approach Crockford to lay a price without arousing any suspicion. Crockford offered 10 to 1, to which Gully took two bets at £10,000 to £1,000: one in which Mameluke would beat ten named horses and in another that he would beat nine.

When Crockford discovered that Gully was the owner, one can imagine his effrontery: he had been tricked by Gully. When money started flowing in from all quarters against Mameluke, Gully must have realised what was going on and took every precaution to protect his horse. But it was the start that settled the outcome. Mameluke was known to be a horse of short temper, and it appeared that every effort was being made to antagonise him. There were several false starts, and when the Starter, who was believed to have been bribed, finally let them go, Matilda was several lengths in front of the field, and Mameluke, who had been facing in the wrong direction, was almost the length of Doncaster High Street behind.

Somehow Sam Chifney managed to get Mameluke into a challenging position. At the distance he actually headed Matilda, but the effort in making up the lost ground was just too much and he finally succumbed by just half-a-length. So convinced was Gully that Mameluke would have won that he challenged Mr Petre, the owner of Matilda, to a match, even offering the mare a seven-pound pull in the weights. But Matilda's trainer, John Scott, was indignant: Matilda had been the luckiest of winners and it would be madness to take on Mameluke again. Unfortunately for Gully, Matilda featured in both lists, but he paid his losses despite knowing that he had been cheated.

It was not only the English who were exercising their expertise in chicanery. The French were implementing their own special blend, as was aptly demonstrated in the 1840 Prix du Jockey Club. The record books will show that the winner was (shall we say, described as) M. Eugène Aumont's filly Tontine, by Tetotum out of Odette, from Lord Henry Seymour's filly Jenny, by Royal Oak out of Kermesse. Before the race rumours abounded, possibly spread by a disgruntled stable lad, that a coup was planned, and preceding Colonel Peel's claim by four years, Lord Henry Seymour objected to the winner, claiming that she was in fact a four-year-old English filly by the name of Herodia, by Aaron out of a mare by Young Election. The case was investigated by both the French Jockey Club and by a tribunal, whose conclusions were contradictory. The stewards of the Jockey Club were not satisfied that Lord Seymour's claim was proven and Tontine's name remains forever as the winner of the Prix du Jockey Club.

Although Lord Seymour's claim was not substantiated, there must have been very strong suspicions that a substitution had taken place. In the *French Stud Book* no progeny appears against Tontine's name, although it was well known that she had bred several foals. One must wonder what happened to her offspring. Would it be too facetious to suggest that they followed their dam in the accomplishment of other coups?

These episodes illustrated that where the thoroughbred racehorse ventured, villainy of one sort or other was sure to follow. And villainy on the Turf – disgraceful as it may be – is an absorbing subject; none more so than the shameful incidents that took place in the Derby of 1844. Each of these could almost justify its own story, but for them to occur at the same time was truly beyond the work of fiction. Rightly, in one of Sir Arthur Conan Doyle's adventures, did Sherlock Holmes remark to Dr Watson: "My dear fellow, life is infinitely stranger than anything which the mind of man could invent."

2
Back to Denton and Malton

Denton! The name is reminiscent of one of those imaginary towns in a hospital television drama, but, no, it's a real place - almost isolated from the rest of the world. The only way out of Denton is the way you came in. At one end of the village is a smattering of cottages and at the other, Denton Park.

I had driven in from Otley, on the twisting, undulating road, to the village, delightfully situated on the banks of the River Wharf, and now I was at the gates of this magnificent eighteenth-century house. What history had passed this way. It was here, in the old house, that the great parliamentarian, Lord Thomas Fairfax, had been born; and the Royalist Prince Rupert had lodged here on his way from Lancashire to York a few days before the battle of Marston Moor. But I was not here to reminisce over these pages from our social history. It was from here that the most infamous scandal in the history of the British Turf had, in part, its origins.

The Ibbetsons had made a fortune as cloth merchants and land investment. They had land at Darlington, Knaresborough Forest and Kirby Overblow, where Henry, the third son of James Ibbetson, had a stud farm with a string of horses.[1] Denton Hall came into their ownership when it was acquired by James Ibbetson in 1717.[2] The old mansion of the Fairfaxes had burned down and Samuel Ibbetson had rebuilt it on a more modest scale in the 1730s.[3] On his death it was inherited by his nephew, Sir James Ibbetson, who, having deemed it unfashionable, pulled it down and had the present elegant structure – designed by the architect John Carr – built.[4]

The Ibbetson family were wealthy and of gentry status. Their family line traced to the Darcys and Wyvills, both influential in the development of the thoroughbred, and further back to the Fairfaxes and Edward III.[5] But they were not without an element of financial and certainly personal problems. In the early years of the nineteenth century Sir Charles Ibbetson was left to bring up three young children when his wife died within a year of moving into Denton[6] – not a trifling task, indeed. And his patience was tried to the extreme by the conduct of his eldest son, Charles Henry. He lived way beyond his means, kept male servants and, despite being frequently in debt, kept a stable of several horses.[7] At the age of 21, in 1835, the young spendthrift took a commission in the 9th Hussars and, adopting the aplomb of a Regency rake, also took a mistress, Harriet Towns, a dancer at the Opera.[8] This behaviour infuriated his Colonel of the regiment, Lord Loughborough, and it must have come as an acute embarrassment to his father to receive a letter from Lord Loughborough, penned in the most insensitive terms, admonishing his conduct and suggesting that Sir Charles should exercise parental control.[9] His extravagances knew no bounds. Despite his dubious financial resources, he had ventured into the world of breeding and racing horses. In 1837 he purchased Muliana,[10] a full sister to Muley Muloch, sire of the much-revered Alice Hawthorn. Muliana produced for him a colt by Sir Hercules,[11] a moderate performer – in fact, few of his cattle were successful, and those that were had only moderate ability. Unfortunately, bad horses were as expensive to maintain as good ones.

He fell deeper into debt and, with a writ out for his arrest, Lord Loughborough insisted that he leave the regiment.[12] He returned to Denton in disgrace, but, despite Lord Loughborough's moralising request, Sir Charles appeared to have little control over his wayward son, who spent much of his time with his fellow officers in the barracks at Leeds or with Miss Towns, whom he had ensconced in the leafy suburb of Headingley.[13]

Sir Charles was becoming increasingly frustrated by his son's dismissive attitude. He realised that on his own death his father's 1775 settlement of the estates would expire, possibly putting his son's self-indulgence beyond reasonable limits. He therefore decided to meet his son's debts on condition that he agreed to make a resettlement of Denton, restricting his interest to a life tenancy, in favour of his younger brother, Frederick.[14]

Sir Charles, worn out with anxiety at his inability to control his son's irresponsibility, died two years later, in April 1839.[15] Even the reading of the will was a melodramatic affair. As the solicitor unrolled the scroll, he illuminated the penalties, down to the minutest detail, that Charles Henry, who had now assumed the baronetcy, would incur should he marry Miss Towns.[16] Resentful of these penal clauses and infuriated at his father's choice of executors, Sir Charles Henry, beside himself with rage, stormed out of the room, accompanied by his cousin, an Anglican parson, who also, surprisingly, exercised disquiet.

It would have been to his father's disappointment that Frederick fared as no better example than his elder brother. A captain in the 2nd Queen's Dragoon Guards, whilst on a tour of duty in Ireland he formed a liaison with a woman of considerable beauty, the wife of a linen draper, fleeing to France when her brother discovered her living with Frederick at Athlone barracks.[17]

Despite Sir Charles Henry's indiscretions and his affinity for debt, he did eventually assume some responsibility, becoming a major in the West Yorkshire militia, and, with the assistance of lawyers controlling affairs, Denton survived. The unfortunate Miss Towns, who had two children by him, was cast aside – although he was obliged to pay her a small annuity – in favour of a new lady, Eden, the widow of Percival Perkins, whom he married in 1847.[18] The annuity to Miss Towns, together with a further annuity to an aunt and mortgage repayments, left him in a perilous financial state. When he died in 1861 at the relatively young age, even in those days, of 46, Denton passed to his sister, Laura (Frederick having died at the age of 31), who in 1845 had married Marmaduke Wyvill of Constable Burton, thereby renewing the alliance of almost two centuries before. Laura lived until 1908, and Denton remained part of the Wyvill Estate until its sale by her grandson in the 1920s. Today it is in the hands of a corporate nonentity, a sad reflection of a once remarkable dynasty.

And so the era of the Ibbetsons, a prolific merchanting and landowning dynasty of nearly two centuries, was at an end. Sir Charles Henry Ibbetson had not left the legacy that his forebears would have desired; his misdemeanours would have no doubt disappointed them. A colourful and flamboyant character, he was a Corinthian - not perhaps in the mould of my Lords March and Bentinck, as his desperate finances did not permit him to aspire to such heights, but a Corinthian nevertheless. As the *Racing Calendar* and *General Stud Book* will convey, during his vibrant years he bred, raced and even rode some of his own horses. He will be remembered for none – with the exception of one. Even this animal, however, would not be considered exceptional. But exceptional or not, its name will be forever etched on the Turf as the illegal winner of the 1844 Derby – Running Rein.

Like Newmarket, Malton is not a particularly inspiring place. It is a typical North Yorkshire country town, with narrow streets, lined with York Stone buildings. At the top of the hill, on Old Malton Gate, is The Lodge, now a hotel but in the nineteenth century a stud farm, where William Allen bred many a noted winner, and where Gladiator, the sire of Running Rein (Maccabeus), stood in his early stud career, and also the Capsicum mare – his dam.

I had got as far as the end of Castlegate and was now heading south across the Derwent. On the Langton Road was the first glimpse of a string coming in from exercise. The riders acknowledged me, as I gave a wide birth, and then the vast expanse of the Wold was before me. It is a place of great solitude, its beauty sculpted by the continual restlessness of the earth. Like the Heath at Newmarket, it triggers a rare excitement that only the thoroughbred racehorse can command. I am mindful of the history of this place. Running horses were bred here before the Arabian forefathers arrived and John Cheny established his first Racing Calendar. In the early days it is probable that the Darley Arabian galloped here; certainly Sampson and his majestic son, Bay Malton, did so, and Lord Rockingham's Allabaculia, the very first winner of the St Leger.

But the greatest era in Malton's history was in the middle of the nineteenth century, with the arrival from Newmarket of John and William Scott. They became the most revered of racing people: John as a trainer and Will as a jockey. During his years at Whitewall John Scott sent out winners with clockwork regularity, including seven Two Thousand Guineas, three One Thousand Guineas, five Derbies, eight Oaks and sixteen St Legers. Will rode the winners of four Derbies, three Oaks and nine St Legers – four in successive years. At his best, no jockey surpassed Will Scott, as was admirably demonstrated in his riding of Satirist in the 1841 St Leger, when he defeated the Derby winner, Coronation, who on his day was at least a stone superior.

That Will should have been the first jockey to win the Triple Crown on Sir Tatton Sykes is an arguable case. Inebriated and abusive to the Starter, he was hopelessly left at the start of the 1846 Derby, but he still managed to finish second, beaten by only a neck by Pyrrhus the First.

One way or another, William I'Anson, who had ventured down to Spring Cottage, Norton, from Gullane in Scotland, had a fair few good 'uns, too. I'Anson was a paragon among owner breeders. What glittering stars were bestowed on him by his peerless broodmare, Queen Mary,[19] her pony-sized daughter, Haricot, and Haricot's wonderful daughter, Caller Ou, a St Leger winner and a winner of 49 of her 98 races, and the amazing Blink Bonny, a winner of both the Derby and the Oaks, and her son Blair Atholl, who I'Anson produced to run as a maiden in the Derby, which he won in a canter.

Although the Scotts and I'Anson were the most renowned of their profession, there were many other breeders and trainers operating on a much smaller scale. One of the small-time breeders in the Malton area was Dr Charles Cobb, whose practice was at Low Street,[20] and who resided at Sutton House,[21] Norton – not too far from I'Anson's place. He had a solitary mare, Mab, which he had acquired from Mr Allen, who had also owned the Capsicum mare before selling her to Sir Charles Henry Ibbetson. Mab was foaled in 1833 and was by Duncan Grey out of a dam by Macbeth, out of Margaret by Hambletonian. She was an uninspiring sort: small, ill-tempered and a bad nurse, with worms.[22] According to the *Racing Calendar*, it would appear that she had never raced. In 1840 she dropped her first foal, a colt by Gladiator, who was cut. On 5 June the same year she was taken by Thomas Lofthouse, an employee of Dr Cobb, to Squire Osbaldeston's stallion, The Saddler, who was at Ebberston Lodge and on 11 May 1841 dropped his bay colt foal, which later turned brown. He was a very thin, small foal, but he had big limbs, although he had cracked heels, a characteristic of his sire, and turned his off-fore foot out considerably.

Gladiator and the Capsicum mare at Mr Allen's, and The Saddler colt at Dr Cobb's – this is where it all began.

3

Abraham Levi Goodman and the Background to the Fraud

Who is this harmless-looking old Jew seated by the fireside of a wayside inn near Six Mile Bottom,[1] whose pronounced Hebrew features invite the butt of three mischievous young sprigs, who have dropped in for 'something hot' to keep out the cold?

"Good morning, Father Abraham!" exclaimed the first. "I hope I see you well?"

"How are you, Father Isaac?" continued the second, with well-counterfeited civility.

"All hail, Father Jacob!" reiterated the third. "I wonder what brings you out so far from home on this raw day?"

Rising humbly from his seat, the old Jew lifts his hat with much mock dignity, and replies in quiet tones, "Gentlemen, you do me too much honour by your courteous enquiries and by the names you have been pleased to bestow upon me. My real name is Saul, the son of Kish; and I have been sent forth in search of my father's asses, which he has lost. I was about to return, despairing of finding them, when - lo and behold! - the God of Abraham, of Isaac, and of Jacob has brought them into this very room; and here I will leave them while I go to report to my father." With these words and doubtless with many a secret chuckle, the old man totters feebly along the passage and leaves the house.[2]

No, this is not one of Aesop's fables; this enchanting anecdote, whether it has any bearing on the truth or is a figment of the imagination, relates to none other than Abraham Levi Goodman, whose celebrity in skulduggery on the Turf is probably unequalled in all its history. He had gone to Newmarket on a touting expedition and had disguised himself as an old and infirm Jew to prevent his being recognised, as he had been warned off the Heath, which to him was forbidden ground.

Very little is known about Goodman other than that he was a

cheap, common criminal, falling foul of the law as early as 1828, when he was one of a gang charged on suspicion of robbing a woman of £300 at Hampton races.[3] He was the proprietor of the Little Nick[4] gambling club in Leicester Square, and was in league with every rogue and ruffian in town. His death certificate indicates that he died of dropsy on 19 November 1863, at 45 Cow Cross, Saffron Hill – in Victorian times a squalid neighbourhood densely inhabited by poor people and thieves. His age is given as 56, which would indicate that he was born in 1807, and his occupation is recorded as 'Gentleman'. There do not appear to be any records in the 1841 Census, although the St Marylebone rate book records him as living at 29 Foley Place in 1842 (now 34 Langham Street). He also owned Hallmead Farm, Sutton.[5]

If you were to pick a team of sharp-practising scoundrels of the Turf, then Abraham Levi Goodman would surely be amongst their number. The anti-hero of the Running Rein Scandal, he became a racehorse owner in 1840, initially acquiring a string of six horses - not for the delight of ownership, but purely for financial gain. Well versed in the art of manipulating the rules of racing in order to bring off a betting coup, it was well known that he was the orchestrator of several unproven glaring robberies on the Turf.

One such event was the Hurst Cup on 25 June 1840,[6] which had the Hampton crowd howling. Six horses started for the four heats, of which Mr S. Smith's Bedford was the favourite at starting, and with Mr V. King's Alsdorf they were backed against the field. Bedford and Mr Collins' bay filly, Drogheda, did not contest the first heat, which was won by Mr King's Alsdorf.

In the second heat Mr Brick's Shuffler and Mr Wells's Tutor were withdrawn, so only four went to post, and it was cleverly won by Mr Collins' Drogheda. Bedford threw a plate, causing him to swerve, but still managed to finish second.

For the third heat Teddy had been withdrawn, so only three went to post: Bedford, Drogheda and Alsdorf. Bedford, who had been backed at 6 to 4 against the field, won with some difficulty. An objection was made against Drogheda, on the grounds that her jockey had carried five pounds over weight without declaring the fact to the stewards before the start, which, under Jockey Club rules, would lead to disqualification. On going to scale, however, it turned out that he was barely two pounds over weight, which he was entitled to carry without declaration, and thus he was permitted to start again. This was rather a poser to some who had been certain that Drogheda would be disqualified and had confidently backed Bedford at long odds, some to the extent of 2 to 1.

Although Bedford, Drogheda and Alsdorf had each won a heat, Mr King believed that Alsdorf did not have much chance and he was withdrawn, leaving just Bedford and Drogheda. There was some confidence in Drogheda, who had been backed to a certain degree, but suddenly offers of 4, 5 and even 6 to 1 were made on Bedford. This rapid shortening of the odds was enough to cause even the most ignorant to surmise that there was obviously a whiff of skulduggery here.

Bedford started and cantered over whilst, to the astonishment of her backers, Drogheda was pulled up and withdrawn. As Mr Collins led her back in front of the stand he was subjected to the most vocal disapproval, to which he responded by making a respectful bow to his tormentors. Their reaction to this was to propose a subscription to pay the expenses of a ducking.

Mr Collins's reason for this irregular behaviour was that he did not wish to run the risk of having his mare claimed for 200 sovereigns had she won. There was an air of dishonesty here, and certainly the backers of Drogheda, who believed that they had been deceived, had an entirely different impression of the situation: why, if Mr Collins had no desire to lose his mare, did he enter her?

Lord Chesterfield, one of the stewards, was of the opinion that an inquiry was necessary and consequently ordered the cup to be withheld. As there had been no start, the bets made on Bedford for the last heat were declared void. However, on the following day the objection was withdrawn, the cup was duly handed over to Mr Smith and, of course, all bets were settled, much to the disgust of the backers of Drogheda.

The editor of *The Sporting Review* was adamant that a robbery had been committed:

Although Messrs. Smith and Collins were the apparent villains of the piece, the true rogues were, however, well known. And what was the result? That the blackguard by whom the robbery was 'put up' was to be seen at every subsequent meeting of the year, laying his money, and racing his horses with the first noblemen and gentleman in the land. Why were no exertions made by the Stewards of the Jockey Club to pursue the swindlers and purge themselves of so notorious a scandal, or command their absence from Newmarket Heath?[7]

Probably aware of the law of libel, he restrained himself from naming the rogues, although it was hard to avoid the suspicion that it was Goodman who had influenced Mr Collins to withdraw his mare.

Where Goodman certainly was involved in an unquestionable cheat was the last event of the Newmarket Houghton Meeting of the same year, which was a match between Mr Litchwald's Shark and Goodman's own Mungo Park.[8] The betting opened at 5 to 4 on Shark but dramatically turned in favour of Mungo Park, eventually closing at 3 to 1 and 4 to 1 on him. This was surely a cheat in the offing. Macdonald, on Shark, could not have made it more obvious that his mount was 'pulled double' the whole way, and seemed able at any part of the race to go on and win. Yet, as with the Bedford affair, there was not a murmur from the stewards.

Was Goodman already attempting a Derby fraud three years prior to the Running Rein affair? Rumours were circulating about the means of making the favourites, Ralph and Coronation, 'safe' in order to clear the way for a victory for Belgrade (chestnut colt Belshazzar-Alice) formerly owned by Goodman but subsequently transferred to Lord Lichfield.

These rumours had little effect other than to induce extra vigilance on the part of the trainers of Ralph and Coronation, who took especial care to prevent the possibility of intrusion into their stables.[9]

Rumours they may have been, but with Goodman's apparent involvement they did not go away and, having exploded the insinuations of making the favourites 'safe', there was further speculation that measures would be taken to reduce the weight of Belgrade's jockey, Wakefield, after weighing out and to restore the weight before weighing in. This would be executed in various ways: by exchanging saddlecloths, by substituting a heavy whip for a light one, or by handing a handkerchief to the jockey containing the necessary weight in quicksilver, which he would hide under his jacket as he rode back to weigh in. However absurd this appeared, Captain Rous deemed it judicious to summon Wakefield and forewarn him of the rumours that had been circulating. Captain Rous did not give credence to these rumours but thought it expedient that Wakefield be acquainted with their existence so that he might guard himself against the possibility of suspicion.

As it was, Belgrade, despite being fourth favourite, finished down the field, thus relieving his connections of any subsequent inquiry.

The ease with which Goodman had pulled off his earlier robberies must have bolstered his confidence to pull off the greatest deception the Turf had ever known – to win the Derby with a four-year-old.

Goodman realised that at level weights, over the Derby distance of one-and-a-half miles, a good four-year-old was almost certain to defeat three-year-olds, especially as in the summer months they would have only just turned three. There were, of course, a number of problems to overcome, but the fortune to be won in bets at Tattersalls made the risk worthwhile. And Goodman, with his ingenuity and understanding of racing, would leave nothing to chance in his desire to overcome these problems.

The major problem was how to make the substitution without arousing any suspicion. It would have been ludicrous to produce an unraced four-year-old on Derby day, especially if large sums of money had been wagered on it during the period leading up to the race. Goodman therefore had to produce his potential Derby winner in two-year-old races, when, in fact, he was a three-year-old. Thus, when he appeared as a runner in the Derby, he would be accepted as the same horse that ran in two-year-old races the previous season.

The task now was for Goodman to find a suitable candidate.

4
The Fraud Begins

Around the time of Sir Charles Ibbetson's death, his son had acquired from Mr Allen, of The Lodge, Malton, a mare by Capsicum out of Acklam Lass. The Capsicum mare was sixteen years old and had produced nine foals, none of which had achieved any great success. It is possible that the mare was already in foal to Gladiator and that this is what enticed Sir Charles Henry Ibbetson to buy her. Gladiator, who was also at Mr Allen's, had run second to Bay Middleton in the 1836 Derby and was described as the ideal of a handsome and powerful racehorse.

In April 1840 Isaac Grey, groom to Sir Charles Ibbetson, made his way with the mare from Denton Park to Mr Smallwood's at Middlethorpe near York, to be put to Physician.[1] On 14 April she dropped her Gladiator foal, which was described as a good-looking bay colt, with no white about him and with a strong-looking head, full in the jowl, a lengthy colt, standing shortish on the legs – rather short in the quarter. After being put to Physician, Isaac Grey returned with the mare and foal to Denton.

Edward Messenger was engaged as stud groom to Sir Charles Henry Ibbetson on 12 June 1840.[2] In July 1841 Messenger instructed Weatherbys, Secretaries of the Jockey Club, by letter to enter the colt for the Derby Stakes to be run at Epsom in 1843 as the nomination of Mr Watson.[3]

Whether it had been Sir Charles Henry Ibbetson's intention to have a runner in the Derby is unknown. Saddled with debt, he may have been forced to disperse some of his stable, and in September 1841 his land agent, George Hayward, gave instructions to Tattersalls that part of his stud, which included the Gladiator colt, was to be sold at auction at the Doncaster sales that September.

The sale took place on 16 September, two days after the Marquis of Westminster's Satirist, trained by John Scott and ridden by his brother, William, had won the St Leger. The Gladiator colt, together with his engagement for the 1843 Derby Stakes, was knocked down to Abraham Levi Goodman for the princely sum of £52 10s – this was going to be Goodman's four-year-old for the 1844 Derby. Goodman also purchased from Sir Charles Ibbetson's stud a black colt by Voltaire out of Saltarella[4] and a brown filly by Muley Muloch out of Melody.[5] He also purchased a chestnut colt by Langar, dam by Cervantes. Messenger and Wharton delivered the Gladiator colt to Goodman and his associate, Henry 'Pickles' Higgins, at the Doncaster Arms stables, and, at the request of Goodman, Messenger directed Wharton to take the colt to the London and Birmingham Railway's, Rotherham, Masborough Station.

George Worley, who farmed 500 acres of his own land at Sywell, near Northampton, was at the 1841 Doncaster St Leger Meeting. Worley knew Higgins, a Northampton coachmaker, and met the latter at the meeting. Higgins informed Worley that he and Goodman were going to buy some colts and that he intended to send one – a colt by Gladiator dam by Capsicum out of Acklam Lass by Prime Minister – to him, to run in his paddock at Sywell. Worley, who had previously kept a colt for Higgins, agreed to this, as he considered himself in debt to Higgins for a few pounds.[6]

Higgins called on Worley on 19 September to inform him that he had got the colt over from Weedon to The George Inn[7] at Northampton, which was run by Higgins' cousins, John Knight Higgins and William Thomas Higgins, and to request him to collect the colt the following day when he came to the cheese fair. Worley drove to Northampton with his man, Benjamin Pinney, and sent the latter to collect the Gladiator colt and take him back to Sywell whilst he attended the fair. When Worley returned, the colt was in his paddock. Worley had not previously seen the colt but was suitably impressed, describing him as a bay yearling, standing straight on his legs – a good-looking, healthy horse.

About a week after the colt arrived at Worley's, Higgins dined with him. The conversation passed to the Gladiator colt. Higgins, in an attempt to demonstrate his intellect, informed Worley that he had been looking in a book, and as the colt was by Gladiator he would call him Spartacus.

George Odell,[8] a Northampton horse dealer, had known Worley for 25 years. He had also known both Goodman and Higgins for some years. Odell had been at Worley's in October 1841 in regard to the sale of some horses, and Worley had shown him the

Gladiator colt. He paid particular attention to it, as Worley informed him that it was an eminent horse – a racehorse that he was looking after for Goodman and Higgins. Odell frequently saw the colt at Worley's; even Higgins took him once or twice to see the colt.

Goodman's plan was now beginning to swing into action. He now required a suitable colt to be impersonated. As the colt to be impersonated would be a year younger, it was not necessary for him to be identical in appearance to the Gladiator colt. All Goodman required was to have another colt whose name he could use, a name that would be registered in the *General Stud Book*.

At Newmarket, in October 1841, a month after he had bought the Gladiator colt, Goodman met Henry Stebbings. The son of a Newmarket barber, Stebbings had worked with horses since he was thirteen, eventually becoming a trainer to Squire Osbaldeston at Ebberston, and later at Hambleton.[9] When it came to scruples, Stebbings was on about the same level as Goodman and was quite prepared to go to any lengths for financial gain. With his knowledge of racehorses and his unscrupulous background and 'no questions asked' attitude, he was just the kind of man that Goodman preferred to deal with.

Goodman expressed an interest in Stebbings buying him a foal or two, if they were cheap, but made no request as to the colour or type of foal he required. With his local knowledge and no specific requirement, Stebbings approached Dr Cobb, and in October 1841 he entered into negotiations for the purchase of his colt by The Saddler out of Mab. Stebbings told Dr Cobb that he wanted it merely as a companion for another colt, and about three weeks afterwards he purchased him for £28. Stebbings sent his servant, William Wilds, to pay for the colt, and on 7 December Robert Stanton, assisted by John Kitchen, a servant of Dr Cobb, who had the care of him after being foaled, took the colt to John King's stables at Grove House.[10] He was turned out in a paddock adjoining the Langton Road with a colt named Kilgram (bay colt 1841, Muley Muloch). King's son, William, attended him whilst he remained there until 17 January 1842.

Stebbings, who had named The Saddler colt Running Rein, now had to get him from Malton to York, in order to deliver him to Goodman in London.

"Here's the keeper, Jim (Stebbings) – he'll be the very man to go to Malton for the colt and meet you at York." The man, whom Henry Stebbings is addressing, looks up from supping his ale, at the Hambleton Inn.

It's a cold January evening – 1842.

"Will you go?" Stebbings emphasises his request to John Watson, gamekeeper to Mr Horsefall of Mount St John, near Thirsk.

"Yes, if you pay me well, but the weather is very bad," Watson replied, indicating he would not take on the task without suitable payment.

"Well, I'll give you a sovereign for the job," said Stebbings, to which Watson replied that he would go.[11]

Stebbings gave instructions to Watson that he must go to John King's and ask for a dark bay or brown colt with a white star on his forehead, which he had bought from Dr Cobb, by The Saddler out of Mab, now called Running Rein. This was too much information for Watson to take in.

"What's the use of telling me all this; I can't think of it all but you needn't be frightened, I shall get the right one," Watson, snapped.

"You'll be sure to go in the morning; I am not going myself but Jim will meet you at Crummack's, The Windmill Inn,[12]" Stebbings, worriedly, replied.

Watson left Hambleton between seven and eight the next morning and stopped about three hours at Hovingham. Travelling was difficult – the weather being very wet.

Watson arrived at King's between six and seven in the evening to be greeted by King's sister, as the former had gone to Malton and not yet returned. Watson explained why he had come and said he would call again in the morning.

Watson returned to King's between seven and eight the next morning. King gave him a cordial welcome. *"Well, how d'ye do, Watson? What have they sent you for – the colt?"*

"Yes, I am going to meet Jim Stebbings, at Crummack's," Watson confirmed.

John King took him to see the colt, which was in a box with another colt. King brought him out. Watson was not impressed. This was certainly not going to be the most convincing of Derby winners. He was very thin, and loose, like a thing that had been kept on the common. His near hind leg was swollen from the hock to the fetlock. As he walked he put his heels and fetlocks on the ground, and the toes were turned up. He was a long-pasterned colt, which made him go down on the fetlocks, and he was a little calf-kneed.

Watson led the colt away at about nine o'clock. He had difficulty leading him, so he put the halter round his neck and drove the colt from behind, with a stick that he had retrieved from the hedge.

He arrived at the Lobster House, between Malton and York, at about twelve o'clock and stopped for about an hour and a half to feed and water the colt, but he ate nothing. Watson continued on his way to York, driving the colt from behind, as before, and met Henry and James Stebbings at about four o'clock, just before he got to Crummack's.

Watson took the colt into a loose box at the bottom of the yard and gave him some hay, corn and water and dressed him over a little. Henry Stebbings locked the door to the box and gave Watson the key, instructing him not to let anyone see him. The next morning the colt was taken to the railway station, where Watson saw the colt onto the train, accompanied by James Stebbings.[13]

On 20 January Daniel White, who was employed by Goodman's brother-in-law, Mr Joseph, went to Euston Square station to collect the colt and deliver it to Goodman's stables in Chapel Mews, Foley Place.

Goodman now had the mechanism to complete the fraud.

During the two days and a night that Running Rein was at Goodman's stables, the trainer, Thomas Coleman, called to look at Mungo Park, whom Goodman was hoping to sell to him. Whilst there, Goodman asked him to come and look at a yearling colt by The Saddler that he had bought out of the north. Coleman was not impressed with the small brown colt that Goodman showed him; it was very poor and rough, had a thin light neck and was pot-bellied.[14]

Daniel White then took the colt to James Pearl's stables in Milton Street, Dorset Square, where it was kept until 30 January, before being collected by William Bean,[15] a Finchley horse dealer, and Henry Saunders, his groom. It was part of Goodman's deception to keep the genuine Running Rein concealed. Had he appeared prematurely at Hallmead Farm, it is possible that embarrassing questions would have arisen as to his identity. Bean's was the ideal place to keep him. A horse dealer for 30 years, who had twice been made bankrupt and twice insolvent, he was part of the network of dishonest acquaintances that Goodman had built up in his pursuit to perpetrate his fraudulent schemes.

Running Rein (The Saddler colt), attended to by Henry Saunders and York, also known as William Harlowe, was initially turned out into a temporary straw yard near Bean's henhouse and at night was kept in a box, with a donkey, beneath the bedroom of Mrs Bean's maidservant, the wonderfully named Fanny Fage, who could have stepped from the pages of a Charlotte Bronte novel. He was a troublesome beast, disturbing Fanny at night, kicking the stable door and generally causing a commotion.[16] In the daytime he frequently strayed into the adjacent field owned by Mr Meeson, Mr Bean's neighbour. Edward Ing, a 16-year-old lad employed by Mr Meeson to dib and set potatoes, and Mr Bailey, Meeson's foreman, frequently drove him from the field.[17]

The Gladiator colt remained at Worley's until the latter end of January 1842, under the care of Benjamin Pinney, who regularly received instruction from Higgins. During January the colt met with an accident: something frightened him and he tried to jump a wall and hedge, cutting himself severely on the near foreleg, just above the knee. The wound extended two to three inches and would clearly leave a scar as long as the horse lived. John Morris Girling,[18] a veterinary surgeon, attended the colt and returned to examine him on one or two occasions, instructing Pinney to administer the necessary remedies.

At the end of January Pinney returned the colt to Higgins at The George.[19] Odell, who had been away attending some fairs, next saw the colt in February, being exercised by Higgins' man, Chapman, at Vigo Cottage,[20] the house that Higgins shared with his two cousins. He was also, for a very short time, at Davis's, a coachmaker in Northampton. Since Odell had last seen the colt, which had been at Worley's, in early January, he noticed the wound on its near foreleg, which Higgins informed him had been caused by jumping a hedge at Worley's. Higgins wanted some place where he could turn out the colt and enquired of Odell if he knew of a suitable paddock. Odell suggested Mr Sanders, Mr Elwes or Benyon Drage, but none of these appeared suitable to Higgins. He eventually made an agreement with Mr Markham,[21] a Northampton solicitor, for the use of his paddock and the colt was taken there by Thomas

Field, who had been engaged by Higgins to take care of the colt. On about 25 June the colt, while trying to jump over a wall at Markham's paddock, met with a similar accident, and in the same place as that incurred at Worley's, although not as serious as the first injury. Girling again attended the colt and the remedies were applied by Field.

Following the accident the colt was taken to The Rose and Crown[22] to recover from the injury. Whilst there, Benyon Drage,[23] who also knew both Goodman and Higgins, was taken by the latter to see the colt for the first time. Higgins, pointing out the large wound on the near foreleg, just above the knee, informed Drage that he was a thoroughbred: his sire Gladiator, and dam by Capsicum out of Acklam Lass. The colt remained at The Rose and Crown for about a week before returning to Markham's paddock, to be broken by Richard Watson, for which Higgins paid him two guineas. The colt remained at Markham's paddock until 21 September 1842, when Higgins, for a single sovereign, requested Watson to take the colt to London. The journey took Watson three days, stopping the first night at Woburn and the second night at St Albans before arriving at Haines's Livery Stables at Foley Place, where he delivered the colt to George Rayner, Haines's foreman.

The following day Goodman met Watson at his Chapel Street Mews stables and asked if he would take the Gladiator colt and a brown filly (probably the filly by Muley Muloch out of Melody) to Smith's at Epsom, but he declined on account of the colt having kicked him on the knee. Goodman suggested that he ride the filly and lead the colt, but Watson said the colt would not suffer himself to be led and he declined. Watson left London at 2 o'clock that day and Goodman placed under his charge a filly foal, requesting him to deliver it to Roade station, Northampton.[24]

The Gladiator colt remained at Goodman's Chapel Street Mews stables until 27 September 1842, when he was taken by William Drewett to William Smith's at Epsom. Despite being supposedly broken by Richard Watson, the colt was extremely wild and would not bear a rider on his back.

5

Gladiator, The Saddler, The Capsicum Mare and Mab

The field for the Derby of 1836 was one of exceptional quality. Bred by Lord Jersey and trained by Tiny Edwards, the winner was the highly strung, bad-tempered, some may even say vicious, Bay Middleton. Before he had even set foot on a racecourse superlatives were lavished on him and he was backed at 8 to 1 for the Derby. His first race (he did not run as a two-year-old) was the Riddlesworth Stakes at the Newmarket Craven Meeting. He easily beat his five opponents, which included Destiny, who was to win the One Thousand Guineas. As expected, he won the Two Thousand Guineas, beating Lord George Bentinck's Elis, who was to subsequently win the St Leger.

Then came the Derby. Bay Middleton was a strong favourite, despite the circulation of detrimental rumours – possibly attributed to his malevolent behaviour. His most formidable opponent appeared to be Danebury's Venison, a son of Partisan, who had finished second to The Athenian in the two-year-old Lavant Stakes at Goodwood. Also in the field was Lord Wilton's Gladiator, an unraced son of Partisan, trained by John Scott and ridden by his brother, Will. Scott had already trained three Derby winners and had considerable confidence in Gladiator.

Edward Moorhouse, in his book *The Romance of the Derby*, records that, after several false starts and considerable delay, a more unsatisfactory start was never witnessed. The Athenian obstinately refused to start, and Gladiator and another two were a considerable distance in the rear. Rounding Tattenham Corner, it was evident that Robinson was riding Bay Middleton with great confidence. At the distance Gladiator, having recovered from his poor start, went up to him, but the favourite had no difficulty in shaking him off and won easily by a couple of lengths.[1]

The performance of Gladiator reflected the Scotts's confidence in him, and maybe a more even start could have yielded a different result. Several of the jockeys believed that the horses ought to have been recalled. Will Scott, on Gladiator, was the worst sufferer, as he did not realise that the start had been initiated until the field had gone some distance.

A favourite for the St Leger, Gladiator proved difficult to train owing to lameness, and he retired to stud at The Lodge, Malton.

Gladiator was the antithesis of Bay Middleton. Whereas Bay Middleton was a long-time disappointment at stud, although he did eventually sire a really good horse, in The Flying Dutchman, and another Derby winner, Andover, Gladiator was one of the outstanding stallions of the nineteenth century.

Bred in Yorkshire by George Walker, Gladiator was by Partisan out of the good race mare, Pauline. He was a very bloodlike dark chestnut, standing at 15.3 hands, and much admired for his shape and vigour. He was said to possess a strong frame with much scope, had good feet and was described as 'the ideal of the handsome and powerful racehorse',[2] yet rather delicate, requiring remarkable nicety in his preparation. John and William Scott gave £100 for him and sold him to Lord Wilton for £200, with a contingency of half of the Derby and St Leger stakes money should he have won either.

Gladiator's sire, Partisan, was a bright bay, by Walton out of Parasol by Pot8O's. Bred by the Duke of Grafton, he stood at 15.2 hands and was said to be 'very muscular in form, without heaviness'. The Druid (pen-name of Henry Hall Dixon) writes of him as a 'beautiful short-legged horse, with a lovely head, straight hocks, and a somewhat clubby off fore-foot'. The trainers of his era were said to refer to him unanimously 'with much fondness, as being like a piece of machinery in his action'.

Although blessed with abundant speed, he was considered backwards at three but much improved at four, when he defeated such good horses as Bourbon (bay colt 1811 Sorcerer), winner of Newmarket's Claret Stakes. He was entered for the Derby but his trainer, Robert Robson, could not get him properly prepared owing to the length and severity of the previous winter. At stud he got the Derby winner, Mameluke (bay colt 1824); Two Thousand Guineas winner, Patron (chestnut colt 1826); One Thousand Guineas winner, Zeal (bay filly 1818); and Oaks winner Cyprian (bay filly 1833).

Gladiator's dam, Pauline (bay filly 1826), was by the Derby winner Moses out of Quadrille by Selim. Pauline was bred by

George Payne, who had inherited Sulby Hall in Northamptonshire and £300,000 in cash and securities. His profligacy was well known in Crockford's and other London clubs, where his inheritance soon drained away. Sulby Hall was sold to Lord Overstone and Pauline was sold to George Walker, who also acquired her dam, Quadrille.

Gladiator was not initially a great success at stud. The infamous Running Rein (Maccabeus) was from his first crop. His best runners were Napier (chestnut colt 1840), who won the Buckingham Palace Stakes at Ascot and the Liverpool St Leger; Prizefighter (chestnut colt 1840), winner of the Great Yorkshire Stakes and third to Nutwith and Cotherstone, beaten by a head and a neck in a tremendous race for the St Leger; and Sweetmeat (brown colt 1842), winner of numerous races including the Queen's Vase and Doncaster Cup, beating the great northern race mare, Alice Hawthorn. Sweetmeat was also his best stallion son in England, being the sire of the Derby winner, Macaroni, who was in turn the sire of Lily Agnes, dam of Ormonde, arguably the greatest racehorse of the nineteenth century.

Gladiator's best daughters were Miss Sarah (bay filly 1842), winner of the Great Yorkshire Stakes and Park Hill Stakes, third in the Oaks and second in the St Leger; Hope (chestnut filly 1842), second in the Oaks; and Dacia (chestnut filly 1845), winner of the Cambridgeshire and second in the Cesarewitch.

Sent to England in 1846 to purchase stallions by the French government, Monsieur de Place, equerry to Louis-Philippe, saw Gladiator at Dean's Hill, Stafford, and was much taken with his elasticity and muscular development. M. de Place had first looked at Lanercost, but Mr Kirby had refused his offer of 3,000 guineas; however, after an initial hesitation, Colonel Anson accepted his offer of £2,000 for Gladiator, and M. de Place secured for France what was to become one of the best bargains of the century.

During his ten years at Haras du Pin, until his death in 1857, Gladiator became one of the most influential sires of the nineteenth century, and although his male line died out his name still appears in most pedigrees to this day. The first of any note sired by him was Fitz-Gladiator, a fair racehorse but more so a tremendously influential stallion, who was the sire of Gabrielle d'Estrees (chestnut filly 1858), winner of the Prix du Jockey Club; Gontran (chestnut colt 1862), winner of the Prix du Jockey Club and the Poule d'Essai for colts; and Nicolet (bay colt 1864), winner of the Poule d'Essai for colts. A grandson of Fitz-Gladiator, Saxifrage (chestnut colt 1872), sired several classic winners, including three winners of the Prix du Cadran and the brilliant Tenebreuse (bay filly 1884), winner of the Poule d'Essai for fillies, Grand Prix de Paris and the Cesarewitch. Other notable Gladiator colts were Celebrity (chestnut colt 1851) and Ventre St Gris (bay colt 1855), who both won the Prix du Jockey Club – in the latter's case his first and only race; and Brocoli (bay colt 1855), winner of the Poule d'Essai for colts.

Gladiator produced some wonderful fillies. Honesty (chestnut filly 1851), Mademoiselle de Chantilly (bay filly 1854) and Surprise (bay filly 1857) all won the Prix Diane. Surprise was the dam of Sornette (chestnut filly 1867), one of best fillies of the nineteenth century, winning the Grand Criterium, the Prix Diane and the Grand Prix de Paris. Sadly, poor Sornette suffered from extreme nervousness. Even before her career started she got away from her lad and escaped into the forest, where she was lost for two days. When she finished her racing career and entered the Haras de Villebon it became apparent that she had lost none of her juvenile habits. Set at liberty, she bolted off across her field in such an excited state that she staked herself and died almost instantaneously – a tremendous loss to the French breeding industry.[3]

By far the most famous of Gladiator's grandsons was Gladiateur (bay colt 1862) by Monarque out of Miss Gladiator. Taunton describes him as rough looking and angular, without any quality; but, amongst his Derby competitors, he stood out like a giant in the midst of pygmies. The Druid remarked, 'With his flying mane and hairy heels, he towered above them like a king.'[4] He was, indeed, one of the great racehorses of the nineteenth century, winning the Triple Crown and the Grand Prix de Paris. Despite his ability on the racecourse, he was, surprisingly, a failure as a stallion.

Had M. de Place arrived in England a couple of years later, it is probable that Gladiator would have been beyond his reach. In 1843 he sired a bay filly out of a mare by the Derby winner, Plenipotentiary. She ran only once, falling in a race at Chester. Unconvincing she may have been as a racehorse, but there never was a matriarch who left such an indelible mark on the Turf through her own produce and that of her descendants, as did Queen Mary.

Bred at Stockton-on-Tees by the well-respected and popular

northern breeder, George Skipsey, The Saddler, sire of the genuine Running Rein, by Waverley out of Castrellina, was a full brother to the good stallion, The Bard (bay colt 1833). He was sold as a three-year-old for £3,000 to Mr Wagstaff and later to George Osbaldeston.

He won one of his two starts as a two-year-old in 1830, a 200 sovereigns sweepstake at Northallerton, beating Lady Fractious (grey filly 1828 Comus), Mr Walker's Victoire (chestnut filly Whisker) and Lady Elizabeth (bay filly 1828 Lottery).

In 1831 he won the York St Leger, defeating several good winners, and the next day he won The Short Stakes, beating Lord Cleveland's Chorister (bay colt 1828 Lottery). In August at York, after a terrific struggle, he won sweepstakes of 30 sovereigns each, beating Lord Scarborough's Brother to Tarrare (bay colt 1828 Catton) and Lady Elizabeth (bay filly 1828 Lottery), winner that year of the Gold Cup at Richmond. Chorister took the shine out of him in the St Leger, Taunton even suggesting that he showed a little of the white feather, with the race almost won. He then won the Doncaster Cup, beating Mr Riddell's Emancipation (bay colt 1827 Whisker), the Hon. E. Petre's Rowton (chestnut colt 1826 Oiseau) and Mr Beardsworth's Birmingham (brown colt 1827 Filho da Puta), the latter two both being St Leger winners. The following day he won a £320 sweepstake, beating Colwick (bay colt 1828 Filho da Puta). He ran without success in his only other engagement that year.

In 1832 he lost a 200 sovereigns match over a half-mile course at Newmarket to Crutch (chestnut colt 1828 Little John), who was regarded as the top sprinter of his day. At the same meeting he won a 500 sovereigns match, beating Hedworth Williamson's Protocol (grey colt 1828 Partisan). At Ascot he fared less well, finishing third in the Oatlands to Rowton (chestnut colt 1826) and third in the Cup to Camarine (chestnut filly 1828 Juniper) after running a dead heat with Rowton. He was then purchased by Mr Osbaldeston.

In 1833 he started seven times. At Newmarket he won a 50 sovereigns each sweepstake, then lost a 100 sovereigns match to the Goodwood Cup winner, Rubini (chestnut colt 1828 St Patrick), and at Doncaster he lost the Fitzwilliam Stakes to Tomboy (bay colt 1829 Jerry) and the Cup to Rockingham (bay colt 1830 Humphrey Clinker). He also ran three times at Heaton Park, ridden by his owner.

In 1834 he won his first race, a match for 200 sovereigns at Newmarket, beating Lord Chesterfield's good runner, Glaucus (bay colt 1830 Partisan). He then finished unplaced for the Goodwood Cup, won by Lord Jersey's Two Thousand Guineas winner, Glencoe (chestnut colt 1831 Sultan), and ran third to Colonel Peel's Nonsense (chestnut colt 1830 Bedlamite) for the Richmond Plate, which was his last race.

Well regarded in the stud, he sired the One Thousand Guineas and Park Hill Stakes winner, Sorella (chestnut filly 1841), who in turn produced the Magyar Egyesitett Nemzeti es Hazafi dij winners, Sabine (chestnut filly 1858 Frantic) and Sagitta (chestnut filly 1862 Arsenal) and also appears as the ninth dam of the July Cup winner, Sir Cosmo (brown colt 1926 The Boss). The Saddler also sired the Woodcote Stakes winner Miles's Boy (bay colt 1844) and the Manchester Cup winner Sylvan (bay colt 1845). His daughters produced the Two Thousand Guineas and Great Yorkshire Stakes winner, Pitsford (chestnut colt 1847 Epirus), the One Thousand Guineas winner, Habena (chestnut filly 1852 Birdcatcher), the Doncaster Cup winner, Hungerford (chestnut colt 1848 John o' Gaunt), the Cesarewitch winner, Vengeance (bay colt 1852 Chanticleer), and the Magyar Kancadij winners, Margarite (chestnut filly 1851 John Bull) and Parva (bay filly 1852 Tourist), the former also a winner in the Egyesitett Nemzeti es Hazafi dij. He is also seen as the sire of the sixth dam of The Boss (chestnut colt 1910 Orby).

The Saddler died in 1847 in passage to Ostend on his way to Bohemia.

The Capsicum mare, dam of Maccabeus, was bred by Mr R. Hudson in 1823, her dam, Acklam Lass by Prime Minister, out of Young Harriet, by Camilus. Probably owing to her lack of a name, she was sometimes referred to as Pepper's dam, her bay filly by St Nicholas. She had the distinction of being the only mare ever to have two sons (Running Rein and Croton Oil) running in the same Derby! None of her offspring gained any distinction on the Turf.

The dam of the genuine Running Rein, Mab, had a similarly undistinguished career. She was covered by the Derby winner Pyrrhus the First and exported to France in 1853. She died in 1857.

6
Enter Goneaway

Goodman recognised that, as he had to run the Gladiator colt – which had now been renamed Maccabeus – as Running Rein in two-year-old races, he would be unable to run in his own name in three-year-old races. If no appearance was made, questions might be raised: certainly Sir Charles Ibbetson would be interested in his absence. But Goodman had a stroke of genius. So daring was his concept that, if the substitution was successful, it occurred to him that it would be possible not only to win the Derby in 1844 but also the preceding and succeeding ones. The plan was to acquire another horse to impersonate Maccabeus.

How was Goodman going to achieve this? It is clear that the impersonator had to bear some resemblance to Maccabeus. Maybe the link was James Jaques, who at times worked for Henry Higgins. He also trained and rode for Thomas Ferguson, a former Irish linen worker and racehorse owner. Maybe, just maybe, in quiet conversation, Higgins somewhat disguisedly mentioned to Jaques their plan and Jaques suggested that Ferguson's horse, Goneaway, could be a likely candidate.

Thomas Ferguson, owner of the famous Harkaway, was at Liverpool races in July 1842 to see his horse Fireaway, ridden by James Jaques, win the Liverpool St Leger. Goodman was also at the meeting and met Ferguson. It is quite probable that as part of his audacious scheme he deliberately sought Ferguson out. One can imagine the mind of 'the wily Jew with several ugly blots and not a few mysteries to account for' (as described by one contemporary) working, as he enquired of Ferguson the colour of his horse Goneaway.[1] Ferguson, probably mystified and obviously unaware of Goodman's plan, replied that he was a bay horse and had a white heel and white star. This is probably exactly what Goodman wanted to hear. Although Goneaway's record was far from impressive, having run only once as a two-year-old, in the name of Mr Whittle in the 1841 Anglesey Stakes, finishing unplaced to Ballinkeele, he was a full brother to Harkaway (who was a chestnut). Goodman had obviously done his homework in securing his four-year-old to impersonate Maccabeus.

Despite his coarse appearance - in fact he looked more like a carthorse than the splendid racer he was, it was when in action that Harkaway's remarkable powers were seen, and the apparent ease to himself with which he galloped, his vast stride and his great rate of going were truly wonderful. If Goneaway were half as good as Harkaway, as a four-year-old, he would probably be good enough to win a Derby. Goodman then asked for the hire of him for 12 months and the terms contained in the following agreement, which was not actually signed until January 1843, were agreed:

Memorandum of Agreement between A.L.Goodman and Thomas Ferguson from the 20th September 1842 to 20th September 1843.
A.L.Goodman gives Thomas Ferguson Five Hundred Pounds for the use or hire of his bay colt called Goneaway, 3 years old, and half of all cups, stakes and public money that the horse may win from September 20th 1842 to 20th September 1843 and then to be returned by A.L.Goodman to Thomas Ferguson. Signed A.L.Goodman.[2]

Mr Ferguson confirmed that there was also a person by the name of Bond with Goodman when he made the agreement. It is not inconceivable that this was Joseph Bond, brother of the notorious Ephraim (who had passed away a year or so earlier), owner of the Athenæum Club. They were typical of persons with whom Goodman would be associated and were not to be trifled with. As an example, Thormanby[3] relates an occasion when Lord Chesterfield lost £5,000. He gave the Bonds his cheque, but when it was presented at Lord Chesterfield's bank they were informed that Lord Chesterfield had given instructions that it was not to be paid. The Bonds immediately repaired to his lordship's abode, where, by persuasive means, they obtained admission to the anteroom to his lordship's bedchamber. The unsuspecting defaulter, sauntering from his room, was to his surprise confronted by the Bonds, who demanded payment. The indignant Earl questioned their impudence and threatened to have them evicted, furiously ringing his bell. But Ephraim Bond, an ex-prizefighter, counter-threatened, stating that he assumed his lordship was only summoning for a glass of water, otherwise he would find himself through the window and into the courtyard below. Chesterfield was no doubt petrified and promptly paid up, as it is almost certain that Ephraim Bond would have carried out his threat.

Before Ferguson sent the horse from Ireland he received a letter from Goodman requesting him to send some of the black hair from Goneaway's leg.[4] Ferguson unquestionably complied. But were his suspicions not aroused: firstly by the question of colour, and now the supply of black hairs from his leg?

Goodman was, if anything, meticulous in his preparation, even resorting to sourcing the correct colour of black dye in order to stain Goneaway's white heel, which he managed to obtain from Louis Rossi, a hairdresser and perfumier, who resided at 254 Regent Street.[5] It is possible that the recommendation to use Rossi came from Adam Glenn, one of Goodman's conspirators, a biscuit maker whose business was at 106 Regent Street.[6]

Ferguson brought Goneaway to Liverpool on 6 January 1843 and met Goodman on the quay. The horse was taken to the Kings Arms and Ferguson and Goodman went to the Mersey Coffee House, where Goodman paid Ferguson £400 and an IOU for £100. Ferguson left the horse with Goodman and returned to Dublin.[7]

Goneaway was first taken to Goodman's stables in London, where it was likely that Goneaway's heel was dyed to make him look a little more like Maccabeus. He was then moved to Hallmead Farm at Sutton, arriving on Tuesday 10 January, accompanied by another horse by the name of Railroad. They were both placed under the care of William Carlin, who had entered service as head groom with Goodman at Hallmead Farm, Sutton, on 2 January 1843. Goneaway's name was unknown to Carlin, who recognised him only as a bay horse, at least 15.3 hands, with a long, bushy, square, heavy tail, which reached nearly to his hocks.[8]

On the Thursday Goodman ordered Carlin to prepare the horse for physic.[9] They had given him two doses in London but could not get either of them to work. Carlin accordingly prepared the horse and gave him a dose of aloes. The physic worked well, but there was no appearance of the two doses lying in him.

The horse, which was then known as Maccabeus (Goneaway), remained with Carlin for about two weeks, before being sent to Stockbridge to be trained for the Derby by William Sadler. Carlin rode Maccabeus (Goneaway) to Kingston, accompanied by Sadler, who road Railroad. He was put in a box and left with William

Sadler, for Stockbridge, and Carlin returned to Sutton with Railroad.

Goodman's disfiguration of Goneaway was completed at Sadler's, by docking his tail. He had engaged John Day junior to ride Maccabeus (Goneaway) in the Derby. Day rode him in a gallop about a fortnight before the Epsom Spring Meeting. When he returned from the gallop, Goodman, surprisingly showing some conscience for the welfare of the horse, asked Day if it hurt young horses to dock their tails previous to a race. Day replied that it didn't. Goodman then asked if it hurt older ones, to which Day again replied that it didn't. Goodman then said: "'Well I think I shall have this horse's tail taken off,'"[10] and he requested Day to do it, which he carried out in the stable.

Day later confessed that he thought it was strange that Goodman should have his tail docked so near to a race. Although it was not an uncommon practice to dock horses' tails, this was normally carried out in October, when they were yearlings. He had asked Goodman why he wanted it done, to which Goodman replied that he would just like to have it done.

Day was of the opinion that the horse was an older one. He had occasion to look into his mouth at the time of docking his tail and he saw that he had tushes.[11] Day queried this with Goodman, who replied, "Oh, it is very common for a three-year-old to have tushes."[12] And Sadler also dismissed it, as he was prepared to accept Goodman's declaration that the horse was of the correct age, and that Sir Charles Ibbetson had also been down to see him and confirmed he was the horse he had bred.

Goodman could not pull the wool over John Day's eyes. Day was a qualified veterinary surgeon and passed on his suspicions to his father, informing him that he would not ride Maccabeus (Goneaway) in the Derby, as he was more than three years old. Instead, he would bet against him, as he did not believe that Maccabeus (Goneaway) would be permitted to run. Hargreaves obliged him, taking a bet of £200 to £3,200.[13]

7
The Epsom Spring Meeting

At around the end of 1842 Higgins informed Odell that the Gladiator colt, which he and Goodman were overseeing together, had gone to London. They had named him Maccabeus and he was entered for the Derby. Higgins said that he would take 200 to 10 for him and strongly recommended that Odell should take it. Odell accepted the offer and authorised Higgins to take the bet for him.[1]

Worley had not seen the Gladiator colt since it had left his premises in January 1842. Whilst out hunting in March the following year, Higgins told Worley that he had changed the name of the Gladiator colt to Maccabeus and proposed to Worley that he should 'stand in about Maccabeus'. Worley's understanding of 'stand in' was that he was not to know the horse and that he would receive a sum of money if the horse won. At that moment the hounds found and the conversation was dropped, but Worley suspected that some trick was to be played.[2]

Maccabeus (Goneaway), had not run as a two-year-old, but during the spring of 1843, on reports of his having been very highly tried at Stockbridge by his trainer Sadler, he became greatly fancied for the Derby; and it was reported that Goodman and his party had backed him for the Derby to win near on £100,000.

As a precursor to the Derby, Goneaway, impersonating Maccabeus, was entered at the Epsom Spring Meeting, for a £50 plate, given by Sir Gilbert Heathcote, added to sweepstakes of five sovereigns each: three-year-olds 7st and four-year-olds 9st, one mile, with 13 subscribers. Goodman and his associates had regarded defeat as so impossible that he was backed at 7 to 4 on – a remarkably short price in a field of 13. There were several in Goodman's party, some of whom may not have been able to restrain their tongues. John Day had passed on his suspicions to his father, and one must wonder to what extent his intentions had evaporated into the bookmaking fraternity. Higgins had already told Benyon Drage that the horse that was to run for Maccabeus was a four-year-old, and that his leg and foot had been stained.[3]

Benyon Drage attended the Epsom Spring Meeting with Higgins and visited William Smith's house. Goodman and William Sadler were also there and they went to Smith's stables to see the horse that was to run for Maccabeus. Drage realised that it was not the horse that Higgins had kept at Northampton, and Higgins later informed Drage that it was Mr Ferguson's horse, Goneaway, and that the horse was dead.[4]

Of course, Ferguson was oblivious as to what was going on with his horse.

William Carlin was also at the meeting. It was the first time that he had seen Maccabeus (Goneaway) since he had taken him to Kingston, with William Sadler, and he could scarcely believe that it was the same horse, so disfigured was his tail, which had been pulled and made to look like a cat's tail.

He was to be ridden by John Day's apprentice, John Howlett, who had also heard rumours regarding the horse's age and had expressed a reluctance to ride him if he was a four-year-old. But Goodman and Sadler's son reassured him that he was a three-year-old.[5]

Several other Derby entrants were on show, so that something like a measure might be taken of two or three of the favourites, and the meeting attracted a full attendance of sporting men of all classes.

The horses were saddled in front of the Grand Stand, and, as 'no false starts' was the order of the day, some time elapsed before they were assembled at the post in an orderable manner. At the word 'go' Patchwork and Maccabeus (Goneaway), went away nearly abreast, followed by Captain Flathooker, St Jean d'Acre and Conquest. In fact, all were laid up except Sirikol, who sprang right across the course immediately on leaving the post and was some lengths astern of the body of horses until they were nearly into the straight.

As the field approached Tattenham Corner, Conquest had taken the inner ground and, probably pressed by the horses on her right, pushed against the railing chains. The chains giving way to the pressure, she lost the straight line and met the corner of the first post with tremendous force, striking it with her chest. As a result, she rebounded into Spiteful's path, causing the horse to fall over her. Epaulette, who had been in their track, jumped over Spiteful but fell immediately after and threw her jockey. The consequences of this accident were that Conquest died within a few minutes, and her rider, Walter Day, was badly cut about the arm and knee. W. Balchin and Evans, the riders of the other mares, were also bruised but were able to ride in the next race. Meanwhile, the race proceeded. Patchwork, who had till then kept his head in advance of the favourite, gave way halfway round the turn, and Maccabeus (Goneaway) went on with the running. Captain Flathooker waited on him to the road, where he reached his girths. He maintained that position until four or five lengths of the chair and then, making his final effort, defeated Maccabeus (Goneaway) by a long neck - cleverly, but not without a touch of Mann's spur. Sirikol made up a good deal of lost ground after crossing the road, passing St Jean D'Acre inside the distance, but was beaten by two or three lengths of the winner. Behind him were Courage (fourth), St Jean d'Acre (fifth) and the Morello filly (sixth), with an interval of about a length between each. The others were beaten off by a long way. Epaulette and Spiteful, after dislodging their riders, ran the course through without any further accident.

The outcome hit Goodman's party like a thunderbolt. Goneaway was a four-year-old (substituting for Maccabeus, a three-year-old) in receipt of two stone from Captain Flathooker, also a four-year-old, and considered to be of limited ability. As one scribe put it: '... not backed for a shilling'.[6] As a consequence, 33 to 1 was readily available on Maccabeus (Goneaway) for the Derby, and on the showing of Sir Gilbert Heathcote's Sirikol, who was thought to be at least seven pounds inferior to Amorino, £500 was laid on the latter to beat Cotherstone.

Worley met Higgins at the Derby and enquired as to the whereabouts of Maccabeus, to which Higgins replied that he was ill and could not run.

Thomas Ferguson returned to England at the end of May with his filly Fanny Callaghan, who had been entered for the Oaks. He met Goodman on the Friday before the Derby and dined and stayed at Hallmead Farm that night. Goodman invited Ferguson into the stables to see the horses, mentioning that Goneaway would be returning to Sutton the following day.

He showed Ferguson a stout, bay horse, who was then eating grass. Ferguson described the horse as having rather a coarse but still good head; a lengthy horse with strong quarters, a good-shaped horse all over, about 15 hands and an inch or inch and a half. Goodman told him, "That is Maccabeus and I mean to run him next year for the Derby," and he asked Ferguson if he thought him similar to Goneaway.[7]

Whilst they were in Running Rein's (Maccabeus's) box, Joseph Anderson, one of Goodman's associates, drove up. The bell rang and Carlin, Goodman's head groom, went into the stable to inform Goodman that Anderson had arrived. For some reason Goodman did not wish Anderson to know that Ferguson was there, and he shut Ferguson in the stable. (It is probable that Goodman wished to maintain as much discretion as possible. Only Goodman and Higgins knew the details of the fraud. Had Anderson met Ferguson, any resulting discussion could have proved embarrassing for Goodman.)

Ferguson remained in the stable for about 15 minutes and took the opportunity to take a good look at the horse. He examined his mouth as well as he could, the horse being rather playful and difficult to control. In Ferguson's judgement, the horse was then three years old. He further commented that Maccabeus had a peculiar-looking head and a mark on one of his forelegs - the result of the accidents incurred whilst at Worley's farm and Markham's paddock.

When Goodman returned he showed Ferguson a colt, which he said was by The Saddler and he planned to run him the year after, meaning that he would run Maccabeus in 1844 and The Saddler colt in 1845. The colt was rather more of a brown – a little darker than Maccabeus. Ferguson visited Goodman at Hallmead Farm about three times during this period, recalling that he saw The Saddler colt on the lawn each day.[8]

William Carlin recalled that Maccabeus (Goneaway) returned to Hallmead Farm on the Saturday afternoon, in a van drawn by post horses, and that Sadler and one of his boys, Tollard, had brought him.

When Ferguson went to see Goneaway he was in for a shock. Goodman took him into the stable and, pointing to a horse, asked him if he knew who it was. Ferguson recognised him immediately as Goneaway, but his tail had been cut and his foot and near-hind pastern had been dyed black. Ferguson replied: "'To be sure. I would know him anywhere. But damn you, you have cut his tail off and what do you mean by that? You might as well cut his head off, or his leg off, and say that would not hurt him."' Ferguson was livid at what Goodman had done to his horse. The leg and foot had been dyed so well that Ferguson had difficulty in telling one from the other and he asked Goodman how he had done it, to which Goodman replied, "'Oh, it was very easy.'"[9]

Surprisingly and, one might think, rather foolishly for someone previously considered astute, Goodman told Ferguson that he was going to run him in the Derby for Maccabeus and that, although the horse had been amiss, he believed he would run pretty well.

Ferguson could not believe Goodman's fraudulent proposal and asked, "'How can you do that? Lord Miltown and Mr Latouche know the horse as well as I do, and if they ask me if it is not my horse Goneaway, I will not tell an untruth for any man living.'" Goodman explained that Lord George Bentinck, who knew Goneaway, had seen the horse at William Sadler's and did not recognise him, and queried why he should say anything about him: "'If anyone asks you, say you have him.'" However, Ferguson was determined not to withhold the truth if anyone asked him, so Goodman reluctantly abandoned his intention of running him for the Derby.[10]

Goodman, of course, was still the lessee of Goneaway and wasn't one to pass up a financial opportunity, so he declared that after the Epsom races he would run the horse at Newmarket and win a great stake on him. He invited Ferguson to go shares with him, but Ferguson declined to have anything to do with financial gains obtained in that way. As far as Ferguson was concerned, the horse was good enough to win plenty of money in a fair way and, if Goodman attempted to play that game, he would not wager a shilling on the horse. In view of Ferguson's uncooperative stance, Goodman told him that he might as well take the horse away, which Ferguson accordingly agreed to do.

Goodman was in for a shock, as Ferguson informed him that before he returned home with Goneaway he was going to enter the horse for the Goodwood Cup and would win it with him if Goneaway continued to improve. Goodman vigorously remonstrated with Ferguson against entering the horse to run in England under his proper name, as he felt sure that he would be recognised as the horse that Goodman had run as Maccabeus at the Epsom Spring Meeting. Ferguson, however, was unfazed by

Goodman's protestations and did indeed enter him for the Goodwood Cup.

Following Ferguson and Goodman's falling out, and prior to the removal of Goneaway, Ferguson returned to Hallmead Farm. On one occasion Goodman entered the stable whilst Ferguson was looking into Goneaway's mouth and asked, "'What are you doing that for?'"

"'I thought you might be playing tricks with his teeth as well as his tail,'" Ferguson annoyingly replied.

"'I knocked the tusks out of him but they are springing again. I have a machine for the purpose and it is easily done,'" Goodman cynically responded.[11]

Armed with this information, one would have thought that Ferguson would have made it known to the stewards – or the newspapers. Had he done so, the fraud would have been nipped in the bud. Surprisingly, however, he collected his horse and returned to Ireland without a murmur.

A van drawn by post horses, provided by William Andrews at The Greyhound in Sutton and driven by the post boy James Dewdney, arrived at about 2 o'clock on the morning of 7 June, to collect Goneaway for what was to be the beginning of his tragic journey. Carlin assisted in loading Goneaway, whom he still believed to be Maccabeus, into the van, and, accompanied by one of Goodman's servants, the horse was taken to a livery stable in Foley Place, where he was fed. Ferguson then accompanied the van to Euston Square station and paid Dewdney for the horses.

At Liverpool the van was loaded onto the Railway and Steam Packet Company's steamer, *Britannia*, trading between Liverpool and Dublin. It left Liverpool at about 6 o'clock that evening, on what was to be an extremely rough passage. Poor Goneaway, having suffered at the hands of Goodman, was now to experience the ravages of Neptune. The terrified horse plunged and kicked, as the vessel, which suffered the loss of its foremast, rolled with the storm. James Taylor, a steward on the *Britannia*, called Mr Ferguson, but nothing could be done to control the frightened animal.[12] The vessel finally arrived in Dublin at about 8.40 on the evening of 8 June.

Dominick Holland, who had previously worked for Ferguson and had taken care of Goneaway during 1842, so knew the horse very well, now worked for Mr Dycer in Dublin and was in charge of the stallion Barkston. It was Barkston who had also covered Fanny Dawson, and he may have been the sire of Goneaway. He recollected that one night, between 12 o'clock and 1 o'clock, Goneaway was dragged up from Dublin harbour on a float and was brought to him at Mr Dycer's veterinary repository in Dublin. Holland was raised from his bed by Ferguson, who had brought the horse up himself, with the aid of some sailors. The horse was lying on the float, soaking wet, weak and so stiff that he was unable to stand. The float was backed to the stable door and then, with the assistance of the sailors, was dragged into the stables.[13] Poor Goneaway never recovered from his ordeal and died between 8 and 9 o'clock the same morning. He was sold to the carrion butcher for five shillings – hardly a fitting end for any racehorse, irrespective of its ability.

Back at Hallmead Farm, Goodman drove into the yard about a week later, declaring that Maccabeus (Goneaway) was dead and that he had died at Bedford.

Shortly after the Derby, Worley, Odell and Higgins were dining at the Kings Arms in Northampton and the topic of conversation turned to Maccabeus. Odell asked Higgins what had become of the colt, to which Higgins replied that he was dead, saying that Sadler had poisoned him! Odell remonstrated, "'Then I have lost £10 and you must put me in something to get it back again.'" Higgins, attempting to pacify Odell's anger, said that he had got another horse, by The Saddler, and if Odell would be guided by him he would make him all right.

Higgins, accompanied by Odell, called on Worley during July. Talking horses, Worley produced the *Guide to the Turf*. On looking down the Derby entries for 1844, Higgins, pointing to the entry of Mr Goodman's Running Rein by The Saddler out of Mab, exclaimed, "'I can tell you who will win the Derby next year.'" Worley immediately suspected that it was the horse he had kept for Higgins and Goodman and expressed his outrage: "'Damn it, Henry, I think that was my horse.'" Higgins hesitated a while and then at last acknowledged: "'There are only us three present. It is the colt you had but that is to go no further.'"[14]

8

Maccabeus Masquerades as Running Rein

Goodman's campaign for Running Rein (Maccabeus) began in October 1842, when he personally gave instructions to James Manning[1] at Weatherbys to enter Running Rein for the Clearwell Stakes at the Second October Meeting at Newmarket in 1843, and also for the Two Thousand Guineas to be run at the First Newmarket Spring Meeting in 1844, although it is unlikely that Goodman had any intention of running him in the latter. Running Rein (Maccabeus) was now firmly ensconced in Smith's stables on the Burgh Heath Road (now known as Priam Lodge)[2] under the care of George Hitchcock, whom Smith had engaged to break him, as Richard Watson had failed to break him completely whilst at Markham's paddock in Northampton. Also under Hitchcock's care were three other of Goodman's yearlings: Dr Phillimore (chestnut colt 1841 Velocipede), a black filly by Camel out of Minikin and a black filly by Sheet Anchor out of Mrs Fry (later named Mrs Opie).

Hitchcock may have been of the opinion that Running Rein was older than the yearling status that he had been advised, but he was careful to hold his tongue. Hitchcock had previously crossed swords with Smith, when he had suggested a three-year-old half-bred colt may have been a four-year-old, and the latter had taken a horsewhip to him.

William Webb, a Newmarket man, had joined Smith as head lad in November 1842 and had overall care of Running Rein after Hitchcock had broken him. Webb described him as a fine, remarkably strong colt, straight on his legs and feet, with large arms and hocks.[3]

On 7 February 1843, as the result of a dispute regarding a bill for £200 that Goodman owed to Smith, the latter ordered Goodman's horses to be taken away. Running Rein (Maccabeus) and the black Camel filly were collected by a man by the name of Cook and taken to Goodman's premises at Sutton, where they were placed under the care of William Carlin. Running Rein remained under Carlin's care until October 1843, when he was taken to Newmarket by Mist, one of Goodman's boys.

The genuine Running Rein enjoyed Bean's hospitality until February 1843,[4] when Goodman sent his servant George White, a short young man who had been ravaged by smallpox, to collect him. Mrs Bean poured a glass of gin and requested Fanny Fage, her maidservant, to give it to George. George, in convivial mood, offered the glass to Fanny, but she declined in case Mrs Bean detected the gin on her breath.

George White took the genuine Running Rein to Hallmead Farm. Goodman informed Carlin that he was a half-bred yearling that had been given to him. He was a very poor and ragged specimen: long in the pastern and he turned his off-fore out considerably. Carlin never heard it called by any name and Goodman did not appear to place any great value on him.[5] The colt was at first quiet and temperate, so Carlin's wife used to attend to him, but he gradually became riotous and masterful with her. He began to look at mares in a manner that Carlin had never known a yearling to do.[6] Carlin suspected that something was wrong with one of his testicles and recommended that Smith have him castrated.[7] This procedure was duly carried out by Mr Coleman, a veterinary surgeon from Cheam, and after this the colt grew. In June Carlin began to break him and he improved surprisingly, although there is no evidence that he was ever put into training.

Nothing more was heard of the genuine Running Rein, with the exception that Goodman had introduced him to Thomas Ferguson as his entry for the 1845 Derby. Neither had any mention been made of Maccabeus, who had been announced as dead, until the Second Newmarket October Meeting. On Monday 9 October the latter, masquerading as Running Rein, made his racecourse debut in a Fifty Pound Plate for two-year-olds. However, before this meeting Higgins had made it known to George Odell that the horse known as Running Rein was Maccabeus, and that the deception that Maccabeus was dead "'was only to keep Mr Worley right'".[8] He also told Benyon Drage that the colt purchased from Dr Cobb was bought for the purpose of being impersonated by the Gladiator colt.

Throughout the year Lord George Bentinck had suspected that Goodman was trying to introduce a ringer, although the reason for his suspicion was not clear. Maybe there had been a few wagging tongues: with so many parties involved, these conspiracies would have been desperately difficult to keep discreet. And Bentinck, as Sylvanus tells us, struck terror into the hearts of the conspirators when, prior to the Second October Meeting, he had met Smith's team on the Heath. Among his lot was Running Rein, whom he immediately pointed out as the older brother of Croton Oil (bay colt Physician-Capsicum mare), his own horse – a three-year-old, knowing him from the likeness of his dam.[9]

Benyon Drage accompanied Higgins to the Second October Meeting at Newmarket and saw Running Rein at exercise, immediately recognising him as the horse he had seen at the Rose and Crown at Northampton. Goodman was also there and, in his presence, Drage pointed to the horse and said that he would take 1,000 to 3 that he would win the Derby. Goodman appeared greatly annoyed at Drage's remark, believing that Higgins had been talking to Drage about the horse. Higgins subsequently told Drage of Goodman's irritation and that he had told Higgins that he was good for nothing and was sure he had been telling Drage about the horse.[10]

The race produced a great deal of speculation. Betting commenced in the morning at 9 and 10 to 1 against Running Rein, but so rapidly did the commissions come into the market that at post-time 3 to 1 was scarcely available. *The Sporting Magazine* recorded that there were some grounds for suspecting that Goodman's horse was a year older than 'he ought to be' to qualify him for a two-year-old race, as he was as well furnished as many bona fide three-year-olds.[11]

In the race there were two false starts, one of them resulting in the Duke of Rutland's Crenoline, who was very restless at the post, bolting nearly half-a-mile before Boyce, her jockey, could bring her under control. In the third, successful start Running Rein took the lead, was never headed and won by three lengths from Crenoline. Buckle rode the winner, who was immediately backed for the Derby at 40 to 1.

After Running Rein's victory The Duke of Rutland, spurred on by Lord George Bentinck, who had been suspicious that Running Rein was a ringer, objected to the winner on the grounds that he was a three-year-old. However, Goodman distinctly denied that there was any foundation for the suspicion raised. As the objection was not made before the race, the onus of proof rested with The Duke of Rutland, and there was some confusion regarding its settling. Captain Rous suggested that bets should be paid 'under protest', which helped to calm the situation somewhat, but payment did not pass over without some unpleasant looks and tolerably broad assertions.

At Higgins's request, Drage had taken on a joint account for himself and Higgins – a bet of 20 to 5 against Running Rein and also an even twenty pounds that Crenoline would not win. The objection was enough for Drage, who knew the horse was over age, and he tried to persuade Higgins to sell his interest in the horse as he would prefer to have nothing more to do with him.[12]

On the following day Running Rein ran again, in the Clearwell Stakes. So certain were the Yorkites of the result that they backed John Scott's Voltri, who was on his first run, down to evens favourite; Running Rein was 3 to 1 and Colonel Peel's filly, Zenobia, 10 to 1.

At starting Running Rein had a slight lead, with Mr Wreford's (bay colt Camel–Wadastra) lying up and Col. Peel's (bay filly Slane–Sea-kale), Goodman's (black filly Camel–Minikin) and Lord George Bentinck's The Devil to pay all in excellent positions, followed by Zenobia. In fact all laid up closely, except the crack, Voltri, who got off well enough but ran raw and awkwardly and did not live with the pace above half-distance and, in the words of one Newmarket trainer, ran as 'slow as a pig'.[13] On getting to the New Ground, Running Rein led Mr Wreford's Wadastra colt and Zenobia. On entering the ropes, Chapple dashed Zenobia past Running Rein and won in a canter by a length from the Camel colt, which came again and defeated Running Rein for second place by a length.

Mr Watt, the owner of Voltri, had objected to Running Rein before the start of the race, but as he did not win the case was not investigated. However, Bentinck was convinced of Goodman's skulduggery – and not without good reason: how could a two-year-old filly beat a three-year-old colt at a difference of only two pounds? He arranged for a veterinary surgeon to examine Running Rein, but Goodman refused to have his horse examined.

The hearing to the Duke of Rutland's objection was postponed for two weeks, until Tuesday 24 October at the Newmarket Houghton Meeting. During these two weeks Lord George Bentinck requested Mr Allen, who had kept Mab and the Capsicum mare at The Lodge in Old Malton Gate, to obtain evidence from Dr. Cobb, the breeder of The Saddler colt, and others who had been involved with him. Mr Allen sought Dr. Cobb's permission to send John Kitchen, the lad who had attended the foaling of the Saddler colt, to Newmarket to attend the hearing. Lord George was out when Kitchen arrived, but his valet looked after him. He was well fed, with bread and cheese and some ale, and was taken to the home of John Kent, Lord George Bentinck's trainer, where he was furnished with quarters for the night.

The following morning the stewards – Lord Stradbroke, Charles Greville, Mr Byng and Mr Thornhill, accompanied by the Duke of Rutland, Goodman, William Smith (who had previously had care of the horse), Lord George Bentinck, Kitchen and Mr Barrow (a veterinary surgeon), went to the Golden Lion stables in Newmarket High Street, to inspect Running Rein. Despite not having seen the colt for almost two years, to the best of his knowledge Kitchen believed that it was The Saddler colt. The Duke of Rutland requested that the horse's mouth should be examined by competent persons, but Goodman refused to permit any examination to be made, instead calling on Bean and other witnesses to support the qualification of the horse. This was a trifle surprising. If Goodman's case was an honest one, why should he refuse to allow such an examination? The investigation could have done no harm whatsoever to Goodman because, even if the examination had indicated that he had the teeth of an older horse, Goodman would still have been able to argue, 'Why, this is all a mistaken judgement on the part of the veterinary surgeon; it is ridiculous to attempt to rely on a notion formed in this way. I have clear distinct evidence with regard to the birth and breeding of the horse, and I can therefore give you satisfactory details respecting it, without resorting to mere opinion and mere speculative judgement.'

At the Jockey Club Rooms Kitchen positively confirmed the identity of Running Rein. The stewards repeatedly urged Goodman to allow the horse's mouth to be examined for the sake of his own character and in order to prevent future objections, the horse having two engagements for the ensuing Spring Meeting, but

Goodman persisted in his refusal to grant permission. The stewards decided that they had no power to compel him to do so, and so the Duke of Rutland's objection was overruled and the stakes were duly paid to Goodman. However, the stewards warned Goodman that he would have to take the consequences of such a refusal, in as much as he would not be allowed to run his horse again unless he acquiesced to such a test.

Unfortunately, the stewards were unaware of an ancient Rule and Order of the Jockey Club, which had been published yearly in the *Racing Calendar* from 1770 to 1818, although omitted thereafter. The Rule stated:

That the Stewards of the Jockey Club shall appoint some proper person to examine every colt or filly, being of the age of two, three or four years, at the Ending Post, immediately after running, the first time any colt or filly shall start for any Plate, Match, Sweepstakes, or Subscription at Newmarket, and the said appointed person is to sign a certificate of such examination, and his opinion thereupon, which certificate is to be hung up before eight o'clock the evening of the said day of running, in the coffee-house at Newmarket. But for all Plates, Matches, Subscriptions, or Sweepstakes, where the colt or filly is required to be shewn before running, the examination as above mentioned shall be made at the time of shewing them, and the certificate of the person appointed shall immediately, in like manner, be fixed up in the coffee-room at Newmarket.

It would appear that this rule had either been repealed or, more likely, fallen into disuse, but had the stewards exercised their powers and enforced an examination of Running Rein's mouth the scandal of the Derby would have been averted. Even though they may have been unaware of this rule, it was not beyond their powers to have introduced a new rule, which they could then implement when considered necessary.

Because of Goodman's refusal to have Running Rein's mouth examined, Bentinck was probably even more convinced of his deception. He may even have formed the opinion that Kitchen was part of the conspiracy. In retrospect, it is not impossible to infer what may have happened. Whatever he was, Goodman was no fool and was more than a match for the apparently witless stewards. He was shrewd enough to realise that, even if the stewards were incompetent, Bentinck certainly wasn't and had realised what was going on. He probably anticipated that Bentinck would procure Kitchen for the inquiry. Even with the gap of two years, it is unlikely that had he been an 'Honest John' Kitchen could have been mistaken in his belief that the shabby, calf-kneed colt at whose birth he was present, could possibly have turned into the fine specimen that was Running Rein. In all probability, through his network of villains (it may even have been Stebbings), Goodman collared Kitchen before the inquiry, cramming him with promises and piecrust, to provide evidence in Goodman's favour.

On the Thursday of the Houghton Meeting, Col. Peel's Zenobia 'walked over' for the 50 Sovereigns Sweepstakes. There were seven subscribers. *The Sporting Magazine* reported that many were hoping to get a further peep at the 'four-year-old' Running Rein, as Goodman facetiously terms him, but were at a loss to know why Mr Goodman paid the forfeit on this occasion for his 'old 'un' was quite well.[14]

After Running Rein returned from the hearing at Newmarket he fell lame. William Webb, who had left Smith's employment at Epsom Races but remained around Epsom and was from time to time employed by Goodman, gave him three doses of aloes at various times. He suspected that Running Rein might be a three-year-old, as he observed that he appeared to be shooting the middle tooth. Unfortunately, he could not positively swear to it, as he did not have the opportunity of examining his mouth in sufficient detail.[15]

So far Goodman's plan had come off triumphantly. His 'four-year-old' had evaded the scrutiny of the stewards and the way was now clear to absorb the generosity of Tattersalls' layers for the Derby: 33 to 1, 20 to 1 – Goodman and his associates took it all. He informed Carlin that he had let Oliver (the steeplechase rider) stand £250 to £5 on the horse for the Derby, and suggested that Carlin should also stand in, but did not say what.[16]

Unlike Bentinck, who had sought all his racing life to win the Derby, Goodman was intent only on landing a massive betting coup. He also probably realised that the Houghton inquiry was a close call and that the rumours circulating about the horse's age were likely to escalate.

With the exception of Lord George, Goodman always seemed to be one jump ahead of the authorities. He had no wish to be the focus of any possible future inquiry and somehow had to divorce himself from Running Rein.

The story that seems to have been perpetuated through Turf history was that, as part of his intrigue, Goodman decided to dispose of his ownership of Running Rein, the ideal candidate being Smith's landlord, Alexander Wood. Goodman was reputedly in debt to Wood, so what better way to liquidate the debt than to suggest to Smith that Wood buy Running Rein in part settlement?

The story continues that, on the good account of the jockey, Jem Chapple, Smith persuaded Wood to buy him. Wood, supposedly unaware of Goodman's chicanery, liquidated the debt and paid Goodman £200 for the balance. Subsequent events would suggest that Mr Wood might have been more involved with the fraud than his innocence portrayed.

On 27 November 1843, delivered by Mist, one of Goodman's boys, Running Rein returned to Smith's stables – now in the ownership of his landlord, Alexander Wood.

At around the same time George White, Goodman's town servant, called to take away the unnamed, brown, half-bred yearling [sic], on whom Goodman placed no value. But George White was no match for The Saddler colt, who twice broke away from him. He was eventually led away by a man named Fiddler. Where he was taken is unknown – possibly to Smith's. However, one thing is certain: The Saddler colt was never seen again.

Running Rein (Maccabeus), now back in training with Smith, became the subject of a number of reports that he was more than three years old. William Butt, a stable lad who had been employed by Smith at various times and who assisted Pearce, Running Rein's lad, was aware of these rumours and repeatedly examined the horse's mouth. He also examined Dr Phillimore, Mountain Dew and Ballinkeele, whom he had care of. He found tusks in Running Rein's mouth, half the length of the nail of his little finger. In Mountain Dew and Dr Phillimore there were none; and in Ballinkeele they were rather longer than his whole fingernail.[17]

The murder was leaking out: Butt had never seen a three-year-old with tusks, or a four-year-old without. He observed that Running Rein had the ways of an older horse, being very spirited and aware of what was required of him.

With the rumours concerning Running Rein's age circulating around Epsom, William Lumley, the licensee at the Spread Eagle in Epsom High Street, asked John Bartlett, a veterinary surgeon residing at Dorking, if he would examine the horse, with respect to his age. About two months after Running Rein's return to Epsom, Bartlett and Lumley went to Smith's stables. Bartlett examined Running Rein's mouth and thought his teeth were those of a three-year-old. He advised Wood of his belief and asked if he had any objection to seeking another opinion. Wood agreed and Bartlett suggested a number of suitable names, which included William Mavor of Bond Street. After examining the horse Bartlett had even more reason to doubt his age, as Wood, apparently as a bribe, offered Bartlett to stand £100 to nothing, which the latter ignored.

On 14 January Bartlett again called at Smith's stable and made a further examination of the horse's mouth. He discovered that all the teeth had been filed, the sharp edges of the last four prominent incisors nearly down to the mouth. When asked why Mavor had not been down, Smith responded that Wood had made up his mind that no more veterinary surgeons should examine his horse. When Bartlett told Smith that Running Rein was definitely a four-year-old, Smith's reaction was to request Bartlett not to say anything about it. This admission was putting the noose around both Wood's and Smith's necks. Bartlett reported his findings to Lumley, who suggested that he go and see Wood. When Bartlett confronted Wood about the findings of his re-examination of Running Rein and his conclusion that he was definitely a four-year-old, Wood begged him not to say a word about it. Bartlett urged him to seek another opinion if he was not satisfied with his inference, but Wood was adamant that he would not allow this and instead would obtain a certificate from the breeder. This, of course, would be entirely unconvincing and would in no way corroborate the true identity of the horse.

On the following day Bartlett went to Smith's to examine the horse again, not because he had any doubt as to the horse's age, but to explain to Smith the difference in the teeth of a three- and four-year-old. Bartlett asked Smith if he had a three-year-old in the stable. After some hesitation he showed Bartlett Dr Phillimore. Smith dismissed the lad in charge of Dr Phillimore's care, as he did not wish him to be present during the examination. Bartlett pointed out the difference between the teeth of Dr Phillimore and Running Rein. Smith was satisfied with the explanation given, but again he begged Bartlett not to say anything about it. Unfortunately, Wood had gone to London and so Bartlett was unable to speak to him directly, but on returning to Dorking he wrote the following letter to Wood:

Dorking, 15th January 1844
Sir,
I have this day again examined your horse Running Rein at Mr. Smith's stables, Epsom, and I am still of the same opinion that I was yesterday respecting the age of the animal. The horse is, I am perfectly satisfied, four-years-old. I assure you there cannot be any mistake in this case.
I am Sir,
John Bartlett.[18]

Bartlett received no reply from Wood. On 22 January he met Lumley on the Downs and expressed his discomfort. He was concerned that his opinion ought to be made known; otherwise it might be considered that he was party to any deception. Lumley recommended that he wait a while. As he had still received no response from Wood, on 24 January he called at the Spread Eagle, informing Lumley of his intention to write to the Jockey Club unless Wood consented to make his (Bartlett's) views known. Lumley sent a message for Wood to come to the Spread Eagle, but he refused, saying that he was otherwise engaged. Therefore, there was no alternative but to challenge Wood at his own premises.

Wood was in his yard when Lumley and Bartlett arrived. Bartlett immediately challenged Wood to make his opinion regarding Running Rein's age known; otherwise he would write to the Jockey Club. Wood became very abusive, accusing Bartlett of being mixed up with a party involved in a conspiracy against him. Bartlett warned him that he had made up his mind to write to the Jockey Club and that if Wood cared to call at the Spread Eagle in a quarter-of-an-hour or twenty minutes he would show him the letter. He also told Wood that if there were any alteration to the letter that he could make in justice to Wood, he would be prepared to do so. However, Wood refused to cooperate, leaving Bartlett with no alternative but to implement his planned action and write the following letter to the Jockey Club.

Dorking, 24th January 1844
To the Honorable Stewards of the Jockey Club.
My Lords and Gentlemen,
Having lately been called up by Mr. Alexander Wood to examine a horse
of his now standing at Mr. Smith's stables at Epsom and which is
entered in the name of Running Rein for the next Derby, particularly
with reference to the age of the horse, I think it my duty to apprise you
that my decided opinion is that the said horse is four-years-old and that
such was my opinion I forwarded in writing to Mr. Wood. I inform you
of this in order that you may take any steps you may deem necessary to
make the fact known to the public,
I am, etc.
John Barlett junr.[19]

Bartlett received no reply, but Wood sent the following letter to
the editor of *Bell's Life*:

Sir,
I shall feel obliged by your giving insertion to the following statement:-
Having been informed that unpleasant rumours were abroad respecting
the age of my horse "Running Rein," I thought it my duty to call in the
veterinary surgeon, for his opinion on the subject; accordingly on 9th
January last I consulted Mr. John Bartlett of Dorking, who, after
having as I supposed carefully examined the horse's mouth, stated
publicly before several persons, "that he was a perfect three-year-old,
that he would lay a thousand pounds to two-pence, that he was no
more," and he previously stated privately to me that he had just seen Sir
Gilbert's (Heathcote) horses, and from the appearance of all their
mouths, there could be but a week or so difference between them all, and
that he would willingly meet any other veterinary surgeon, and give his
reasons for his opinion; Mr. Bartlett then left me, and I fancied the
matter settled, and at rest.
Five days afterwards, namely the fourteenth, Mr. Bartlett went to
Smith's stable (without my knowledge), and requested to see the horse,
and he then stated that "the horse was four-years-old, and that his teeth
had been filed."
On the following day, the fifteenth, he again examined him, and then
stated he was four, but that his teeth had not been filed.
Feeling greatly annoyed at the contradictory statements of Mr. Bartlett,
I applied to the breeder, from whom I have received sufficient evidence

to prove the horse's identity, and also that he is not yet quite three-years-old.

Alex Wood.[20]

Bartlett's reply to the editor of *Bell's Life* was published a week later, as follows:

Sir, – Observing in your number of Sunday last a letter signed "Alex Wood," purporting to give you the particulars of the circumstances attending my late examination of the horse Running Rein, I beg you will, in justice to myself, give my most unqualified contradiction to the correctness of the statement. As I am aware that the matter is now before the proper tribunal, I think it unnecessary to go into any detailed statement of the facts, but shall at the proper time (if called upon) be quite ready to verify the opinion I have expressed, and in the mean time will content myself by denying that the statement is accurate in many particulars; and that with regard to the gentleman's horses whose name he mentions in the letter, I neither did, and it is impossible I could, have made any such remark as the one he stated I privately *made to him, as I have never on any occasion looked into the mouths of that Gentleman's Derby colts.*

I still retain a decided opinion the horse is four-years-old, as stated in my letter to Mr. Wood; but if he is dissatisfied with that opinion, as the horse still remains in his stables, he will, if incorrect, have no difficulty in getting a competent person to refute it.

John Bartlett, Veterinary Surgeon.

Dorking, Feb.7, 1844.[21]

As a consequence of Wood's letter, he also wrote the following letter to Weatherbys:

Dorking, 4th February 1844

Gentlemen,

On the 24th day of January last I conceived it my duty to write to The Honourable Members of the Jockey Club stating that having been called upon by Mr. Alexander Wood of Epsom to examine the horse, Running Rein, entered for the next Derby, with a view to ascertain the age of the horse, I formed a decided opinion that the horse was 4-years-old and that such was my opinion I informed Mr. Wood my object in writing this letter was in order that the public might not be deceived in the matter.

51

In today's Bell's Life *in London there is a letter from Mr. Alexander Wood on the subject in which after giving a most incorrect version of the circumstances attending my giving the opinion in question he concludes by saying that he has applied to the Breeder from whom he has received sufficient evidence to prove that the horse is not yet quite three years old. I still retain the same decided opinion as before and as the correctness of it is thus unfeigned it would be satisfactory to all parties if my opinion was refuted or confirmed and I shall esteem it a favour if you will inform me whether supposing Mr. Wood to assent the Jockey Club would appoint a competent person to examine the horse or what steps would be taken by them in the matter. I trust you will excuse my troubling you with this and will favour me with a line by Monday or Tuesday's post.*

I remain, Gentlemen, your obedient servant,

John Bartlett junr.

Veterinary Surgeon.[22]

Bartlett received the following answer from Weatherbys:

Old Burlington Street

5th February 1844

Sir,

I am directed by the Stewards of the Jockey Club to acknowledge the receipt of your letters of 24th January and the 4th Inst. to inform you in reply that the question of the age of the horse called Running Rein is not at present before in such a shape as to give them any power to interfere in the matter.

I am etc.

C. Weatherby[23]

This was an astonishing admission by the stewards. Having requested Running Rein's mouth to be examined but being refused by Goodman, at Newmarket, they were being offered a gift by Bartlett, whereby they could have scuppered the fraud at a single stroke – talk about looking a gift horse in the mouth! One must wonder at the indifference of the stewards; but if the stewards had their heads in the sand, Bentinck certainly didn't. Wood, and Goodman of course – who still maintained an interest in the horse and frequently visited Smith's stables accompanied by Wood, were now off the hook, at least for the time being, although they took the precaution of removing Running Rein just in case Bentinck seized on Bartlett's inference and, as Goodman would no doubt have put it, 'come snooping around'. The venue was first to Goodman's stables at Sutton, and then to Haynes' stables in Foley Place, where he remained from 5 February until 8 February.

Wood, however, seemed determined to have the last word, and in response to Bartlett's letter he again wrote to the editor of *Bell's Life*:

> *Sir, – As the leading vehicle of communication to the sporting world, I beg again to trouble you. Having had a high opinion of Mr. Bartlett, I am rather surprised at his apparent want of memory, as shewn in his letter to you last week. His assertion as to the age, &c., of Running Rein, having been made in the presence of* disinterested *and respectable individuals, I shall have no difficulty when the proper time arrives, of contradicting his statements.*
> *Being but a very small better myself, the position the horse may have in the betting is a matter of indifference to me; but should he be fortunate enough to win his engagements, I am possessed of corroborative proof of his age and identity quite sufficient to convince the tribunal to whom Mr. Bartlett has written. Begging to apologise for taking up so much of your valuable space.*
> *I remain, yours truly,*
> *Epsom, Feb.14, 1844.   Alexander Wood.*[24]

This must have been a bluff by Wood. He knew that the horse was a four-year-old and that the 'corroborative proof' would have been of little use to him, as the pedigree of the genuine Running Rein would have specified his year of birth as 1841.

Carlin saw Running Rein at Smith's towards the end of February 1844, when Goodman had him stripped in order that Carlin could give an opinion of him. Goodman again suggested that Carlin should 'stand in' with the horse, but again did not specify any terms.[25]

9

Ratan, The Ugly Buck, Orlando and Leander

The year is 1775. George III has been on the throne for 15 years and Lord North is Prime Minister. We are at war with the colonies and Captain Cook has just completed his second expedition of the southern oceans. It is six years since the old woman, bearing her load of faggots on Epsom Downs, had seen a horse (who was to have such an impact on the breed of the thoroughbred racehorse) with a white leg being chased by another, whom she did not think would catch the horse with the white leg, even if he pursued him to the end of the world; and the first Derby is five years away.

The young man who entered this world in the winter of this year, the son of a humble Fleet Street fishmonger, was to become one of the magnificos of the gambling and gaming clique. William Crockford was born in the shadow of Temple Bar – the gateway from the west into the City of London, at the division of Fleet Street and the Strand. It was a harsh and sometimes brutal environment for a child's upbringing. He was fortunate in that his father's business was reasonably prosperous in an area of abject poverty; it was relatively lawless, what little law there was being heeded by few. This was the home of the footpad, the thief, the burglar and the cut-throat, ready to relieve the unwary who ventured into this violent theatre of his purse – and possibly his life. As a child he must have witnessed the horrific sight of public executions at Newgate gaol: criminals hanged as a public spectacle, the ghoulish crowd baying and screaming curses as the victims pleaded for their lives. While growing up in this environment, where a man had to live by his cunning and wit, there was little about life and human nature that the young Crockford failed to learn – a perfect grounding for his adult life.

From an early age Crockford developed a deep interest and understanding of gambling. In the myriad of lanes and passages surrounding Temple Bar he witnessed in the gambling dens the shortcomings of those willing to continually risk their meagre wages on such a chancy business. In his youth he watched, listened and learned the trade and tricks of the card sharp and dice thrower. He was able to memorise cards that had been played, and, like many a good player of games involving numbers, he had a remarkable head for figures. He may not have fully understood the mathematical theories of probability or been aware of all the permutations and combinations, but nevertheless, in a game of dice or cards, he was able to make a skilled assessment of whether the odds were in his favour. It is almost certain that he would have learned, and perfected, the three-card trick; and he was a master of whist and cribbage. Probably well before his adult life he would also have acquired a cool temperament towards gambling; he would have had confidence without rashness, the ability to understand the minds of his opponents and, above all, an acute awareness of when to wager, choosing to do so only when his agile mind had decided that the odds were in his favour, and backing off when they were against him.

Once the young Crockford had served his apprenticeship it was time for him to depart from the pervasive stench of Billingsgate, venture into the vortex of the West End gambling dens and put his skills to lucrative account. And it did not take long for the fishmonger's son to show the rakes and dandies who frequented these gambling dens that he was more than a force to be reckoned with.

On one of his forays into the West End he lured an egotistical butcher – a wealthy man – into a game of cribbage.[1] It was like a lamb being led to the slaughter: Crockford, the professional yet still no more than a boy, against the boastful amateur. This whippersnapper was certainly going to be taught a lesson – or so the latter thought! The game lasted the whole night, and by the time dawn had risen over the West End the whippersnapper had relieved the braggart of £1,700. It was the prize that Crockford needed to establish his own gambling den and what was the start of the most remarkable gambling business in the West End.

However, Crockford's gambling ambitions were not limited to dice and the card table. The turf beckoned. He had probably ventured to Newmarket and Epsom in his youth; he may even have witnessed the great match over the Beacon Course, when Hambletonian, cut to ribbons by Buckle's spurs, just managed to hold off the challenge of Fitzpatrick, on Diamond, by a short neck. By all accounts half the country was there, either drawn by the excitement of the great contest, or to make their fortunes. One can only imagine how they got there, as in the late eighteenth century the rail network had not even found its way to Cambridge, let alone Newmarket, and it would not arrive until almost a half-century later. The stagecoach, phaeton (an open horse-drawn carriage) or post horse were the preserve of the more wealthy; the poor probably had to make it on foot.

But there was money to be won – and lost. In those far-off days there were very few layers. Bets would generally have been between gentlemen. Crockford, with his head for figures, would have recognised that there was a market here; not necessarily on the great match, but this was a four-day Meeting. It was probably at a Meeting such as this that the premise of creating a 'book' and laying all horses in a race arose: bettors would get reasonable odds, and he would still yield a profit, irrespective of which horse won.

Crockford became the first of the great Turf speculators, leading the way for the likes of Bill Davis and Fred Swindell, at the beginning of the Victorian era. His club in St James's was flourishing; in addition to facilities for cards and dice, his clients could back their fancies on the Turf. He purchased a large house in Newmarket and opened a gambling club to accommodate his clients during races at Newmarket, finally becoming a man of substance in the Newmarket set when he became an owner, starting modestly in 1811 with just two horses.

It would have been nice for Crockford to record that his horses were the equal of any other on the Heath, and that his colours of white and red cap were as famous as those of the Earl of Egremont and the Duke of Grafton. Alas, however, though a dab hand at running his gambling businesses, as an owner of racehorses he was unsuccessful. His knowledge of horses was poor and consequently he made bad purchases. Most would probably have given up, but Crockford persevered, never surrendering his ambition that one day the Derby would fall to him.

That opportunity almost came in 1819 with a horse he was lucky enough to breed himself, Sultan.

There were really only two contenders: Sultan, and the Duke of Portland's Tiresias, who had won the Newmarket Stakes and Palace Stakes and was, justifiably, marginally the favourite. Crockford, abandoning the principles he had learned in the gambling dens, backed Sultan; and the ex-bare-knuckle pugilist, John Gully, who was a great rival of Crockford and intensely despised him (in fact, the feeling was mutual) was happy to lay Sultan.

The end of the story was a disappointment for Crockford. Tiresias made all the running, with Sultan lying immediately behind. Sultan made his challenge in the last hundred yards, failing by only half-a-neck to catch the winner.

No doubt the nobility welcomed the Duke of Portland's success. It was all very well a fishmonger becoming a 'leg' – even for the nobility to do business with him – but to be a winner of the Derby! M'dear, *what* would the people of St James's say?

It was somewhat understandable that Crockford was not considered a likeable person. If it were fair to judge a person from their appearance, then there is something unpleasant in Rowlandson's sketch of Crockford. He does not have the urbane appearance that one would expect of a successful businessman, but is almost idiot-like – a figure of fun. He has a large mouth, large flabby-looking lips, puffy cheeks and a peculiarly shaped, snout-like nose, almost merging with his upper lip. Yes, it would be difficult to like such a man, although the appearance belied the man and it certainly paid to be on the right side of old Crocky.

The St Leger fared no better for the hell-master. His magnificent Sultan was made favourite; with Tiresias not entered, it seemed at his mercy. But poor old Crocky's luck deserted him once again. Sultan broke down in his final preparation and Doncaster was deprived of his presence.

In those bygone days, with the lack of speedy communications, those fortunate enough to see Sultan hobbling off the Heath were able to hedge their bets. Unfortunately, Crockford was not one of them; he continued to accept the over-generous odds on Sultan, not realising, until he had finally heard of Sultan's injury, that he had fallen into a trap.

Crockford was even denied the brilliance of Sultan in the breeding shed, having sold him to Lord Foley. But it was Crockford's own fault that, despite his winning 14 races, he could not recognise some quality of greatness in Sultan, unlike a contributor to the *Old Sporting Magazine*, who said of him: 'I saw Sultan run all his races; but, if defeated, I never saw him run a jaded, shuffling, spirit-broken horse. He had his favourite courses, in which, though carrying very heavy weights, he never had his equal.'[2]

The Druid described him as having a lovely head, long back ribs and muscular quarters. He was a long horse, and many were wont to compare him to the print of the Darley Arabian:[3] certainly, Herring's artistic brush depicts a striking similarity.

Yes, brilliant he was. He was champion sire from 1832 to 1837, and in the nineteenth century he was only excelled by Sir Peter Teazle, his great grandson Stockwell, Hermit and St Simon. From his loins sprung forth Green Mantle (bay filly 1926), winner of the Oaks; Augustus (chestnut colt 1827), Ibrahim (brown colt 1832) and Achmet (bay colt 1834), all winners of the Two Thousand Guineas; Galata (brown filly 1829), winner of the One Thousand Guineas, the Oaks and Ascot Gold Cup; Destiny (chestnut filly 1833), winner of the One Thousand Guineas; Glencoe (chestnut colt 1831), winner of the Two Thousand Guineas and Ascot Gold Cup; and, of course, Bay Middleton (bay colt 1833,) winner of the Two Thousand Guineas and the Derby. The latter two would have been enough to earn Sultan immortality. Glencoe, apart from becoming a leading sire in America, was the sire of Pochahontas, one of the great matriarchs in Turf history, who was the dam of Stockwell, his full brother Rataplan, and King Tom. Bay Middleton was the sire of The Flying Dutchman and Andover, both Derby winners.

Crockford, probably disillusioned with the dishonesty of racing (although when it came to honesty, he was certainly no saint himself), abandoned his interest in being an owner and in 1826 withdrew his horses from training in order to concentrate on his gambling clubs. Newmarket, Epsom and Doncaster were, however, not denied his presence. There were, of course, old scores to settle: Crockford could not forget how he was cheated over Sultan's withdrawal from the St Leger and he had every intention of seeking retribution. The St Leger of 1827 was his opportunity to even the score with Gully. As disgraceful as this episode may have been (as we have seen in our first chapter), in a dog-eat-dog age, where cheating was the norm, Crockford's actions were understandable – at least, they were to Crockford. He was prepared to become involved in any scheme, no matter how disreputable, if it could yield a profit – especially if it meant getting one over on Gully. And here lay the paradox: on the one hand there is this contemptible cheat in the betting-ring, and on the other, a distinguished proprietor of the most fashionable gambling institution in London, who expected his patrons to conduct themselves with the utmost propriety.

The years rolled by and Crockford earned millionaire status as his St James's institution flourished. But by now old Crocky was looking, and feeling, like an old man. His desire to sit at his Hazard table, where he was once prepared to take on any man at the game of which he was master, was waning, and in 1840 he finally called it a day and retired.

There was, of course, one ambition that had not been fulfilled: to win the Derby.

Probably inspired by the success of Sultan, Crockford's interest in winning the Derby was rekindled. Although he had not had a horse in training since 1826, he had maintained his breeding interests, and in 1841 he bred a chestnut colt named Ratan by Buzzard (not to be confused with the celebrated son of Woodpecker) out of a mare by Picton. There was no reason to believe that Ratan was going to be anything other than a moderate performer. His sire, Buzzard, was a reasonable animal, having won several minor sweepstakes, but was nothing out of the ordinary. He had sired the speedy Bentley, who ran away with most of the good two-year-old races in 1833, but had cut a wretched figure in the Two Thousand Guineas; and Gorhambury, who ran second in Cotherstone's Derby (this was the one that Goodman had hoped to win with Goneaway impersonating Maccabeus) and won the Ascot Gold Vase. It does not appear that his dam ever raced, but her sire, Picton, won a couple of minor races at Much Wenlock and Shrewsbury.

However, Joe Rogers, in whose capable hands Crockford had placed Ratan, recognised a latent talent in the horse, and before he made his first appearance in the New Stakes, at Ascot, Rogers had put a few of his select friends on the right scent, not only for the Ascot race but also for the Derby.

The Sporting Magazine considered the field for the New Stakes to be 'of a most superior order':[4] Assay (bay filly by The Prime Warden) had beaten a large field for the Park Stakes at Gorhambury, including Johnny Broome (bay colt by Defence or Venison) – then thought something of – and started even-money favourite. Also in the field was Charming Kate (chestnut or roan filly by Sir Hercules), a sister to the Derby winner Coronation, who had won the Weston Stakes at Bath.

Almost from the start the race was confined to Ratan and the two fillies, Charming Kate having the lead, with Ratan and Assay hard up. At the road Assay joined the leader and they ran together to the distance, at which point Ratan headed them, had it all to himself, and won easily by three lengths from Assay, with Charming Kate a moderate third.

The result was of itself enough to raise Ratan to the top of the Derby betting, but if any doubt remained as to his abilities it was quite removed by his victory in the Criterion Stakes at the Newmarket Houghton Meeting. He was an easy winner by four lengths from the Duke of Richmond's Pastoral (who won a £50 sweepstake the following day by two lengths), with the Days' Seaport a 'bad third'. Seven others exposed themselves shamefully, amongst them the Duke of Rutland's Crenoline, who had run second to Running Rein in a £50 sweepstake a couple of weeks earlier, and Mr Watt's renowned Voltri, whose supporters, not content with the woeful figure he cut in his race for the Clearwell Stakes, came forward once more to his support and paid for their folly.

If there had been an element of doubt concerning Ratan's breeding, this certainly did not apply to The Ugly Buck. Beautifully bred, he was a bay colt by Venison out of Lord George Bentinck's Plenipotentiary mare, Monstrosity. He was purchased by John Day as a yearling. Day was so impressed with his speed when he put him in training that he purchased the dam. Unfortunately she proved barren, and was again unlucky in 1844, 'slipping' twins to Venison. Lord Chesterfield considered The Ugly Buck to be finest horse he had ever seen, and Isaac Day described him as just the size he would choose for a racehorse – in fact, like his sire Venison but on a larger scale. Unlike many of Day's two-year-olds, most of whom would have had the stuffing knocked out of them before they saw their third birthday, The Ugly Buck had an extremely light programme, only appearing once in public, in the Molecombe Stakes at Goodwood. So certain was 'Honest John' that, after all the 2 to 1 and 3 to 1 had been got on quietly, the odds at starting had run up to 5 to 1 on. And his child duly obliged, winning cleverly by a length from Mr Gratwicke's bay filly, by Elis out of The Margravine. Lord Chesterfield's The Dog Billy (chestnut colt by Ratcatcher), who had finished second to Mr

Wreford's Wadastra colt in The Lavant Stakes two days earlier, whipped round just as the flag was dropped and was left behind, but made amends a couple of days later by beating Mr Gratwicke's filly by a head in a sweepstake at Brighton.

It had been expected that The Ugly Buck would make a stand against Ratan in the Criterion Stakes, but John Day, acting on the advice of others, withdrew him. One reason for his decision was the immense sum got on in the Derby market at 20 to 1; another was that they had Seaport in the race in order to gauge Ratan's measure. On this point they failed miserably, as Seaport was a bad third.

The Peel family had at least an arguable case to consider themselves one of the most eminent families of the nineteenth century. The first Sir Robert Peel, a wealthy mill owner and Member of Parliament for Tamworth, was a passionate Englishman; so passionate, in fact, that as a personal contribution to the struggle with Napoleon, at his own cost, he raised and equipped a regiment of volunteers from his own workforce. His eldest son, the second Sir Robert Peel, had been groomed by his father for a political career and entered Parliament in 1809. He became Home Secretary in 1822, introducing far-ranging criminal and penal reforms, which resulted in far fewer crimes being punishable by death, as well as creating the Metropolitan Police Force. In 1834 he was appointed to the highest office, becoming one of the country's greatest Prime Ministers.

The business and political talents of the father and elder son were matched in sport by the fifth son, Jonathan, later General Peel. He was a lifelong friend of Admiral Rous and the great gambling eccentric George Payne, sharing with them a devotion to the Turf. He joined the army as the lowly rank of ensign just before Waterloo, but the peace that followed the Napoleonic Wars prevented him from seeing active service.

In the autumn of his life you could probably observe Jonathan Peel's hardy figure on a bitterly cold April day, with the wind snarling across the Heath, the term 'Spring Meeting' representing a cruel irony. He would spurn the comfort of even the lightest overcoat, as if to make a point to Lord Panmure that this was a sufficient display of fortitude to validate his request to join the British army at Sebastapol, which had been repeatedly denied him.

On the Turf he bred a number of successful horses: Fille de Joie had run second in the 1824 Oaks to Cobweb and, five years later Archibald (bay colt Paulowitz-Garcia), named after his father-in-law, the Marquis of Ailsa, won the Two Thousand Guineas.

If the Danebury confederacy and Crockford (and a snap of the fingers to Goodman and his clique) thought they were going to be without rivals, then they had reckoned without Colonel Peel's two-year-olds. Most owners would have been pleased to have one decent horse, but Colonel Peel had three: Zenobia, described as a fine, dashing bay filly (Slane-Hester) and a sister to Murat, unbeaten as a three-year-old in 1843, including a victory over Lord George Bentinck's, Gaper, who had been strongly fancied for the Derby; Ionian, a bay colt (Ion-Malibran); and a bay colt (Touchstone-Vulture) named Sandwich.[5] Could a horse with such a name win the Derby? Perhaps not. He was duly renamed Orlando.

Orlando's pedigree was classical to the core; maybe one or two blemishes here and there, but generally laced with speed and stamina. His dam, Vulture, was described by The Druid as the speediest animal that ever trod the Turf.[6] She was a winner of six races as a three-year-old and was only beaten in the St Leger – a distance far too far for her.

Orlando's sire, Touchstone, was one of the great racehorses of the mid-nineteenth century. He was a shock, but easy, winner of the 1834 St Leger, starting at 40 to 1. Whether he would have fairly beaten the Derby winner Plenipotentiary, who was poisoned, is always going to be a point of discussion. But Touchstone showed that this was no fluke, twice winning the Doncaster and Ascot Gold Cups. The Druid described him as a very peculiar horse. He turned his hocks out so much, and went so wide behind, that a barrel might have been placed between his hindlegs when he was galloping. Neither distance nor the state of the ground made any difference to him. He never began well, but he could stay forever and his immense speed soon brought him to the fore.[7] Apart from Orlando, he was the sire of Cotherstone (bay colt 1840), winner of the Two Thousand Guineas and Derby; Surplice (bay colt 1845), winner of the Derby and St Leger; Mendicant (brown filly 1843), winner of the One Thousand Guineas and the Oaks; the Two Thousand Guineas winners Flatcatcher (bay colt 1845), Lord of the Isles (bay colt 1852) and Nunnykirk (black colt 1846); and the St Leger winners Blue Bonnet (bay filly 1839) and Newminster (bay colt 1848). He was the maternal grandsire of West Australian, the first winner of the Triple Crown, in 1851. The Derby winners Hyperion, Owen Tudor, St Paddy and Empery, the Two Thousand Guineas winner Tudor Minstrel and the Prix de L'Arc de Triomphe winner Vaguely Noble are just a few of the latter-day marvels that trace back to him in male line, through his son Newminster.

Orlando's first race was for the Produce Stakes at Ascot, for which he started at 5 to 4. On the way to post – The Druid recalls[8] – young John Day (riding Mr Wreford's bay filly by Sultan Junior-Monimia) overheard Nat Flatman (on Orlando) propose to Sam Rogers (riding Lord George Bentinck's ridiculously named filly, Here I Go With My Eye Out) to hedge rides.

> John observed to Nat, "What's good for Sam must be good for me, so let me stand in as well."
> "A very likely thing," said Nat, "your pigmy of a pony has no chance."
> "Never mind," retorted young John, "I can stay with you, though you are on such a grand one."
> Mr Davis started them, but, at the word "Go", each stopped and looked at the others.
> "Mind, I've started you," bellowed Mr Davis, and then left them.
> On they walked for over two hundred yards.
> "Are none of you going to take the lead?" asked John; "because, if not, I shall take it for you."
> Then Jem Robinson (riding Panther) chimed in with, "For goodness' sake, John, canter or gallop; otherwise my horse will bolt."
> Day, responding to Robinson's request, led off at a slow canter; but on nearing the brick kilns he gave his filly a taste of the spur, and stole fifty yards in a twinkling. Nat somewhat upset Orlando in his haste to follow her. Day gave Mr Wreford's filly a gentle pull at the distance, when Orlando reached her girths; and Day, hearing the sound of Nat's whip, knew that he was driving the crack, so he urged on his filly and just beat Orlando by a short head.

One can only wonder at such a farcical occurrence today – the stewards would have had a field day.

Starting at 2 to 1 on, Orlando next ran for the July Stakes at Newmarket, winning very easily by a length from Lord Orford's grey colt, Boots, and five others, including Mr Ford's unkindly named filly, She Is Not Worth a Name. At the same meeting

Orlando beat Lord Kilburne's brown filly (Retainer-Purity) in a match, and Ionian won the Chesterfield Stakes.

Three weeks later, at the Goodwood Meeting, Orlando won the Ham Stakes, reversing the placings at Ascot, with Mr Wreford's filly also beating Zenobia and another of Lord George Bentinck's oddly named horses, All Round My Hat. Two days later Orlando, starting at 5 to 2 on, won a 25 sovereigns sweepstake, easily beating Mr Litchwald's bay colt, Leander (Scamander-Sister to Mussulman), by a length, and on the same afternoon Leander suffered another defeat, finishing behind Mr Gregory's black filly, Barricade (Defence-Europa), and Zenobia.

Leander, trained by Forth at Michel Grove, had opened his account by winning a 50 sovereigns sweepstake at the same Ascot meeting in which Orlando had run an unlucky second to Mr Wreford's Monomia filly. As with Running Rein, there were whispers concerning his size. Several observers were of the opinion that he looked more like a three- or even a four-year-old than a two-year-old. These opinions did not go unheard to Forth's son, Henry. Naturally, both he and his father felt offended. It was if these aspersions were being cast at them, personally.

Forth relayed the comments, heard at Ascot, to the Litchwalds, stating that if there was something wrong about the horse he should not remain in his stables. The Litchwalds protested to him that he was the correct age, that they had bred him and had a certificate to prove his age, and that Forth should not concern himself.

Most would have written Leander off after his Goodwood performances, having been beaten by Colonel Peel's pair. But old Forth was not unduly worried. Leander had been amiss following the Ascot race and could not be fully prepared, and in consequence ran poorly in his two races at Goodwood. After Goodwood he improved and, when tried again, Forth found him to be an 'extraordinary good horse',[9] but owing to his repeatedly being lame he strongly advised the Litchwalds not to back him for the Derby but to let him go through the winter.

It was intended to run Leander in the Criterion Stakes at Newmarket, but he ran away with his boy and fell lame in his hock. On receipt of this news from Forth's son, the Litchwalds were disappointed; they had backed their horse and wanted him to run if the injury was not serious. They travelled down to Michel Grove and, against the advice of Forth's son and his head man, John Norman, decided that he should start. On his return from Newmarket to London, Forth met the van; he found Leander to be very lame and ordered the post boy to return to Hockeril. Forth continued to London, stating firmly to the Litchwalds that to run him would be the ruination of the horse. The Litchwalds took his heed – at least they didn't destroy that part of the drama that was to come.

10
The Derby

In its March issue *The Sporting Magazine* informed its readers: 'We are about to commence one of the most brilliant Racing Seasons ever known in the memory of man ....' They were certainly not anticipating the forthcoming scandal; like the stewards of the Jockey Club, they probably expected the Running Rein problem to disappear.

But would it disappear?

In Northampton Higgins was showing signs of anxiety. Word had got to him that Worley had been talking about the horse, telling various persons that the horse called Running Rein was the horse Maccabeus, which Worley had kept in his paddock. Higgins confronted Worley on the subject. Worley made no denial, as Higgins had been telling him a parcel of lies, and he would continue to tell people what he knew.

Higgins was aware of Odell's relationship with Worley and asked him to intercede, so that they may be reconciled – if not, he would be ruined.

Odell was cognisant of Worley's refusal to speak to Higgins, on account of Higgins having deceived Worley by saying that Maccabeus was dead and trying to make him believe that the colt he (Higgins) had was by The Saddler. Accordingly, Odell drove Higgins over to Worley's to apologise. Higgins cried. He was very sorry for having attempted to deceive Worley and admitted that the horse called Running Rein was Maccabeus, the horse that Worley had kept in his paddock. Worley held out his hand to Higgins and told him that he forgave him.[1]

About ten days before the Epsom Spring Meeting Higgins met Odell near The George, in Northampton, and requested Odell to invite Mr Worley to go to the Spring Meeting to see Running Rein, at Smith's. Higgins offered to pay the expenses and a further inducement of £1,000 if Worley would hold his tongue. Odell was also offered something, but Higgins did not specify an amount. He informed Worley of Higgins's offers, but Worley declined to go to the Epsom Spring Meeting or have anything to do with a bribe.[2]

At the beginning of spring *Bell's Life* reported on the progress of the Classic candidates.[3] By the style of his victories in the New Stakes at Ascot and the Criterion Stakes at Newmarket, Crockford's Ratan had established himself as the best two-year-old of 1843, without revealing the extent of his ability, and was at the head of the Derby market. He was described as a remarkably neat horse, about 15¾ in height, with a sweet temper and sound constitution. Of the other Newmarket runners, William Cooper, whose stables were behind the Golden Lion,[4] had Colonel Peel's Orlando and Ionian, although there was little between the two, and there was some confidence in Mr Thornhill's Apprentice and Elemi. Sherwood, private trainer to Sir Gilbert Heathcote at Epsom, had Campunero and Akbar, the latter having opened his three-year-old account by easily beating Lord George Bentinck's Emma in the Epsom Trial Stakes; and Goodman's friend, Mr Maugham, had Dr Phillimore, thought to be pretty good despite having paid forfeit in his three engagements as a two-year-old. Down at Goodwood Lord George Bentinck had almost 40 horses in training with John Kent, some rather oddly named, such as All Round My Hat and Here I Go with My Eye Out, although none of his three-year-olds could be considered little more than moderate. John Scott, who had won the last two renewals of the Derby with Attila and Cotherstone, had the beautifully bred Bay Momus (bay colt Bay Middleton – Sister to Grey Momus) and, as *The Sporting Magazine* put it, the cruel impostor Voltri, who at one time had stood at 9 to 1 for the Derby. Foig-a-Ballagh and Leander, trained by Forth at Michel Grove, were both reported to have been backed to a heavy amount. *The Sporting Magazine* appeared quite surprised that some 'evil disposed persons' believed Leander to be five years old,[5] whilst *Bell's Life* presumed it remained a mystery to all, except his backers, as to why Leander should have found support at 15 to 1 for the Derby. Running Rein, likewise, belonged to a similar category, his odds of 20 to 1 for the Derby being due to the speculations of his immediate party. Both were facetiously termed 'the modern antiques'. John Day was represented by The Ugly Buck, who had been backed to win an immense stake; the Wadastra colt; and Theseus and Juvenal, both of whom had been supported at long odds. And there was considerable interest in the Irish horse

Loadstone (bay colt Touchstone – Ildegarda), who had won all his races in the style of Mr O'Kelly's famous proverb.

At the Newmarket Craven Meeting Ratan was entered for a Sweepstakes over the Ditch Mile, for three-year-olds not engaged in the Riddlesworth, the 2,000 Guineas or the 1,000 Guineas.

Bell's Life takes up the story of the race: Ratan was backed down to 5 to 2 on and in some cases 3 to 1 on, with 4 to 1 against Lord Albemarle's Delapre, and 7 to 1 against Ratan winning this race and the Derby. The Blusterer, an indifferent specimen of a thoroughbred racehorse, was enabled by the smallness of the pace to make play for the first quarter of a mile, Numskull, for the same reason, lying up with him, and the others in a line; the crack then shot ahead, made the pace good, and, to cut the matter short, made the running to the end, and with a little rousing before he entered the cords, won in a canter by a couple of lengths. Delapre, who had followed him on The Blusterer's retreat, obtained second place. The style of Ratan's victory was such that it was difficult to imagine how he could be defeated in the Derby. Lord George was especially pleased. Ever since Ratan had won the New Stakes at Ascot the previous year he had believed him to be the best two-year-old in England and had backed him heavily for the Derby throughout the winter.

On the following day Colonel Peel's Orlando won The Eleventh Tuesday's Riddlesworth Stakes in a canter, by a length from Mr Watt's Baveno. The victory was held so cheap that 25 to 1 was immediately laid against Orlando for the Derby, and 1,500 to 500 on The Ugly Buck against him, although two days later Orlando's reputation was somewhat restored when he defeated the Duke of Portland's Beiram filly in a match. Half an hour later he walked over for a 200 sovereigns sweepstake. Although his victory over the Duke of Portland's filly was encouraging for his supporters, it failed to dislodge Ratan and The Ugly Buck at the head of the Derby betting.

The First Newmarket Spring Meeting opened two weeks later, on 22 April, in the most glorious weather. On the first day Colonel Peel's Crenoline, who had crossed swords with Running Rein, won the Palace Filly Stakes. The 2,000 Guineas was on the following day. As described by Lord Chesterfield, The Ugly Buck looked absolutely magnificent, and he started as favourite at odds of 7 to 2 on to beat his six rivals in what was a moderate field. Mr Thornhill's

Elemi was second favourite at 11 to 2. Running Rein had been entered by Goodman but unsurprisingly did not feature amongst the starters. Although he was now in the ownership of Mr Wood, it is not implausible that Goodman had enticed the apparently innocent gentleman not to run him; had he done so, Goodman's plans for the Derby would have probably evaporated.

The start had been fixed for 2.30 p.m. and precisely at that time the runners were at the post, but Lord Exeter's Algernon caused a delay by remaining behind when the first signal was given. The second start proved successful, with all getting away favourably. Sam Rogers, on Lord George Bentinck's The Devil to pay, had received orders to make the Buck gallop, if possible, and obeyed them to the letter, in an instant urging his horse into a five-length lead before the others had got running. The Ugly Buck followed, with the Wadastra colt on his girth; next came Dr Phillimore, Joe Lovell, Algernon and finally Elemi. Great as the speed was, the Devil's lead lessened after the first quarter-mile such that, on rising to the Bushes, The Ugly Buck had got within half-a-length, and, Rogers having eased his horse, they were almost level at the top. The Wadastra colt here gave way, and Joe Lovell took third place, but without the slightest chance of getting up. The race was left to the Buck and the Devil. The Buck got his head in front, but the Devil was not to be shaken off; he stuck to him to the last, and after a most exciting contest was defeated only by a neck. About four lengths back was Joe Lovell, who was about the same in front of the Wadastra colt. Mr Maugham's Dr Phillimore was last.

Later in the afternoon Red Deer, carrying 8st 7lb and at 3 to 1 on, won the Coffee Room Stakes, beating the unfortunate Voltri. This proved to be a marvellous trial for the Chester Cup, in which Red Deer was handicapped to carry only four stone and, ridden by the diminutive Kitchener, duly beat the great Alice Hawthorn – who was conceding no less than 5st 8lb – in a canter by five lengths, to establish a minimum weight-carrying record that still stands to this day.

The dismal performance of Voltri prompted the following amusing letter in *Bell's Life*, headed 'A Kind Hint to J. Scott':

Judging from appearances, your Derby nag (Voltri) seems to want strength to enable him to last. I think that may be given him, by giving daily a portion of bone jelly; the best is made from ivory shavings. This

would give him strength of bone and sinew. This may appear new; but when lime is given fowls, it increases the size and strength of their bones, and enables them to make shell faster. For God's sake take some means to bring him on the day at post, or I shall be in Queer Street, as I am heavy on him.
Yours most respectively, E.L.[6]

It would appear that John Scott did not take E.L.'s advice. Voltri was a lost cause and he passed to John Day.

John Day thought that The Ugly Buck had done enough in the 2,000 Guineas, as did a scribe from *The Sporting Magazine*, whose confidence was not shaken, as everyone knew that Venison blood could 'stay a distance', and who had no hesitation in stating that if the race had been run Across the Flat (1¼ miles) instead of the Rowley Mile, The Ugly Buck would have won in a canter. The public, however, did not share this opinion, their point being that he had beaten a bad horse by only a neck. Lord George agreed with the public view: he knew that The Devil to pay was not a top-class horse and that The Ugly Buck had only just managed to beat him. This made Lord George even more unshaken in his belief that Ratan was a certainty for the Derby, and he continued to back him.

But there was an element of disquiet in Lord George's mind. Why were some bookmakers prepared to lay against Ratan? As the horse had been working well, he could not understand the market. This was becoming a dirty business – first Running Rein, and now Ratan. These disturbing harbingers were not lost on the mind of Lord George Bentinck, and he was resolute in determining what was behind them.

He was fortunate enough to enlist the support of John Bowes and John Scott, and on the Saturday before the Derby a formal protest was handed to the stewards at Epsom against Running Rein:

Vale Lodge, near Leatherhead, May 18, 1844.
We the undersigned owners of horses engaged in, and intended to run for the approaching Derby, having strong reasons for believing that the horse meant to be started as Mr. Goodman's Running Rein, is not the b.c. by The Saddler, out of Mab, by which pedigree Running Rein is described in his earlier nominations, but some other horse, and one above three years of age, which has been substituted for the colt by The Saddler, out of Mab, request you as stewards of races to investigate the

*matter, and to oblige the owner or owners of the horse to prove his
identity by evidence; and above all by a proper examination of his mouth
by veterinary surgeons of character and eminence of your selection, to
satisfy you before he is permitted to start that he is not more than three
years old.*

*And we, the undersigned, hereby engage and undertake to bear you
harmless of all expense incurred by any such investigation and further
to indemnify you against any consequences of any action at law which
might be brought against you, should you in the discharge of your duty
as stewards think proper to hinder the colt in question from starting,
until you shall have satisfied that the colt intended to be started as Mr.
Goodman's Running Rein is no more than three years old, and the
identical animal described in the entry for the Derby. We have the
honour to be, gentlemen, your obedient humble servants,*

G.Bentinck.
John Bowes.
John Scott.[7]

To the Stewards of Epsom Races

It is interesting to note that the letter refers to Mr Goodman's
Running Rein, with no reference being made to Mr Wood, to
whom Goodman had transferred ownership.

The presentation of this protest was announced at Tattersalls on
the Saturday, but despite this there was still an inclination to back
Running Rein.

It was likewise intimated that a similar objection would be made
to Leander, owned by Mr Litchwald. This was made on the Monday
by Lord Maidstone, who entered a protest against him to the
Jockey Club on the ground of his being a four-year-old:

Stratton Street, London,
May 20th 1844
Gentlemen,
*Sinister reports have been prevalent with regard to the identity of
Leander and Running Rein.*
*I therefore think it highly important to give the respective owners an
opportunity of proving their pedigrees, and their ages.*
*Under these circumstances I think it right to enter an objection to both
of them for the Derby and beg to say that I shall cheerfully bear all or
any part of the expenses which may be incurred by the Stewards in
prosecuting an enquiry, so essential to the very existence of Horse*

Racing.
Maidstone.[8]

In the meantime Dr Cobb, the breeder of the Saddler colt, the genuine Running Rein, sent the following letter to Sir Gilbert Heathcote, the senior steward at Epsom:

Malton, 21st May 1844.
Sir,
The colt foal by The Saddler out of Mab, which I sold to Mr. King, was, when he left my stables, brown with a small white star on his forehead. I cannot say whether his ears were set in close or not – nor do I know whether he had a white heel – the groom who was in my service last year says, he had not.
I am sir,
Yours respectfully,
Chas. Rob. Cobb.[9]

It was fully expected that both cases would have been gone into by the stewards prior to the race, but such was not the case, the stewards considering that sufficient evidence had been provided by the owners of Running Rein and Leander on production of their certificates showing their breeding, to permit them to start. There was, however, an understanding that should either of them win the Derby, the stakes would be withheld and the objection investigated in more detail. It was the same half-hearted attitude that had been embraced at the Houghton Meeting investigation the previous year, probably in the vain hope that neither would win and therefore the problem would cease to exist. They could not even have foreseen the possibility – and hence the predicament they would be in – should Leander and Running Rein occupy the first two places, for the owners of the other placed horses could not have objected to the winner unless they had the co-operation of the owner of the second, which they certainly would not have got.

On the Monday before the great contest there was the usual hive of activity on the Downs, extensive arrangements being made by architects of every class busily engaged in the erecting of their stalls, booths and sideshows. Proceeding with their labours, in the afternoon they were dismayed by the distribution of the following notification from Scotland Yard:

All persons playing or betting in any booth or public place, at any table or instrument of gaming, or at any game or pretended game of chance, will be taken into custody by the police, and may be committed to the House of Correction, and there kept to hard labour for three months. By order of the Commissioners of the Police in the Metropolis, Thomas Bicknell, Superintendent of Police, Metropolitan Police Office, Scotland Yard, May 20, 1844.[10]

As the issuing of this formidable proclamation was so close to the festival date, it was assumed that it would not extend to Epsom Downs, but enquiries soon established that the Secretary of State for the Home Office, Sir James Graham, was well aware of the forthcoming meeting. An immediate appeal was made to those in authority, but they were in ignorance of any such notice being issued, as were local magistrates. The immediate concern was the financial loss to the inhabitants of the town, and it was felt that Sir James Graham, who must have made his decision well in advance, should have had the good grace to issue his notice at an earlier period, thereby saving some degree of loss to the sufferers. No time was lost in preparing a memorial to induce Sir James Graham to suspend his ruling, at least for the present meeting.

A deputation of the memorialists converged on the Home Office to present their memorial. Unsurprisingly, and condescendingly received by the under-secretary, Mr Manners Sutton, their memorial was met with obstinate refusal, the pompous Manners Sutton curtly informing them that their memorial could not be considered, as Sir James Graham's determination to suppress gambling on racecourses was irrevocable. The furore against this apparently venomous decision reverberated through the racing industry: the revenue raised by letting part of the racecourses' grounds, and the resulting admissions, would be considerably curtailed, which would inevitably diminish the number of stakes, plates and prize money, and the effect would necessarily be more injurious than at first imagined. This had not gone unnoticed at nearby Ascot, where Lord Rosslyn declared that he would of necessity be obliged to reduce the amount of prize money.

On this Monday more drama was to follow. It had become evident that Sam Rogers was a confederate of a Newmarket low-life by the name of Bream, who on occasion used the name Braham. He had succeeded in persuading Sam to bet against Ratan.

Whether out of an intensity of guilt, or fear that Lord George was on the case, Sam went to Crockford's son and disclosed the fact that he had been offered a large sum to 'make Ratan safe'. Crockford junior immediately communicated this to Lord George, who demanded that Rogers surrender his betting book. Would Sam refuse this? Indeed not; and it was demurely handed over to the honorable member for Kings Lynn.

There were some unsavoury names against the bets, which confirmed Lord George's reservations.

So, on the Monday evening, Lord George, with Rogers's betting book in his hand, mounted the steps of the Spread Eagle Hotel in Epsom. Sylvanus recalled:

> It was a rich scene with the motley crowd surrounding the aristocratic catechiser, grinning surprise or intelligence.
>
> It was proposed that Pedley (John Gully's son-in-law) should call over the names, but his lordship, with a whip under his arm and a gold pencilcase in his hand and dressed in his old Welbeck hides, commenced proceedings by tranquilly announcing: "Gentlemen, I am going to call over my jockey, Samuel Rogers's book, and I will thank you to answer your names and bets."
>
> "Mr. Gul—ly!" shouted Lord George, from his rostrum.
>
> "Here!" growled the ex-pugilist, quietly removing the cigar from his lips to give place to a sardonic, catch-me-if-you-can, implied smile. "Here!" he replied.
>
> "You have bet Samuel Rogers 350 to 25 against Ratan, I perceive, (Why this is alright; he seems to be backing his own horse, said Lord George aside). Ah! (turning the page) but he stands in a pony with you on The Ugly Buck (no terms named). This has an ugly look. Are those all your bets with Samuel Rogers, Mr. Gully?"
>
> "If you have any more in my name, and will specify, my lord, I shall be better able to answer you," responded the cautious old bruiser.[11]

Lord George proceeded through Rogers's book, carefully ticking off the names: Tom Crommelin, Jerry Ives and a whole list of other worthy betting men, dwelling particularly on some of the bets he was anxious to emphasise. But there was generally believed to be one bet that nobody claimed. This was £10,000 to £2,000, said to be laid by Sam Rogers against Ratan, to a gentleman of high character in the betting ring. Whoever the gentleman was, he did not answer.

It might well have been surmised from this latter bet that Sam had betted against his own horse, putting him under strong suspicion. No doubt thought was given to Sam's integrity; but, even so, it could scarcely have been expected that he would have registered, in his own betting book, evidence that would have discredited him.

Lord George then closed the book and retired into the Spread Eagle, probably no wiser and giving no inkling to his inner thoughts. But misgivings he must have had: was the transaction Gully's? It seemed perceptible that Gully knew more than he cared to admit. Perhaps if Lord George had rephrased his question to Gully's evasive response, it may have elicited a more definitive reply. As it was, Gully was off the hook, although the volume of money placed on The Ugly Buck by Gully and the Danebury confederacy, whom Lord George despised, left him plenty to dwell on.

He had every reason to believe that skulduggery was afoot to make Ratan safe and must have viewed Ratan's chance of success with rapidly diminishing enthusiasm. But there was little he could do, save to give instructions that Rogers was to be locked up for the night in the adjoining stall to Ratan, and the guard doubled.

The ailing Crockford, at home in Carlton House Terrace, was also beside himself with worry. He loathed Gully and all that he stood for. Cheated over Sultan's withdrawal from the St Leger, Crockford so desired to win the Derby. He could then have gone to the shades, happy in the knowledge that Ratan had realised his dream, but his failing body left him too dispirited to consider the fate of Ratan.

Betting on the Monday was far from brisk, the Buck and Ratan both ending at 5 to 2. Orlando, lacking any support, receded to 12 to 1, and Running Rein, in the teeth of another objection, this one lodged by Mr Crockford, was at 17 to 1. Other bets laid were 15 to 1 against Ratan winning the Derby and St Leger, and 1,200 to 100 against Forth's lot winning the Derby, Oaks and St Leger. Lord Glasgow, who was emphatically against the Buck, offered 90,000 to 30,000 against him. This sum frightened backers, and the best the noble lord could achieve was 3,000 to 1,000, taken by a single gentleman. He also laid 10,000 to 2,000 against the Buck for the St Leger.

As the big day approached, Higgins was ill at ease. Worley's refusal of £1,000 concerned him and on 20 May he wrote to Odell:

London, May 20th 1844.
Sir,
I can plainly see the qualification of Running Rein rests solely with Mr.
Worley, therefore trust you will keep him right as I would not be found
to be a party to the concern for all the world. He must say that the horse
he had was larger than this when called upon, which I expect he will be
before the race as the protest is put in and parties wish it settled before
the race. I think he is sure to win and every one wants to back him.
Trusting you will keep him all right.
I am, Dear Sir,
Yours Truly.
H. Higgins
P.S. Come to me at Epsom as soon as you get there.[12]

Testimony to Sir James Graham's ruling was evident by the partly
erected and unfinished gaming booths and stalls and the resulting
extremely thin attendance on the first day of the Meeting. *Bell's Life*
reported that there was not a single variety of gambling, from
French hazard to throwing for pincushions, to be seen.

The unusual continuation of dry weather had rendered the
ground as hard as iron. Light showers had fallen, but these were
insufficient to affect the hardness of the ground, and so the
stewards ordered the distribution of a large quantity of tan over its
surface from end to end. Attendance in the betting ring was
principally confined to professionals, but, even among these, little
business was done either on the day's races or on the great contest
the following day. The only serious movement in the market was
that of Running Rein: the announcement that the stewards had
declared him qualified to run gave him an immense lift in the odds.
A subsequent announcement by Captain Rous that the stewards
had merely declared him qualified 'to start', without giving any
opinion on the case, did not shake his position and he closed at 12
to 1 with backers.

The morning of the great day opened favourably, encouraging a
sharp contrast to the meagre attendance on the previous day. At an
early hour throngs poured towards Epsom. The South Western
and Croydon Railways provided a constant succession of trains to
Kingston and Stoat's Nest (now Coulsdon). Vast numbers were

76

then conveyed to the course by carriages provided for the occasion, prices varying from four to ten shillings a head, depending on the demand, and the more economically inclined chose to walk. The turnpike roads were crowded with vehicles of all descriptions, creating suffocating clouds of dust. The roadside houses took full advantage of this, their liquid offerings absorbing a fair proportion of patronage from the passing throngs.

In Epsom town an immense crowd had gathered in front of the Spread Eagle, anxiously seeking whispers of information that could provide clues as to the probable outcome of the approaching race. But, despite the occasional changes in the betting, the Buck and Ratan maintained their positions at the head of the field. The admirers of Running Rein were no less anxious to show their support and he was backed for large sums at 9 and 10 to 1.

Each side of the course was lined with vehicles of every imaginable class. The stands, especially the Grand Stand, with the exception of the privileged terraces, were crammed to excess. An immense body of police was in attendance, not only to preserve order on the course but also to execute the resolutions of the Home Secretary to suppress every possible description of gambling. The consequence of this rigorous monitoring was that patrons were deprived of any form of amusement to while away their time between races, confining themselves to indulge, without due intermission, the cuisine and libations on offer.

The 65th renewal of the Derby Stakes was the first race of the day, with 29 runners, as detailed in Table 1.

Table 1: Derby Stakes Runners

Owner	Horse	Jockey
Mr J. Day	The Ugly Buck	J. Day Junior
Sir Gilbert Heathcote	Akbar	J. Chapple
Mr W. Crockford	Ratan	S. Rogers
Mr J. Day	Voltri	W. Day
Mr J. Bowes	T'Auld Squire	Holmes
Sir Gilbert Heathcote	Campunero	Perrin
Mr A. Wood	Running Rein	S. Mann
Colonel Peel	Orlando	N. Flatman
Colonel Peel	Ionian	G. Edwards
Colonel Anson	Bay Momus	F. Butler
Mr Ford	Qui Tam	Robinson

Mr J. Osborne	Mount Charles	Bumby
Mr Ford	Phalaris	Whitehouse
Lord George Bentinck	Croton Oil	W. Howlett
Mr Litchwald	Leander	Bell
Mr Hill	Beaumont	Calloway
Mr Gratwicke	Needful	Cotton
Mr J. Forth	The Ashtead Pet	Boyce
Mr Herbert	Colt by Elis	Sly
Lord Glasgow	Colt by Velocipede	Hessletine
Mr Gregory	Loadstone	Darling
Lord Westminster	Lancet	S. Templeman
Mr St Paul	Telemachus	J. Marson
Mr F. Ongley	King of the Gypsies	J. Marlowe
Mr M. Jones	British Tar	Jones
Mr Cuthbert	Beaufront	J. Howlett
Lord Maidstone	Cockamaroo	Simpson
Mr Dixon	Dick Thornton	Darling Junior
Mr Thornhill	Elemi	Chifney

Odell and Worley had made their way to Epsom and met Higgins at the inn where he was residing. Worley asked Higgins who was to ride the horse, to which Higgins replied that they had hoped to get Job Marson to ride but someone had interfered and he would not ride, so they had settled for Sam Mann, whom Worley knew personally. Higgins reminded Odell: "'I hope you will stay with Mr. Worley and keep him alright.'"[13]

On the morning of the race William Carlin met Goodman and, reminding him of their meeting at Smith's, asked what he stood on the horse. Goodman, with more serious matters on his mind, replied: "'Never mind. You stand along with me. Let us first get over it.'"[14]

Soon after 2 o'clock a vast crowd had gathered at the saddling ground below the starting post to await the runners. Superlatives were lavished on the condition of the two cracks, Ratan and The Ugly Buck, by their respective admirers – the former looking exceedingly blooming, and the latter in the way that John Day's accustomed strong preparation was calculated to produce. John Scott's Bay Momus, an elegant speedy-looking animal, was as bright as satin; Colonel Peel's Orlando, a small horse with a somewhat extravagant action, and Ionian each doing credit to their trainer, William Cooper. *The Sporting Magazine*'s scribe reported that it was only justice to mention that Running Rein evinced the bloom and perfection of condition to quite as great an extent as any horse on the course.[15]

One can only imagine Goodman's apprehension. Providing that Running Rein was to win, within a few minutes he stood to pull off the most daring fraud in the annals of the Turf – he and his associates would be wealthy men. But there was Worley. Higgins would have kept him (Goodman) informed of Worley's reservations, and if an inquiry did materialise Goodman would find himself in an extremely compromising position. He would have been even more concerned had he observed Worley and Odell closely scrutinising the colt in the saddling enclosure. Worley was convinced that it was the same colt he had kept on his farm. Odell concurred: it was definitely the same colt that he had seen at Worley's and later at Markham's paddock.[16]

What was even more amusing, and an unfortunate coincidence from Goodman's perspective, was the appearance of Lord George Bentinck's own horse, Croton Oil. Croton Oil had not run as a two-year-old and in his only previous race he had won both heats of a five sovereigns sweepstake at the Epsom Spring Meeting. The *General Stud Book* records him as being bred by Lord George Bentinck, but he was, in fact, the result of Sir Charles Henry Ibbetson's mating of the Capsicum mare with Physician, therefore providing the only incidence of half-brothers running in the same Derby. Lord George had, of course, facetiously made this remark about Running Rein at the previous year's Second October Meeting at Newmarket, when he had spotted Smith's lot on the Heath.

The jockeys, having been weighed out, were summoned before the stewards, Sir Gilbert Heathcote and Baron de Tessier, from whom they received a robust lesson on the inappropriate nature of seeking to take undue advantage of each other at starting, blended with the warning that the laws of racing would be rigorously enforced; and, should there be any exhibition of unacceptable behaviour and disregard for the mandates of the Starter, fines would be levied for any disobedience.

Bell's Life reported the extraordinary scene from the top of the Grand Stand, over the immense area of the course, rendered still more imposing by the almost breathless silence that prevailed, pending the anticipated commencement of the great struggle. There were two failures before Mr Perren, the Starter, got the field of 29 runners up to the post. At the third attempt the flag dropped and the largest field for three years was under way. The running was at once taken up by Leander, followed for a few strides by Voltri, and then by Akbar, with The Ugly Buck third, Orlando behind on his right, and Ratan on the left. Running Rein was next, in The Ugly Buck's track, and to his rear were Ionian and Bay Momus. The pace was so severe that Dick Thornton, Beaumont, the Velocipede colt, Cockamaroo and two or three others could not live with even the second ruck. After running in this way for nearly half-a-mile, Running Rein made his way to the front and took his place at Leander's quarters on the whip hand. They remained in this order until the top of the hill, at which point Running Rein struck Leander's off-hind leg just above the fetlock, smashing the bone down to the pastern. Bell, although unaware of the extent of the injury his horse had received, immediately pulled him back, and the lead was taken by Running Rein, with Akbar and The Ugly Buck still retaining the positions they had held at the start of the race. Running Rein went on with a lead of upwards of two lengths to Tattenham Corner, where a tremendous tail was visible. In the front rank, too, symptoms of distress were apparent: Akbar was in trouble, and before he was well round the turn he was passed by The Ugly Buck, but the Buck himself had also had enough of it, and he gradually receded on the run down the hill and at the road was beaten to a standstill. Colonel Peel's two and Bay Momus then passed him in succession; Orlando with three parts of a length in advance, Ionian second, and Bay Momus at his quarters. They ran in this way to the distance, where Orlando got within a length of the leader. Halfway up it Orlando made a final effort and reached Running Rein's quarters, where he remained to the end, without even making it necessary for Sam Mann to call on his horse. Running Rein won the race with consummate ease by three parts of a length. Orlando beat Ionian by two lengths, which would probably have been less had Edwards persevered to the last. Bay Momus finished at Ionian's shoulder.

The stewards, who were anxious to guard against the results of any possible protests – and to avoid the consequences of the recent Eglinton Park Steeple Chases, where the winner had been disqualified and the Judge had neglected to place a second horse, directed the Judge to place the first four. The Ugly Buck came in fifth, two or three lengths from Bay Momus, with Akbar a further half-length behind. Ratan, who had been emphatically beaten before he reached Tattenham Corner, was a bad seventh, Elemi eighth, T'Auld Squire ninth and Mr Herbert's Elis colt tenth. Poor Leander stopped and managed to hobble along to the distance, where he was dismounted. It was discovered that the bone in his off-hind leg was terribly splintered and he was taken to the Rubbing House stables. Mr Litchwald wanted him shot immediately, but Forth thought it best to have the opinion of a veterinary surgeon. He managed to get Leander back to Ashtead in a van, where Mr Coleman gave the opinion that the leg was so hopelessly damaged that it was impossible to save him. Mr Litchwald gave the order: "Let him be killed." And the poor beast was shot in the presence of about 20 people.[17]

The Litchwalds left without Forth's knowledge and owing nearly £1,000 in training bills. They had promised to see him the next morning, but instead they started off the same afternoon, sending him the following note from Gravesend:

My Dear Sir,
Things look very bad for me, and could not see how to arrange it for the moment, and think it best to go first to Germany to get it settled. Now you do with the mare (Julia) as you please and run her where you like, and don't forget the Goodwood Cup. Write me how every thing is going on; but let your son write, as I cannot read your hand. Time will bring it all to rights.
 G. Litchwald.[18]

After the race, as Worley and Odell were riding towards the Grand Stand, Goodman rode up to them and asked them: "'Well, did you know him?'" To which Worley replied: "'To be sure, I did.'" Goodman was obviously aggravated by Worley's comment, and out of Worley's earshot told Odell: "'Take old Worley, away.'"

They afterwards met Higgins and Benyon Drage at the inn at Epsom, where Higgins was staying. Higgins gave them a bottle of champagne, rejoicing that he had had many people congratulating him on his success. At a convenient moment Odell told Higgins what Goodman had said to Worley, to which his reply was: "'He

[Goodman] was a very great fool.'"[19]

Worley's comments no doubt concerned Goodman. If an inquiry was held, he would need all the assistance possible to undermine any claim that Worley may make.

On the day after the race Goodman met Carlin again, and appealed to him: "'Perhaps we shall want you.'" "'I will save you if the teeth will do anything for you.'" Carlin answered.[20]

Mr Gill, Mr Wood's attorney, accompanied by a Malton tout named Grey, was also despatched to Malton to seek out John Watson, who had taken the genuine Running Rein from Malton to London. Mr Gill, surprisingly for a man of his profession, was about as principled as a libertine - just the type of gentleman to bring discredit on such an honourable profession.

Gill appealed to Watson: "'I want to see if you can identify the horse for us; you know what I mean; you can do it if you like.'" Gill continued that they would not come to him (Watson) in a scrubby manner. Money was no object to their party and they would not send him £10 or £20 to bring him up to London, but £40 or £50, and when he got to London £100 or £150 was no object to them.[21]

Higgins also agonised over their dilemma: everything hinged on Worley; whatever protests were raised, it would be exceedingly difficult to prove the case against Running Rein if Worley were to vindicate Higgins.'"

After the Oaks was run Higgins again came to Odell, requesting him to beg Worley not to tell what he knew about the horse.

Higgins called on Worley early on the Saturday morning, after the race, even before Worley had risen. He wanted to know if Worley had received any letters from anyone.

"'Not a syllable," Worley sharply replied, "but what if I had?"

"All you have got to do is not know the horse," Higgins pleaded.'[22]

Higgins then made his way over to Odell to enquire if he had seen Worley. Odell answered in the negative. Higgins again appealed to Odell that he hoped he would keep Worley quiet.

One could not accuse Higgins of giving up: on the following Wednesday he again met Worley at a cattle show at the Barrack Yard in Northampton, informing Worley that on Tuesday he (Higgins) had been to London for the settling day – as far as he was concerned the Orlando party could not make a case without witnesses.

Odell divulged to Worley Higgins's request to keep Worley quiet, to which Worley worriedly replied that it was a bad job – it would never do.

If Higgins had the slightest notion that he could expect some support from Worley, it was soon shattered when Odell informed him that Worley would tell the truth about the horse whenever he was called on to do so. Higgins contemptuously replied that they had plenty of witnesses to outswear Worley, adding: "'What a damned fool I was to persuade you and Worley to go and see the Derby. If you had not gone you could not have sworn to the colt. Nobody won't see him no more, I'll take care.'"[23]

11
After the Derby

Hoorah! Mr Wood had won the Derby. Victory for the 'little man'. Not quite yet, however. Mr Wood had been sent for by the stewards, but apparently he had gone home. Imagine the confusion on Epsom Downs. Here was a Derby without a winner. The immediate concern must have been how bets were going to be settled. Despite their dilly-dallying before the race, the stewards had made it perfectly clear that should Running Rein or Leander win the Derby the stakes would be withheld. Immediately, a letter was despatched to Weatherbys:

> We the Stewards of Epsom desire you will not pay the Derby Stake to the owner of Running Rein. Such stakes being claimed by Col. Peel as owner of the second horse until another directive to do so by us.
> May 22 1844   De Tessier
> Gilbert Heathcote[1]

Mr Wood – poor, innocent Mr Wood – could not understand why the stakes had been denied him and issued an action for the stakes against Weatherbys in the Court of Common Pleas, his costs being guaranteed by one J. Dixon,[2] a cheesemonger, well known defaulter and ... an associate of Goodman. Colonel Peel also objected and claimed the stakes, but he was not confident that decisive action would be taken by the Jockey Club: if some of the latter had backed the impostor, there would surely be an element of reluctance to investigate. With this in mind, and counter to Mr Wood, Colonel Peel also obtained an order from the Court of Exchequer, prohibiting the stakes from being given up until the case had been decided by law.

However, it was not Colonel Peel but Lord George who amassed the evidence against Goodman. He was aware of the correspondence in *Bell's Life*, between the veterinary surgeon John Bartlett and Wood, and he had also got wind of Goodman hiring

Goneaway from Thomas Ferguson.

It was well known to Lord George's commissioner, Harry Hill, that there was a mutual acquaintance between him (Harry Hill) and Thomas Ferguson. This was Charles Coughlin,[3] a constant companion of Francis Ignatius Coyle. On the evening of the Derby Harry Hill called on Coughlin, who was dining with Coyle on corned pork and pease pudding. Coughlin offered Hill dinner. A bottle of champagne and the finest Irish whiskey (given to Coughlin by Tom Ferguson) later, and Hill had cajoled Coughlin into writing to Ferguson in order to obtain information as to the substitution for Maccabeus with Goneaway. Harry Hill stood to win a large stake on Colonel Peel's Orlando and faithfully promised Coughlin that he would put him on a large sum to nothing if he assisted in unveiling the fraud. In addition, Hill gave an assurance that Ferguson's reply would be kept secret and shown to no one.

Three or four days later Harry Hill called to see if Ferguson's response had been received. Coughlin naively handed over the letter to Hill, on the promise that it would be returned that same evening. Hill immediately took Ferguson's letter to Lord George, who saw that the information contained in it would inevitably award the Derby to Orlando.

The information locked in Ferguson's letter was promising enough for Lord George to make post-haste to Ireland. When he reached Ferguson's abode at Rossmore Lodge, Ferguson refused the pleasure of meeting Lord George as he was suffering from a severe attack of gout and was too ill to accommodate him. However, Lord George refused to be put off so easily. Waving the letter from Ferguson, which he now had in his possession, he demanded an audience. Ferguson had no choice but to see Lord George, and when the latter emerged from Ferguson's bedchamber he knew enough about Running Rein to seal Goodman's fate.

Ferguson had revealed to Lord George, Goodman's request for the colour of Goneaway and some of the black hairs from his leg. This led Lord George to believe that Goneaway's leg had been dyed, but was this of any consequence since poor Goneaway was dead? However, if he could determine where Goodman had purchased the elixir he would be part way to unravelling the plot.

It did not take a great deal of detective work to assume that Goodman had probably purchased the dye in the vicinity of his home in Foley Place – possibly on his way to the Little Nick. Lord

George visited all the chemist shops in Regent Street and the surrounding vicinity but drew a complete blank. He then turned his attention to the hairdressers in the same locality. By chance, he discovered a woman serving behind a counter at Louis Rossi's, a hairdresser and perfumier, at 254 Regent Street,[4] who remembered selling a large quantity of hair dye to a gentleman whom she was particularly able to describe, as he had ordered a second jar and had forgotten to pay for it. To boot, the woman's husband – none other than Mr Rossi himself – had prepared the dye from instructions provided by the customer. Lord George asked Mr Rossi if he would accompany him in a cab to an establishment that Goodman was known to frequent. This was Glenn's bakery at 106 Regent Street.[5] When Goodman exited the premises Mr Rossi was able to identify him.

At Tattersalls settling was in complete confusion. Most of the Saturday and Sunday after the Derby was spent discussing various opinions as to how the bets should be settled. Some proposed that the settlement should be postponed altogether until it had been legally decided whether Running Rein or Orlando was the winner. Others contended that bets involving Running Rein and Leander should be held over, but that all bets not involving them should be settled in the usual way. This latter proposal was generally accepted, and on Monday Tattersalls issued the following resolution, enabling settlement to commence:

> *At a meeting of the most influential subscribers to Tattersalls interested in the Derby and Oaks settlement, it was unanimously agreed that no possible impediment could exist to the settlement of all accounts on the Derby, in which the names of Running Rein and Orlando do not occur, and that, therefore, the settling will take place as usual, with the above exceptions.*[6]

The reference to the Oaks concerned Mr Litchwald's filly Julia (nothing like going the whole hog), who had been objected to by Colonel Anson, Mr Gregory and Squire Osbaldeston on the grounds that she, like Leander, was a four-year-old; or, as the *Bell's Life* scribe, with an obvious knowledge of Greek mythology, so wonderfully put it: 'that she swam the Hellespont with Leander, like that veteran, she might have obtained a riper age than would have entitled her to compete against her juvenile companions.'[7]

There was, of course, a further problem – the death of William Crockford.

There was an accepted practice whereby if the party whose account was to be settled had died all parties were absolved from payment. However, a precedent had been created when a Mr Stonehewer had died on the Saturday after the Derby. His account, which stood to the amount of £15,000, was settled on the following Monday by Captain Rous, at the request of the executors. On the same day, and after this precedent was set, the following letter was received by Tattersalls from Mrs Crockford, William Crockford's widow.

Sir – I trust that the circumstances which cause me to address you will be sufficient apology for so doing. Being ignorant of the custom in use at Tattersalls in situations parallel to the one I now find myself placed in, I consider it best for me at once to place in your hands the betting book of my deceased husband. You will perceive that, in case Running Rein shall receive the stakes, there will be a loss of £604, and in case Orlando shall receive them, of £724. I enclose you, therefore, a draught for the larger sum, and would wish you to apply this sum, together with the receipts from the several losers, to pay as far as may be the claims of the several winners. It is possible that, in a case of this sort, it is not customary to settle the book; should it be so, I am not anxious to establish a precedent. With a deep sense of the trouble I am about to impose on you, I have the honour to be, sir, yours most respectfully.
S.F. Crockford
Carlton House Terrace, May 27, 1844.[8]

The letter was handed to the stewards of the Jockey Club, who gave their opinion as follows:

We are of the opinion that every person indebted to the late Mr. Crockford on his Epsom account is bound to pay the amount due to the person deputed to settle the same.
May 27, 1844   *Stradbroke*
                                    George Byng.[9]

By the above practice of death absolving payment of debt, a wonderful story was created, which has been perpetuated in legend. This was that Crockford died before the Derby, and that his

87

corpse was propped up in a window of his club in St James's, where passers-by would see it and therefore assume he was in an apparent state of rude health, thus making him liable for any debt.

Prior to settling, the stewards had received a letter, dated 24 May 1844, from Thomas Gill, Mr Wood's solicitor:

To the Honorable The Stewards of Epsom Races.
Gentleman – As solicitor for, and on the part and behalf of, Mr. Alexander Wood, the owner of Running Rein, I beg the favour of your appointing twelve o'clock on Monday next to proceed on the objection of the Hon. George Anson, to the qualification of Running Rein; and also to fix the hour of two o'clock of the same day to proceed on the evidence of disqualification to the same colt to be offered on the part of Colonel Peel.
I am, Gentlemen, your obedient servant,
Thomas Gill.
To Sir Gilbert Heathcote, Bart., and the Baron de Tessier.[10]

Mr Gill personally delivered the above letter to Baron de Tessier on the Friday morning following the Derby, and he was directed to return to attend a meeting with the stewards at 4 o'clock in the afternoon for an answer. Mr Gill arrived at the appointed time only for Baron de Tessier to inform him that Colonel Peel had unfortunately left the racecourse, but that Colonel Anson had promised to see Colonel Peel and send an answer in time for a meeting at 1 o'clock on Saturday at Epsom – which again failed to provide an answer. A revised time of 7 o'clock in the evening was given to Mr Gill. At that time Mr Gill, curbing his frustration, and on this occasion accompanied by Mr Wood, again met Baron de Tessier, who advised them that he had received a letter from Colonel Peel, offering to refer the matter to a barrister, to be selected by the Lord Chief Justice, and stating that he had commenced an action against Messrs Weatherby for the stakes. Mr Wood declined to agree to Colonel Peel's proposal and the objection of Colonel Anson, whereupon Baron de Tessier considered, as far as the stewards were concerned, that the matter was at an end, subsequently sending the following letter to Mr Gill:

25th May, 1844.

Sir – Having received an intimation from Colonel Peel that he has caused notice of action to be served on Mr. Weatherby, we decline further interference with the question of the qualification of the horse, Running Rein – and remain, Sir, your obedient servants.

De Tessier.

Gilbert Heathcote.

To Mr. Gill, solicitor to Mr. A. Wood.[11]

It was inevitable that there would be numerous opinions speculating on the outcome of the case. Rumours were rife, one coming from 'Craven', a scribe for *The Standard*, claiming that Mr Sloane Stanley, a member of The Jockey Club, admitted that there was not a leg for the protest to stand on and regretted that it had ever been urged.

Mr Sloane Stanley responded that their correspondent was misinformed. He had in fact called on Mr Goodman to produce the horse, in order that his mouth could be examined, which Mr Goodman refused to do, consequently throwing the race for the Derby into its state of litigation and embarrassment.[12]

Lord George continued his pursuit of evidence with a meticulous perceptiveness that would have done credit to a TV detective. In fact, Sylvanus informs us that one of the oldest London solicitors remarked that it was impossible for any man brought up to the profession to have prepared a chain of evidence more clear of flaw or doubt than the case got up entirely by his Lordship on this extraordinary trial. One of the people from whom he sought information was the trainer Thomas Coleman, who kept the Turf Hotel at St Albans, writing to him: 'Find out who painted Goneaway's leg. Was it Goodman or William Sadler? It was painted in London.'[13]

Another letter runs:

Can the ostler at Bryant's recollect a dirty, mean-looking little fellow, with light-brown or sandy thin whiskers, with a bad knee, kicked by the horse he was leading up, stopping at the Red Lion to bait, on Saturday the 24th September 1842, and asking his way either to Haines's livery-stables in Langham Place, or else to Mr. Goodman's stables in Foley Place? The colt he was leading up was a high-couraged, unbroke, or rather half-broke bay, entire thoroughbred two-year-old colt with black legs, and not a white speck about him, and a long tail. The colt had also, at that time, a small scar scarcely healed up, on his near arm, just above the knee on the outside. The scar would be about this size [sketch]. *The man and colt were on their way to Epsom to Smith's training stables. The man's name was Richard Watson.*[14]

12

The Litchwalds and the Exhumation of Leander

Apart from the investigation into Running Rein, there was also the question of the unfortunate Leander. According to Bell, Leander was full of running when he was struck into, and had he not suffered a fatality there was every possibility that he may have won – or finished second to Running Rein. Had Leander won, Mr Wood, probably completely ignorant of the suspicions surrounding the Litchwalds' horse, would not have objected to the winner. Even if it had occurred to him to do so, Goodman would have probably advised him against it. And had Leander finished second, the Litchwalds would likewise not have stepped forward to support their old 'un.

There was even a suggestion – and this is not at all surprising in view of the farce at the 1840 Houghton Meeting – that Goodman and the Litchwalds were in collusion and that it had been predetermined that Leander should win and Running Rein should finish second, but this has never been substantiated. Had either of these scenarios materialised, there would have been no inquiry, no trial, and the result would have been perpetuated throughout Turf history.

The Litchwalds were well known as large purchasers of thoroughbred stock for the German market. One of their purchases, Blue Pill, who had finished second in the 1840 Croxton Park Gold Cup, had been winning some good races in Germany. Nimrod, reviewing the racing season in *The Sportsman*,[1] seized on the opportunity to articulate his view that Mr Litchwald was of dubious character and had thought proper to 'come Tom Paine'[2] over his countrymen by starting horses under false pedigrees. The upshot of this charge was that all his horses had to run under certain conditions, which implied that, although winners, the stakes would be held in abeyance until he proved that the accusations against him were unfounded. His case was submitted to the

Committee of Racing, once in Micklenburgh and twice in Prussia, and the outcome was that Mr Litchwald was no longer allowed to start a horse in those countries.

During the Goodwood race week of 1842 the Litchwalds sent three horses to John Forth's stables at Michel Grove to be broken and trained, with their pedigrees signed by themselves: a brown filly by Muley Moloch, out of Barbara, subsequently named Julia; a bay colt by Scamander, out of sister to Mussulman, subsequently named Leander; and a bay colt by Velocipede, out of Fair Jane. *The General Stud Book* records that the brown filly by Muley Moloch, out of Barbara, was bred by John Scott in 1841 and sold with her dam to Mr Litchwald. But was this the same filly that ran in the name of Julia in the Oaks? The stewards, after due examination of her mouth, obviously thought not.

Owing to ill health, Forth did not see Leander until December of 1842, when he described him as a large, coarse-looking colt, but possessing the appearance and points of a racehorse; possibly a remarkable description for an apparent yearling.

Following his Goodwood races Forth tried him in August, with Venus (bay filly Sir Hercules-Echo) at three pounds, she being then three years old. Venus was not a bad sort, having finished second in the Woodcote Stakes. Leander won the trial by two or three lengths, leading Forth to suspect that the Ascot observers may not have been incorrect in suspecting he was a three-year-old.

Did Mr Forth immediately call in a veterinary expert to dispel his concern and come clean? No. He waited until the following February, when he had two sick horses in his stable. Mr Wood, veterinary surgeon of Arundel (not to be confused with Running Rein's Mr Wood), was called in to attend to them, and was asked to take a look at Leander at the same time: "Oh, and by the way, Mr. Wood. Whilst you are here would you examine this horse's mouth, as I am a little uncertain of his age? His name is Leander." Mr Wood conveniently pronounced him a backward three-year-old.

Forth asked for a certificate to substantiate Leander's age.[3] But why would he need this? Surely, if he really believed Leander to be three years old, he would need no certificate. However, Mr Wood's signature, and that of his clerk as witness, provided a convenient endorsement to enable Forth to carry on training Leander for the Derby with a clear conscience and counter any awkward questions that might be asked at a later date. *Bell's Life* even queried whether the horse submitted to Mr Wood for examination was the identical Leander, or an animal professing to be Leander, of the age mentioned in the certificate.

The certificate read as follows:

I hereby certify that in the month of February last I examined privately, at Mr. Forth's request, the horse "Leander," and pronounced him to be three-years-old at that time. He had a decided three years' old mouth, and its tusks had not shown themselves.
J.Wood.
Arundel, 27thMay, 1844.   S.T. Hartman

The events surrounding the death of Leander were truly astonishing. After he was shot, and before he was buried at Ashtead, Mr James Mitchell, a veterinary surgeon and sometime butcher and driver of the Worthing to London coach, who was obviously aware of the suspicions surrounding Leander's age, asked Forth if he could take off the jaw, as it had the appearance of a very young mouth and it would be a satisfaction for Mr Forth to show his friends. Initially, Forth declined, but he later agreed that it was better to do so.

Mitchell sawed off the lower jaw and John Cuthbert,[4] who had buried the horse, boiled it to remove the flesh and preserve the teeth. The jaw was then sealed up in order for it to be inspected by the veterinary surgeon, Mr Field, of Oxford Street.[5]

Two nights later, to celebrate the victory in the Oaks of Colonel Anson's The Princess (chestnut filly Slane – sister to Cobweb), a high-spirited party was held at John Scott's at Leatherhead. The protest against the Litchwald's filly Julia became a topic of discussion, and it extended to Leander and his secret interment. By way of a caper, the merrymakers decided that it would be a good idea to venture into the night and dig Leander up, thereby discovering, to their amazement, the absence of the lower jaw. This only confirmed previous suspicions. The drunken revellers then decided to go the whole hog and have his head off.

The unfortunate Leander was suitably butchered and on the Saturday morning his head was submitted to John Bartlett, the veterinary surgeon of Dorking. Mr Bartlett was an expert when it came to the examination of horses' teeth in order to determine their age, and it was he who was so incessant in his belief that Running Rein was a four-year-old. After examining Leander's upper jaw he pronounced that it was definitely that of a four-year-old. This was farcical enough, but the comedy did not end here. On the same day Forth acknowledged that the missing lower jaw was in his possession – that it had been cut off by Mr Mitchell and boiled for the purpose of removing the flesh and preserving the teeth.

Armed with his trophy, old Forth made his way up to London to deliver it to Mr Field. Picture the scene in Mr Field's office. Here was Mr Forth, confidently presenting the jaw to Mr Field and expecting to be fully vindicated. However, instead Mr Field was not at all obliging, announcing that this was not the jaw of a three-year-old but that of a four-year-old.

Being entirely displeased with Mr Field's anatomical knowledge, Forth stormed off to Weatherbys in Burlington Street, where he accidentally happened on Lord Stradbroke. He expounded his belief to Lord Stradbroke that – despite the opinions of the veterinary surgeons Messrs Field and Bartlett and however eminent they may be – Leander was a three-year-old.

After listening to Forth's verbal onslaught the noble Lord gave prominence to the fact that the Litchwalds were not available to denounce these accusations, having returned to Germany. *Bell's Life* was not so delicate, however, pointing out that the Litchwalds had 'made themselves scarce' and were nowhere to be found. It was indeed unfortunate that the Litchwalds were not present to relieve themselves from the suspicion of having any inducement to sanction such extraordinary proceedings. *Bell's Life* went on to express facetiously their surprise that as well as removing the jaw Mr Litchwald had not sold the carcass to make German sausages![6]

On Tuesday 28 May Mr Forth appeared at Tattersalls, reiterating his assertion that Leander was of the correct age, and produced the certificate signed by Mr Wood and the following certificate from James Mitchell:

I hereby solemnly declare that I cut the under jaw from Leander in the presence of several persons, not at the request of Mr. Forth, but thinking, as the horse lay, it was the youngest mouth I had ever seen. I thought it would be a satisfaction to Mr. Forth to show his friends.
Jas. Mitchell
Worthing, 28th May, 1844.[7]

Bearing in mind the controversy surrounding Leander and a further accusation that Mr Forth meant to refuse to pay his bets on Leander – an accusation that he most profusely denied had the slightest foundation, claiming that he would cheerfully pay every bet he lost – Mr Forth deemed it judicious to send a lengthy missive to the editors of the morning papers, comprehensively detailing the history of Leander, from the time the Litchwalds had sent him to Michel Grove, until Mr Wood had apparently confirmed him to be three years old.

The epistle according to Mr Forth continued:

... My son, in the early part of the present month, happening to be in town, saw Messrs. Litchwald, and spoke to them of the unpleasant remarks which were continually made in the weekly sporting papers relative to the horse's age, and said that they ought to put a stop to them, as they had it in their power to do so; they then declared to him that they could swear he was the right age, and before several persons showed him the "German Stud Book," which appeared to be perfectly correct, and it was his opinion, as well as mine, that the Messrs. Litchwald knew their horse to be a three-year-old, and could prove it, otherwise I would not have trained him.

In your report of the case in Monday's paper, it stated that I said, 'I had been grossly imposed upon by the Messrs. Litchwald, and it was only the vicious temper of the horse that had prevented an earlier discovery,' etc., etc. I beg to say this is erroneous. I should not be justified in saying that I had been imposed upon by the Messrs. Litchwald, until I am convinced that he was a four-year-old, and that they knew him to be so; and I certainly am not at present convinced on that head, and most sincerely hope that they will yet send over a complete refutation of the charges brought against them; and with regard to the vicious temper of the horse, etc., and the subsequent remark "that it is strange so experienced a trainer should have been so slow in satisfying himself upon the point," I must observe that his temper was not at all vicious, and that he would have allowed any person to look at his mouth. But I contend that it is not the duty of a trainer to examine the mouth of any horse that is sent to his stables, but merely to manage him to the best of his abilities, and that this is the only instance in my life of my sending for a veterinary surgeon to examine a horse's mouth belonging to another party, and I even go so far as to say that I exceeded my duty in this instance, and my only excuse is that I did so in consequence of remarks most annoying to my feelings which had from time to time appeared in the newspapers.

In your paper of this day there appears to be a doubt entertained whether Mr. Wood examined the identical Leander or an animal professedly Leander. To clear up any such doubt I herewith send a copy of a declaration made by me this day before Mr. Hardwick, a magistrate of Marlborough street police office. I am, Sir, your very obedient humble servant.   John Forth.

240 Oxford Street, May 29

Mr Forth's enclosed declaration read as follows:

I, John Forth, of Michel Grove, in the county of Sussex, do hereby solemnly declare, that in the month of February last, in consequence of certain rumours as to the age of the colt Leander, the property of Mr. Litchwald, which I then had in training for the Derby, I caused the said colt to be examined by Mr. Wood, the veterinary surgeon of Arundel, in the said county of Sussex, and that the colt which Mr. Wood did examine and alluded to in the annexed certificate, was the same colt Leander that run for the Derby in the present year; and I do further declare, that in consequence of the said rumours I questioned Mr. Litchwald as to the fact of the said colt's age, and he always positively asserted that the said colt was no more than three-years-old, and that there would be no difficulty whatever in proving the same; and I do hereby further declare, that I believed the assertions so made by the said Mr. Litchwald to be true; and I make this solemn declaration consciously believing the same to be true, and by virtue of the provisions of an Act made and passed in the sixth year of the reign of his late Majesty King William IV, intituled "An Act to repeal an Act of the present session of Parliament, intituled 'An Act for the more effectual abolition of the oaths and affirmations taken and made in various departments of the State, and to substitute declarations in lieu thereof, and for the more entire suppression of voluntary and extra judicial oaths and affidavits, and to make other provisions for the abolition of unnecessary oaths'.

John Forth.

Declared at the Police-Court, Great Marlborough Street, this 29th day of May, 1844, before me,

J. Hardwick

Magistrate for the Metropolitan Police District.[8]

Mr Forth had such a penchant for writing to the press, continually bleating as to how unfairly he had been treated and justifying his actions, that one must wonder if he had time to train his horses. Two days later he fired off another letter, this time to *Bell's Life*, concerning the withdrawal of Foig-a-Ballagh from the Derby:

Sir – As there were paragraphs in your papers of Sunday last and the previous Sunday relative to the horse Foig a Ballagh, I hope you will do me the justice of inserting the following explanation, which I had written to be inserted in the morning papers after my letter about "Leander's age," but it was considered by the editors to take up too much space, and that not having made any charge, it was not necessary that they should insert my explanation. To convince you how uncalled for and how very unjust the remarks were, I will as briefly as possible state the circumstances. On Thursday, the 9th Inst, I wrote to Mr. Irwin in Ireland to inform him that his horse had gone amiss, and recommended him in that letter to write up to Messrs. Weatherby and strike him out, telling him it was a mode of procedure which I had invariably adopted with my own horses. My acquaintance with Mr. Irwin was not of such long standing that I could be certain that he would adopt my recommendation without first seeing his horse, and I contend that I should not have been justified in stating to any individual that a horse belonging to another person, and merely trained by me, was or was not likely to start, but that I should have far exceeded my duty in even saying anything about his being amiss, as Mr. Irwin might have come over to England and determined on running his horse lame or not lame.

In consequence of the remarks that were made on that occasion Mr Irwin has publicly stated that he will never make another declaration of the sort – nor will I. No man has endeavoured to avoid the censure of the world more than myself, and no man has been more unfairly treated. I don't ask the public either to back my horse or to lay against them; they must do as they think proper, allowing me the same right that is conceded to all others, of whatever profession or business they may be. Viz., that of what I please with my own property.

In conclusion, Sir, I beg to say that I well know a certain party who, from a feeling of jealousy, have used their utmost endeavours and strained their every nerve to injure my character, and to crush me for many years past, but had they only remained quiet a short time longer it was my full determination that next Doncaster Races should have

*terminated my career on the Turf by them, relying as I do in full
confidence, on the countenance and support of all honourable and just
men."*
*I am, Sir, your very obedient servant,
240, Oxford Street, May 31, 1844.   John Forth.*[9]

The 'certain party' referred to was obviously the Jockey Club;
Forth was becoming a thorn in their side, inundating them with
letters.

In consequence of the damnable practice of gentlemen mistaking
the age of their horses, a general meeting of the Jockey Club was
held at Weatherbys, Old Burlington Street, on 15 June 1844. The
members present are given in Table 2.

Table 2: Attendees at Jockey Club meeting of 15 June 1844

Right Hon. G.S. Byng		
The Earl of Stradbroke	=	Stewards
The Marquis of Exeter		

The Earl of Albemarle	Col. Peel
The Hon. Col. Anson	George Payne, Esq.
Sir David Baird	Hon. Capt. Rous
S. Batson, Esq.	Earl of Rosslyn
Duke of Beaufort	J.V. Shelley, Esq.
Lord George Bentinck	W. Sloane Stanley, Esq.
C.C. Greville	John Stanley, Esq.
George Grosvenor	The Earl of Verulam
John Mills, Esq.	Sir W.W. Wynn, Bart
W.A. Roberts, Esq.	

The manner in which Sir Gilbert Heathcote and Baron de Tessier
had managed the protest against Running Rein and Leander did
not sit well with all the members, and the letter from Baron de
Tessier, stating his full concurrence in the desire expressed that
Epsom races should in future be under the control and
management of the Epsom stewards, conjointly with the stewards
of the Jockey Club, for the time being, did little to satisfy them.

Several resolutions were discussed, including the refusal of the
Epsom stewards to allow Colonel Peel's solicitor to see the

declarations provided by Mr Wood, by virtue of which they had allowed Running Rein to start for the Derby. Charles Greville believed that the stewards had acted erroneously and that the declarations should have been made available to Colonel Peel and other gentlemen who had objected to the qualification of Running Rein. Three of the members - The Marquis of Exeter, The Earl of Rosslyn and Mr J.V. Shelley - opposed the resolution, although some members had left the meeting and The Earl of Albermarle had declined to vote.

Mr Weatherby sent copies of the resolution to the Epsom stewards, and Baron de Tessier sent the following reply:

Corpus Christi Coll. Oxford
June 18th 1844
Your letter containing the copy of a resolution proposed by the Jockey Club at a meeting of the 15th was forwarded to me here, and reached me in the afternoon of yesterday.
I beg you to communicate my reply to the Stewards of the Club, to whom I presume it is properly addressed.
I have every wish, as one of the Stewards at Epsom, to defer to the opinions of the Jockey Club, but I fear I cannot in the present instance do so consistently with what is due to myself. The declarations in my keeping were placed before the Stewards of Epsom as a basis on which to found a further and more extended investigation.
If the Gentlemen who objected to Running Rein, before and after the Race, had deemed it advisable to investigate the question of his qualification before the Stewards of Epsom, as a preliminary to ulterior proceedings in a Court of Law if they deemed necessary, they would have been in full possession of the matters contained in those Declarations and also would, so far as depended on the Stewards, have been able to examine in person the parties by whom the declarations were made.
But it was thought more advisable to take the case at once into a Court of Law and so soon as the decision was formally stated to the Stewards of Epsom, they considered their functions had wholly ceased, and that they had no right to detain the Declarations, and certainly they had no wish to do so, save only with a view to justify their proceedings up to that time, if the propriety of such proceedings were called in question.
With this in view, solely, and for this purpose solely, I detained the Declarations with the consent of Mr. Wood's Attorney, and therefore I

feel that without his consent I cannot with propriety make them public
pending the present proceedings at Law.
I am, Sirs,
Yours faithfully,
De Tessier[10]

Several other resolutions were proposed and, after some discussion, their further consideration was postponed until Monday 17 June. The members present are given in Table 3.

Table 3: Attendees at Jockey Club meeting of 17 June 1844

The Right Hon. G.S. Byng
The Earl of Stradbroke   =   Stewards
The Marquis of Exeter

The Hon. Col. Anson	The Hon. Capt. Rous
S. Batson, Esq.	J.V. Shelley, Esq.
C.C. Greville	W.Sloane Stanley, Esq.
Viscount Maidstone	The Earl of Verulam
Lord C. Manners	Viscount Villiers
The Marquis of Normanby	Sir W.W. Wynn, Bart.
George Payne, Esq.	

Having taken into consideration the circumstances that had lately occurred on the Turf, which seemed to require the urgent attention of the Jockey Club, the following resolutions were proposed:

1st. That cases have occurred in which persons have fraudulently
entered to run for stakes, which, by the published conditions, were
limited to horses of a specified age, horse above the age so specified;
gaining for the horses so entered an unfair advantage over their
competitors, and thus races have been won by horses which were in
reality not qualified to start.

2nd. It appears to the Club that such proceedings not only tend to
defraud the owners of those horses which would otherwise have been
winners, but are calculated to inflict an injury upon the Turf by
bringing racing into disrepute, and by deterring honorable men from
entering into a competition in which they run the risk of being

encountered by such dishonest rivals.

3rd. That the Club, as patrons of racing, have in this matter a direct interest separate from that of the individuals who may happen to be sufferers by such frauds; and that it behoves them to take care that in all such cases the law by which such frauds are punishable should be duly enforced. But it may frequently happen that the individuals upon whom such frauds have been practised may, on application to the Stewards of the race, obtain redress, so far as regards the payment of the stakes, and being content with this, may not choose to incur the trouble and expense of prosecuting the offending parties, and thus such parties, or other parties of a similar description, may be induced by the expression of impunity to repeat attempts of the same kind.

4th. That in all cases in which it shall be established to the satisfaction of the Jockey Club that a fraud has been practised, or attempted, by any person, in regard to the entering or running any horse for any race, or that any other fraudulent proceeding which is punishable by law has taken place in regard to any race, the Jockey Club shall, if they think fit, with the consent of the party aggrieved (in case such party should decline to prosecute), take such steps as may be recommended by proper legal advisers, for the purpose of inflicting on the offenders the punishment to which they have rendered themselves liable.

5th. When the age of qualification of a horse is objected to, either before or after running, for any race in which he is engaged, the Stewards, or those whom they may appoint, being Members of the Jockey Club, shall have power to order an examination of the horse's mouth by competent persons, and to call for all such evidence as they may require, and their decision shall be final; unless they shall think fit to recommend that the question in dispute be carried into a Court of Law.

6th. If a horse shall run in any race in England, or elsewhere, and it shall be proved to the satisfaction of the Stewards, or of those whom they may appoint, that the horse was not of the age represented, the owner, or part owner, trainer, groom, or person having the care of such horse at the time, shall be for ever disqualified from running or training any horse where the rules of the Jockey Club apply, and from being employed by any member of the said Club.

7th. No horse foaled out of the United Kingdom shall be entered for any race where the rules of the Jockey Club prevail, unless the owner shall at the time of naming produce to the person appointed to receive such nomination, and leave with him, a certificate from some racing club of the country where the horse was foaled, or from the mayor or other public officer of the district, stating the age, pedigree, and colour of the horse, and the marks by which it is distinguished.

A further meeting was held on 22 June, to consider the question of the age of Leander. The members present are given in Table 4.

Table 4: Attendees at Jockey Club meeting of 22 June 1844

Right Honourable G.S. Byng	=	Stewards
The Earl of Stradbroke		

The Hon. Col. Anson	T. Houldsworth, Esq.	J.V. Shelley, Esq.
Earl of Chesterfield	Colonel Peel	W.S. Stanley, Esq.
C.C. Greville, Esq.	Earl of Rosslyn	J.R. Udny, Esq.
General Grosvenor		

The persons examined on this occasion were the Forths, father and son; Mr Wood, the veterinary surgeon of Arundel; and Mr Field, Mr Bartlett and Mr Mitchell.

Mr Forth Snr repeated his version of the affair, admitting that he had had some suspicion that the horse was a three- instead of a two-year-old when he first joined his string, but that he was satisfied with Mr Wood's opinion and took no further steps in the matter, although he now really had no doubt that Leander was four years old when he ran for the Derby.

Mr Wood, veterinary surgeon at Arundel, stated:

I was desired to examine the mouth of a horse, in February 1844. He was a dark bay horse, with black legs. I declared him to be three-years-old. Mr. Forth told me afterwards that the horse whose mouth I examined was Leander. Mr. Forth asked me to give a certificate that Leander was three-years-old, which I did.

Mr Wood was then shown the lower jaw of a horse. He said at

once that it was the jaw of a three-year-old. He was then asked to examine the jaw and to state to the club why he thought it was that of a three-year-old. He did so, and then declared that it was the jaw of a four-year-old: "'The lower teeth do not reach that length till a horse is four-years-old; or nearly so.'"

The jaw produced was Leander's jaw, which had been in Mr Field's custody since the Epsom races.

Mr Wood continued:

I examined the horse in February, rather carelessly, and thought he was three-years-old. I think that in the space of three months such an alteration as that between the horse I examined in February and the jaw now produced could hardly have taken place.

Mr Field stated:

Forth called on me after Epsom races, and left in my care the lower jaw of a horse which I now produce, which he said was Leander's jaw. It is decidedly the jaw of a four-year-old horse. The upper jaw now produced is also that of a four-year-old. The whole being put together, exactly fits. I can always decide between a three and a four-year-old without doubt.

Mr Bartlett stated:

The head of a horse, which I now produce, was examined by me at Leatherhead, on the 25th of May. The lower jaw had previously been cut off. The head has been in my possession ever since. It is the head of a four-year-old horse. The lower jaw, now produced, exactly fits and belongs to the head. Colonel Anson told me on the 25th May, when I examined the head, that it was Leander's head. I cannot be mistaken between the age of a three-year-old and a four-year-old, nor can I between a two and a three-year-old, unless some trick has been played.[11]

Mr Mitchell stated that he saw Leander after he was shot and, thinking he had the mouth of a very young three-year-old, had his lower jaw cut off for the satisfaction of Mr Forth, and Mr Mitchell on his cross-examination admitted that he "didn't know a two-year-old from a three-year-old, a three-year-old from a four-year-old, or in fact anything at all about the age of a horse".

The Sporting Magazine could not hold themselves back from

commenting on this comedy:

> *We ought to have been boiling over with indignation instead of laughter*
> *– to have commented on it in strong and bitter terms; but, really, the case*
> *for the defence was too much for us. Such a compound of affirmation*
> *and contradiction was, perhaps, never seen before in a court of honour*
> *or a court of justice.[12]*

Having heard the evidence, the Jockey Club members were fully
satisfied that Leander was four years old when he ran in the Derby,
and they therefore resolved:

> *1. That Messrs. Litchwald, the owners of Leander, shall be for ever*
> *disqualified from entering or running any horse in their own name, or*
> *in the name of any other person, at any race where the rules of the*
> *Jockey Club are recognised.*
> *2. That Mr. Ley, whose horse ran second for a two-years-old stakes at*
> *Ascot, in 1843, when Leander came in first, is entitled to those stakes.*

Mr Wood considered the treatment he had received to be
undeserved and sent the following letter to *The Morning Post*:

> *Having read in your paper of yesterday my evidence before the Jockey*
> *Club on Saturday last, and considering it to be a most unfair and*
> *partial statement, I hope you will insert this letter. I find that there are*
> *several things omitted which would have materially altered the evidence;*
> *as for instance, when I said it had* then *the appearance of the jaw of a*
> *four-year-old horse, I stated also that its having been boiled would make*
> *a material difference in its appearance, from what it had when the*
> *animal was alive, and the flesh and gums on the jaw. The evidence too,*
> *as printed in your paper, would imply a doubt that the horse I saw in*
> *February was Leander, when, in fact, I had no such doubt. I know the*
> *horse that I then examined was Leander, and I considered him to be*
> *three-years-old, and told Mr. Forth so at the time. There are many other*
> *statements that are very unfair, and, as I am a plain countryman, quite*
> *unaccustomed to being questioned and cross-examined, but know my*
> *own business very well, only want justice done to me.*
> *I am, Sir, your obedient servant,   John Wood.*
> *Arundel, June 27th 1844.[13]*

The Jockey Club inquiry had not absolved Mr Forth, nor found against him of any wrongdoing. Their failure to indulge him provoked yet a further response in an attempt to restore his reputation, which was posted in both *The Morning Post* and *Bell's Life*:

Gentlemen – It is with much surprise that I read in the Racing Calendar, of Tuesday the 25th instant, a statement which purported to be a statement of the evidence given before a meeting of the Jockey Club, on the 22nd inst. with reference to the horse 'Leander.' Now, I do positively assert that such statement notices only the evidence of some of the persons examined, and that in so compressed a form that the statement so published is calculated to produce a false impression as to my conduct, and I appeal to the recollection of those honorable members who were present at such meeting as to the truth of my assertion.

I court the fullest investigation by the Jockey Club, and I now positively assert, as I have already on oath affirmed, that I believed the colt 'Leander' was the proper age when he ran for the Derby.

I am, Gentlemen, your most obedient, humble servant,

29th June, 1844.[14]   John Forth

He also posted a copy of a letter he had received from Mr Litchwald, who persisted in his assertion that Leander was three years old, which would appear to indicate that Mr Forth had no knowledge to the contrary prior to the horse starting for the Derby, save for his own suspicion based on the trial with Venus:

Lankwitz, Berlin, June 24th.

My Dear Sir – I am very sorry I could not answer your letter sooner, as I have been a fortnight from home; but I am very easy about the Leander affair, and do not care what the people say in the newspapers. We cannot help it; but I can only assure you he was a three-year-old. What Field or anybody else says about his mouth is all nonsense; but I shall be able to send you, by and by, some more proof, &c. (signed) G.Litchwald.

Another letter from Mr Litchwald, to the editor of *Bell's Life*, reads as follows:

Seeing in the different London papers various accounts respecting my horse Leander and the mare Julia, I think it proper to give the public the following facts:–

The statement of Mr. Forth about Leander is perfectly true in all respects. The colt was brought over by one of my men. I likewise sent afterwards a German lad to Mr. Forth to look after the horse, who well knew the horse, and was with Mr. Forth for a year. But in consequence of Mr. Forth being dissatisfied with the boy, I thought proper to remove him from his stables. I likewise have sufficient proof which would prove Leander not only his right age, but that he was bred by me in 1841. It may be asked why I do not produce these proofs? Had he won the Derby, of course I would have been compelled to bring the proof forward; but as he is now dead, in what way can I prove it? My witnesses must have seen the horse in England before they could prove a decision.

Respecting Julia, I bought her and her dam of Mr. T. Scott [sic], in Malton, in the spring of 1841, who sent them both to Hull to be shipped to Hamburg. I then sold the same mare and foal to Baron Seckendorf at Broocks, near Demmin. Some time afterwards in consequence of the foal pleasing me so much, I made an agreement with the Baron that the filly should be named in the Oaks and other races between us.

She was, therefore, sent to England to Mr. Forth to be trained for her engagements, and, of course, I must call on Mr. Scott to give me a certificate, and which I have done.

Your remarks respecting 'making ourselves scarce, and were nowhere to be found' could only be to create more prejudice in honest men's minds, it being well known I bought a great number of horses in England for Gastrow races, which took place on the 31st of May, and I only arrived there just in time. I must further add, my remaining in England could prove nothing.

I am, Sir, your very obedient servant.

G. Litchwald

Lankwitz. June 20th 1844[15]

Perhaps old Litchwald had the last laugh. According to Sylvanus, having been accused of knowing that Leander was a four-year-old, he scornfully replied: "'What lies they tell in England! Mein Got, he was more than six!'"[16]

13
The Trial

On Saturday 25 May Mr Wood, who thought he had every reason to believe that he was the innocent party, and supposedly not realising that he had been duped by Goodman, initiated a legal action against Weatherbys, the holders of the stake money. The case came before the Court of Common Pleas on Tuesday 4 June.

A few days previously Messrs Weatherby had obtained a rule nisi, calling on Mr Wood and Colonel Peel to interplead and relieve the stakeholders from the expense and anxiety of litigation.

Mr Serjeant Byles, appearing for Mr Wood, the plaintiff, stated that he was willing for the rule to be made absolute. But Mr Serjeant Talfourd, appearing for Colonel Peel, objected to any step being taken in the absence of Mr Serjeant Shee, on whose application the rule had been obtained. Their Lordships were aware that a separate action had been brought against Messrs Weatherby, in the Court of Exchequer, by Colonel Peel. Interpleader rules had been obtained in each court, and Colonel Peel was very anxious that an issue should be directed by the Court of Exchequer, as the state of the cause paper in the Common Pleas precluded all hope of the case being tried there during the sittings after the present term.

Mr Serjeant Byles said that Mr Wood was equally anxious to have the cause tried in the Common Pleas, and therefore he wished to press it on as fast as possible. The form of the issue had been agreed on between the parties, and all that Mr Wood desired was that an issue should be directed. But Mr Justice Creswell wondered how the court could allow Mr Serjeant Byles to make the rule absolute in the absence of Mr Serjeant Shee.

Mr Serjeant Byles said that Mr Wood had been called on to appear and show cause, and he had no cause to show, but was ready to have the rule made absolute. A contest would probably arise hereafter with reference to one of the actions abiding the issue of the other, and it was necessary to prepare for that struggle by pressing on the case without delay.

It appeared to Mr Justice Creswell that the Court of Exchequer had got possession of the case first. Mr Serjeant Byles claimed, "'Our horse came in first, my Lord,'" and Mr Serjeant Talfourd responded, "'Ah! But we say that it was not your horse: that he was a four-year-old.'"[1]

The separate action brought by Colonel Peel was heard in the Court of Exchequer on Thursday 6 June. Mr Ogle, having obtained the usual interpleader rule in this action, called on Colonel Peel and Mr Wood to come in and state their respective claims, in order that the case might be dealt with by the court, in its discretion, according to the very 'justice thereof'.

Mr Martin then appeared on behalf of Colonel Peel and expressed his readiness to submit to any issue that might be framed under the sanction of the court, provided that an opportunity was given therein to him to make use of the acts, declarations and statements of Mr Goodman, in whose name 'Running Rein' had been entered for the Derby, and certain other races, in the same way as if he were a party to the issue. The main issue might then have been whether Running Rein was a colt foaled in 1841, whose sire was The Saddler and dam Mab. The other question, as suggested by Mr Martin, was raised by the affidavit of Colonel Peel, which set forth that Running Rein had been entered for various stakes in the sole name of Mr Goodman, and that he was part-owner of the horse.

Mr Baron Alderson asked who had paid the Derby Stakes and who the subscriber was. Mr Martin countered that the real question was: 'Who was the party to the contract out of which the claim of Mr. Wood arose?'

It was also proposed by Colonel Peel that a second issue be added, to include Mr Goodman's conduct and statements respecting 'Running Rein' as evidence in the same cause between Colonel Peel and Mr Wood, who was now the owner of Running Rein. There was no wish whatever on the part of Colonel Peel to raise any technical questions. He would suggest an issue as to whether Mr Wood was entitled to recover the stakes.

Mr Platt, who appeared with Mr James for Mr Wood, said that Mr Martin's proposition was an attempt to obtain an advantage over Mr Wood. He would turn the tables on Mr Martin and propose that the issue between the parties would be whether

Colonel Peel *was* entitled to the stakes.

Mr Baron Alderson said that the court would decide what was just between the rival claimants, and if Mr Goodman was the real party, and Mr Wood sought to recover under his title, surely his acts ought to be given in evidence.

Mr Platt reminded the court that this was not the only rule on the subject, for there was another in the section by Mr Wood, in the Court of Common Pleas, and he asked why Colonel Peel should not be the defendant in that suit.

Mr Martin answered that he would accept an issue in any form that the opposition wished. He would be either the plaintiff or the defendant in an action for money had and received, provided that the case was just on the issues of the identity and age of the horse and excluded any allegations of fraud or of any other person's entitlement to the stakes.

Mr Platt had no hesitation in giving his assurance, proposing that the venue should be located in Surrey. Mr Martin objected to having the trial in Surrey, as this would incur far greater costs.

Mr James drew to the court's attention that it had been stated that Colonel Peel had sworn that Running Rein had been entered in the name of Mr Goodman, but that was contradicted by the fact that in Mr Weatherby's *Racing Calendar* Mr Wood appeared as the owner of the horse and the payer of the stake. He continued that the entry was of no consequence, as a horse would be entered as soon as it was dropped and very often would change hands before the race took place. It was clear that in this action the plaintiff sought to 'jockey' Mr Wood out of the stakes by proving at the trial that Running Rein belonged to more than one party, which may have been very likely, so that he could then counter as to whether Mr Wood alone was entitled to the stakes.

Mr Martin assured the court that he wished no such thing and would not set up the rights of a second party to defeat Mr Wood's claim, but claimed that he ought at the same time to have the power of using Mr Goodman's acts as evidence in respect to the real issue in the case.

What Mr James objected to was Mr Martin's assumption, as fact, that Mr Goodman was a party to the cause by the terms of the issue, and that this ought to be proved before he used his acts and statements. Mr Martin agreed to this.

Mr Baron Parke, from the bench, decided that the issue should be framed: Colonel Peel should be the plaintiff and Mr Wood the defendant, and the plaintiff should be at liberty to give evidence of Mr Goodman's conduct and statements if he showed any interest by that party in the horse.

Mr James brought laughter to the court when he stated that the case came from Tattersalls and the court should take care that the plaintiff did not evade the real question, which was the identity of the horse called Running Rein, and that was the only question raised in the protest that had been delivered by Lord George Bentinck on behalf of Colonel Peel to the stewards of the race, and that the Colonel ought not to be allowed to raise any other objection.

Mr Martin begged to be allowed, most emphatically, to deny, on the part of Colonel Peel, the insinuation that he had any wish to try any point other than the substantial one between the parties.

Mr Baron Alderson agreed that the issue would be whether Running Rein was a colt foaled in 1841, whose sire was The Saddler and dam Mab. That involved two propositions in one issue - namely, the identity and age of the horse - and to it should be appended permission to the plaintiff, Colonel Peel, to give in evidence the acts and declarations done or made by Mr Goodman.

When Mr Baron Alderson enquired about his Christian name, asking if it was Thomas, Mr Martin's response of, "'Oh, no. Abraham Levi,'"[2] drew a roar of laughter from the court. He continued by asking Mr Martin whether, if he proved to the satisfaction of the judge that Abraham Levi Goodman was the owner, part-owner, or was interested in 'Running Rein' at the time of his doing or making such acts or declarations, that would be satisfactory. Mr Martin answered in the affirmative.

Mr James said that there should then be another issue: whether Colonel Peel himself was entitled to the stakes. Mr Baron Parke responded that this should be a separate issue altogether.

Mr Martin said that, if there were to be such an issue, Colonel Peel should begin. Mr James strongly objected to this, but Mr Baron Alderson stepped in: "'Equal justice requires that it should be so. If you begin in the present issue, so ought Colonel Peel to begin in that now proposed by you; and it ought certainly to be introduced into another record altogether.'"[3]

Mr Martin felt so confident of Colonel Peel's rights on such an issue that it was quite immaterial to him who began.

Mr Platt strongly urged the propriety of the trial being held in Surrey, as Mr Wood's action had been laid there, and if an issue arose out of that proceeding then it should be tried there as a matter of right.

After some further discussion between the bench and the bar it was ultimately agreed that the issue, framed as suggested above, should be tried in the Court of Exchequer before one of the puisne Barons and a jury.

On Saturday 8 June Mr Martin moved to have the affidavit of Mr Wood, which declared Mr Goodman to be the owner of Running Rein, filed. After some discussion the court decided that an affidavit as to the real claimant of Running Rein should be submitted, and until that was done the court could not proceed further in the case.

Mr Platt applied to the court on behalf of Mr Wood, in consequence of a misunderstanding that had arisen relating to the filing of a certain affidavit. After the rule had been disposed of on the Thursday, and the terms of the issue framed between Colonel Peel and Mr Wood, it would appear that Mr Martin had applied to the court to order that both of the affidavits that had been used by the counsel for Mr Wood should be filed. This, however, although the usual practice, had not been complied with, and as a result Mr Martin had declined to assent to the issue as arranged by the court. Mr Platt assured the court that no affidavit had been used by him on the hearing of the rule other than that of Mr Gill, the attorney of Mr Wood, and that this had been filed.

Mr Martin had not meant to say that Mr Platt had used the affidavit of Mr Wood himself, which related to the ownership of 'Running Rein'. That affidavit, however, had been expressly referred to by Mr Platt's learned 'junior' (Mr James), who had stated, in answer to Mr Martin's assertion relating to the contents of Colonel Peel's affidavit, that "that was contradicted". That contradiction could only be made available by Mr Wood's affidavit, and that affidavit ought to be filed.

Mr Platt stated that he had no recollection of any affidavit having been used other than that to which he had himself referred.

The court, on examining the briefs that had been handed in by the learned counsel for Mr Wood, remarked that something must have been withdrawn, as the page numbers had been altered - page 4 being the first page and the number having been erased and converted to page 1 - and asked whether there had been any affidavit other than that of Mr Gill, Mr Wood's attorney.

Mr Gill (who spoke from the floor of the court), in answer to the question, admitted that counsel had been supplied with another affidavit, but added that its use had been abandoned.

Mr Platt explained that the erasures had been made on consultation with Mr James (Mr Platt's junior); that it had been agreed that Mr Wood's affidavit was unnecessary and should not be used on the hearing of the interpleader rule; and that, as far as he was concerned, no allusion had been made to it.

Mr Baron Alderson stated that it had not been questioned that it had been used, but he certainly had a recollection of Mr James having made use of the expression relied on by Mr Martin, and he presumed at the time that he referred to some affidavit.

Mr Platt submitted that, as he was the leader of the cause and was responsible for its result to the party, he ought not to be fettered by any unguarded expression that might be used by his junior in the heat of the discussion. He stressed that no affidavit had been used, for none ought to have been used or was intended by him to be used.

Mr Baron Alderson confessed that, although Mr James had alluded to an affidavit, he had some doubt as to whether Mr Platt, as leader, should be bound to it.

Mr Martin submitted that, if it was to be taken as though the affidavit had not been used, the issue should be altered by rejecting aspects that imposed on Colonel Peel the necessity of proving that Mr Goodman was the owner, or part-owner of 'Running Rein' at the time he made any declarations or did any acts that Colonel Peel might wish to give in evidence against Mr Wood. That proviso had been dictated expressly by Mr Baron Parke on the Thursday and had only been assented to by Mr Martin on the assumption that the affidavit of Mr Wood had been used and would be filed.

Mr Baron Alderson asked Mr Martin if he had a right, as the representative of Colonel Peel, to insist on Mr Goodman's title, and suggested that it should rather be a question for the stakeholder (Weatherbys), if they disputed Mr Wood's claim?

Mr Martin claimed that it was perfectly acceptable for him to resort to Mr Goodman's acts and declarations, but that the questions now assumed a somewhat different aspect, as there was no affidavit of ownership at all on the part of Mr Wood, who had been called in by the court to state his claim, pointing out that this could only be done by an affidavit. Mr Martin thus submitted that, unless some such affidavit was made, the claimant ought to be barred.

Mr Platt deemed it to be wholly unnecessary for the claimant to make any affidavit, stating that Mr Wood had come into this court in obeyance of the rule, it had called on him to state his claim, and he had done so. What more could he do?

Mr Baron Alderson went on to say that this proceeding was in fact a substitute for a bill of interpleader and ought to be governed by the same principles. Thus, he maintained, there most decidedly should be an affidavit of ownership by a claimant in these courts and, unless one were made and used, Mr Martin was correct in saying that Mr Wood ought to be barred.

Mr Platt responded that, if his lordship thought it necessary, there would be no difficulty in providing such an affidavit.

Mr Baron Alderson closed the proceedings for the day, concluding that there ought to be an affidavit of ownership on which to ground Mr Wood's claim, and that once it had been made it would then be the responsibility of the court to decide whether it was sufficient for the purpose.

On Monday 10 June Mr Platt said that in this "everlasting case" he was now in possession of an affidavit that he believed would be satisfactory to his learned friend.

Mr Martin said he had seen the proposed affidavit of ownership, and he supposed he must be content with it. It stated that Mr Wood became the owner of Running Rein in November 1843, and that he had since that period paid all his stakes and borne all his expenses. The deponent did not actually say whether he was part- or full owner, but Mr Martin supposed that the affidavit provided should satisfy the court, and Mr Baron Alderson concurred that it would be acceptable.

The case was again mentioned in the Court of Common Pleas on the Tuesday, when Lord Chief Justice Tindal stated that when the Court of Exchequer had decided the matter there would be an end to it.

On the Monday before the trial an application on behalf of Colonel Peel, the defendant, was made for a judge's order on Mr Wood, the plaintiff, to permit certain persons to see the horse, for the purpose of identification and with a view to examining his mouth so as to ascertain his age. The judge's order directed that Mr

Wood should permit the defendant's attorney, together with certain persons named, to see the horse between the hours of 10 a.m. and 2 p.m. on the Thursday. Those included in the order were George Worley, George Odell, Benyon Drage, Benjamin Pinney and Edward Messenger, to ascertain the identity of the horse, whether Running Rein or any other horse; the Epsom trainers, Messrs Dockray, Sherwood and Wright, to decide whether the horse that was to be shown was the horse that ran and came in first for the Derby or some other horse substituted for him; and, lastly, veterinary surgeons Field, Mavor (whom John Bartlett had recommended to Mr Wood for a second opinion), Turner and Spooner, who were to examine the horse's mouth to determine his age.

A copy of the order was served on Mr Wood, so that he could not plead ignorance of the directions of the judge or of the time at which a compliance with its directions was expected. Accordingly, on the Thursday, accompanied by Colonel Peel's attorney and Lord George Bentinck, the delegation proceeded to Epsom. At 10 o'clock they arrived at Mr Wood's house; unsurprisingly, he was not at home. They then proceeded to Smith's – the trainer of Running Rein – who refused to show the horse without an order from Mr Wood. They then returned to Mr Wood's house and saw his wife. Colonel Peel's attorney read the judge's order and explained its purpose, but she refused to interfere in the matter in the absence of her husband.

Despite frequent applications being made during the subsequent hours covered by the order, at both Mr Smith's and Mr Wood's, it was clear that the order would not be obeyed and the delegation returned to London as much in the dark as before. This blatant refusal could have been construed as contempt, but Mr Wood, under legal advice, may have felt that the course taken was justified. What his refusal did, however, was to give greater confidence to the supporters of Orlando.

With the advent of the trial, Goodman and his associates were feeling the heat and were pursuing potential witnesses to sway them in their favour. One such witness was William Carlin, who had joined Goodman as head groom in January 1843 and had continued with him until March 1844. Carlin knew what was going on and it was in Goodman's and his associates' interest to induce Carlin to keep out of the way. George Veal, proprietor of the

Denton Hall, near Otley, Yorkshire, birthplace of Thomas, Lord Fairfax (1612-1671), which was acquired by the Ibbetson family in 1716

The converted stable block at Denton Hall. It was here Sir Charles Henry Ibbetson bred Maccabeus, the winning impostor of the "Running Rein Derby"

The Lodge, at Old Malton Gate, where Gladiator started his career as a stallion

Sutton House at Norton-on-Derwent in North Yorkshire, where Dr Charles Cobb bred the genuine Running Rein and his full sister, Genuine

Gladiator ran only once, being second to Bay Middleton, in the 1836 Derby.
He was one of the great stallions of the nineteenth century, and a tremendous
influence in France through his son, Fitz-Gladiator

The Saddler, sire of the real Running Rein, with his trainer Leonard Hessletine
and jockey Jem Chapple, at Doncaster

Running Rein, who finished first in the Derby,
as portrayed in Bell's Life by John Herring

Maccabeus, alias Running Rein, alias Zanoni. illegal winner of the 1844 Derby

Sywell House, Northamptonshire, George Worley's home
(Courtesy of Philip and Kate Bletsoe Brown)

Left: The Golden Lion, in Newmarket High Street. Running Rein was taken to the stables at the rear, to be examined, following the objection to his victory in the Fifty Pound Plate

Below: The start of the memorable Derby of 1844, as depicted by John Herring (courtesy of Fores Gallery)

Orlando, the ultimate winner of the 1844 Derby
(courtesy of Fores Gallery)

Touchstone, sire of Orlando, was one of the great racehorses of the mid-19th century.
He won the St.Leger and was twice a winner of the Doncaster and Ascot Gold Cups
(courtesy of Fores Gallery)

Baron Alderson, who oversaw the Trial
at the Court of Exchequer
*(courtesy of the Honourable Society
of the Inner Temple)*

Sir Alexander Cockburn,
who represented Mr.Wood

Left: Sir Frederick Thesiger, the Solicitor General, who represented Colonel Peel

Right: Lord George Bentinck, who was the real force behind pursuing the Running Rein fraud

Left: Colonel, later General, Jonathan Peel, the owner of the eventual Derby winner, Orlando

The lane passing Sywell House. Legend has it that the ghost of
Maccabeus is said to haunt the lane

Left: Count Branicki, who imported Zanoni into
Russia. He had a vast stud, with approximately
700 mares *(courtesy of Dr.Jacek Lojek)*

Below: Priam Lodge Stables, on Burgh Heath
Road, Epsom, where Running Rein was trained
by William Smith

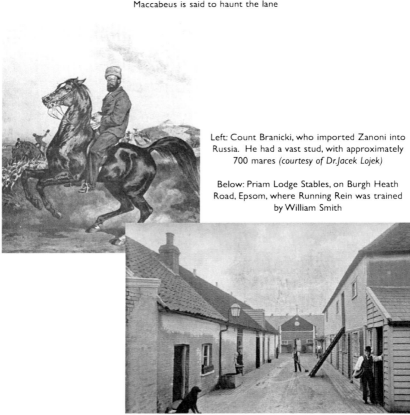

Montague Arms in Upper Montague Street, and one of Goodman's associates, had repeatedly told Carlin that he would take him to a party who would give him £1,000 to lie low. Veal did not reveal the identity of the party, but Carlin suspected that it was probably Goodman and Oliver.

On Saturday 29 June, two days before the trial, Oliver, Coyle and other strangers called on Mrs Carlin, asking to see her husband, and requested that he go to Veal's at 10 o'clock. Carlin complied, but Goodman and Oliver never showed up and after 20 minutes he left. He arranged with Veal to meet them at 12 o'clock the next day, but he did not keep the appointment, instead going to his brother-in-law's, John Butler, at the Golden Lion in Dean Street. At 2 o'clock Oliver, who had been employed by Goodman and was on fairly intimate terms with Carlin, came to him and tried to persuade him to accept the money. Oliver left him to consider the proposition and said that he would call again at 8.30 to see if Carlin had changed his mind. Accordingly, at the appointed time, Oliver returned and renewed the offer.

Oliver was concerned about Running Rein. He had been a great winner on the horse and he asked Carlin what he should do about hedging. Carlin told him that he must lay 3 to 1 and, if he could do that, lay 4 to 1, but not to stop laying at any price on Orlando.

Oliver then asked Carlin to go with him to the Grand Hotel in King Street, Covent Garden, but before they had got to the end of Old Compton Street Goodman pounced on them. He pretended that this had happened by pure accident, but Carlin observed to Goodman, "'How strange you seem to make it as if you did not come with him.'"

Goodman wanted to know what Carlin was going to do, questioning whether he was going to turn round on him (Goodman), because if so he was one of the cruellest men he had ever met, seeing that they had lived together for 15 months and never a wrong word had been exchanged. He continued, trying to sow doubts in Carlin's mind.

[Goodman:] *"What would Lord George think of you if you turn round upon a man you had never had a wrong word with?*

"When Lord George has got his turn served he will care no more for you [snapping his fingers]."

[Carlin:] *"I am a poor man and can but remain so."*

115

[Goodman:] *"If you will get into a cab and go along with me to Harrington Street* [probably the house of Thomas Gill, Wood's attorney, who lived at 12 Harrington Street] *in the Hampstead Road, I will get you the money."*[4]

Goodman cared for nothing that Carlin wanted to speak the truth. He did, however, still have some lingering doubts as to which way he would turn. Carlin could have walked away, but instead he accepted Goodman's invitation.

Goodman knocked on the door and asked the boy who answered it whether Glenn was there. The boy replied that he would see.

When the boy returned Goodman went in, while Oliver and Carlin waited outside. Goodman came out after about two minutes, indicating that Glenn would follow them to Goodman's house.

There was sherry on the table at Goodman's. They had not been there long when Glenn and Anderson arrived.

[Glenn:] *"How do you do, gentlemen? What is to be done about Mr. Carlin?"*

[Oliver:] *"I must have the money down this night; this is a man I have known a many years and I cannot have no tricks played with him."*

[Glenn:] *"Mr. Oliver, I have not got all the money but I will give you the biggest part of it."*[5]

Glenn called for a pen and ink. He pulled a salmon-coloured cheque from his pocket and wrote, 'Pay to Mr. Oliver or the Bearer Four Hundred and Forty Pounds'. Both Oliver and Anderson took the cheque and read the words he had written out loud.

Glenn signed the cheque and then produced money to the value of £40: £35 in notes and five sovereigns. Oliver was to call at Glenn's the next morning to get £20 more to make up the money.

While at Goodman's house many suggestions were thrown out as to where it would be best for Carlin to meet Oliver to go away with him on the following morning, when the trial was due to start. The foot of Westminster Bridge or Cannings Statue (then at the end of West Palace Yard) were suggested by Goodman and Glenn. However, Anderson suddenly interposed and, concerned that Oliver would make a mess of it, instructed him to wait for Carlin in a cab under the clock of Saint Margaret's church.

Although Carlin had so far gone along with them, he was having serious reservations. He considered that he would be putting himself in great danger should he attempt to flee. He did not fear for his life, but was concerned that he would never be able to face Lord George again and would have to leave his native land, England, for good, with no hope of return. Glenn tried hard to prevail on Carlin that all he could possibly face was a £100 fine, and that if this happened then Glenn himself would pay it. He also tried to assure him that if Colonel Peel won the trial he and Lord George would no longer trouble their heads about him if he were to return to England. Anderson emphasised that if Carlin would accept their offer he would never want for money; it would not take them £20 apiece to make up £1,000. Oliver picked up the cheque and money, and they bade Goodman, Glenn and Anderson goodnight and left.

They afterwards fell in with Mrs Carlin at the top of Dean Street. Oliver, rapping his pocket, said, "'I have got the swag in my pocket for Bill, tomorrow morning.'" Carlin and his wife then walked home, put Oliver in a cab and sent him to Gardner's at the Kings Head.

On the morning of the trial one of the Whitfields met Carlin, informing him, "'You are wanted under the church clock.'" Carlin made no reply but walked on till he met Mr Holmes, who took him into court. There they met with Mr William Clarke, a cigar merchant of Leamington, and in Mr Holmes's presence he said, "'Oliver wants you.'" Carlin defiantly replied, "'He can't have me.'"[6]

Another witness whom the conspirators attempted to spirit away was Thomas Ferguson, who was offered £2,000 to make himself absent.[7]

The case of Wood versus Peel came on trial at the Court of Exchequer, Westminster, on Monday 1 July 1844, before Baron Alderson and the following special jury:

Edmund Antrobus, Piccadilly (Foreman)
Richard Williams, Endsleigh Street
Charles William Moore, Wilton Road
Charles James Cotterill, 7 Warren Street, Pancras
Robert Bentley, 4 Cavendish Road
Joseph Bowman, 19 Mecklenburgh Square
Henry Watson, John Street
Isaac Haywood, Newington Green, Islington

Frederic Bryant, 5 Holloway Place, Islington
William Cotes, Tyndal Place, Islington
Thomas Ashton, Nottingham Place
Hodgson Dickson, Nottingham Place
John Taverner Miller, Millbank Street

The counsel for the plaintiff comprised Mr Cockburn, Mr James and Mr Lush, with attorney Mr Gill; and the counsel for the defendant comprised solicitor general (Sir Frederick Thesiger), Mr Kelly, Mr Martin, Mr Wortley and Mr Peacock, with attorneys Messrs Baxendale, Tatham, Upton and Johnson.

At an early hour the avenues of the court were crowded with people, all eager to gain admission to the main body of the court; the cause being called for at 9.50 a.m.

Once the jury had been sworn in, Mr Cockburn, counsel for Mr Wood, opened the proceedings by requesting Baron Alderson to order the witnesses on both sides out of court. The solicitor general, for Colonel Peel, appealed to Baron Alderson as to why Lord George Bentinck should leave the court, as he had been subpoenaed by the plaintiff. Mr Cockburn's reason was that Lord George Bentinck was a hostile witness and was in fact the real defendant. Baron Alderson would not consent to Mr Cockburn turning out his own witnesses if the other side consented to their presence, but he agreed that the solicitor general would not be allowed to call Lord George as his witness. Mr Cockburn would not press the issue, bringing laughter to the court when requesting that Lord George - who had taken his seat within the bar between the counsel for the plaintiff and the defendant - should go and sit elsewhere. Lord George repaired to the back row of the court.

Mr Lush opened the pleadings, addressing the jury and stating that Alexander Wood was the plaintiff and Jonathan Peel, Esq. the defendant, and that the issue directed by the court was to try "'whether a certain colt called Running Rein which came in first at a certain race at Epsom, this year, was or was not a colt foaled in the year 1841, whose sire was The Saddler, and dam Mab'". The plaintiff had alleged that it was, and the defendant that it was not, and that was the issue that they had to try.

Mr Cockburn rose to address the jury for the plaintiff, stating that at first sight it might appear to be a simple inquiry but that circumstances had arisen such that it was not surprising that it should excite such an extraordinary degree of interest, not only in sporting circles but also among all classes of society. Apart from the direct interest, there was a pecuniary interest, owing not only to the stake but also to the vast amount of bets dependent on the result. He understood this interest but could not conceal his apprehension that the plaintiff in this issue had to contend with individuals connected with the Turf of very great influence, of very great activity and energy, who had enormous sums depending on the outcome. It had become the engrossing topic of conversation in all classes, the effect of which had been to produce a vast amount of prejudice in the minds of many on the question at issue. But he was sure that the gentlemen of the jury would divest their minds of anything they had heard on the subject and had not the slightest apprehension as to the issue under their consideration. The question was not one of opinion, or of science; it was a simple question of *fact* and a mere question of identity, and, although questions of *identity* sometimes presented considerable difficulty, he believed that the case would be found to be a simple question of identity, capable of as simple proof as ever was offered on such a question in a court of justice.

Mr Cockburn continued that, having objected to the winner on account of his age, Colonel Peel would, under ordinary circumstances and according to the usual course of proceedings in matters connected with the Turf, have brought the question before the stewards of the race, and according to the rules and laws of the Turf would have been bound to prove the disqualification of the horse. But Colonel Peel, rather than adopting this course, thought proper to institute legal proceedings, thereby throwing the onus of proof on the plaintiff, Mr Wood.

The solicitor general interjected that he and Colonel Peel would have been very willing to have been plaintiffs, and the learned judge told him not to complain of a grievance that he courted.

Mr Cockburn countered that he complained of no grievance, continuing that the plaintiff had voluntarily undertaken to prove to the jury's satisfaction the affirmative of the issue, and he was prepared with proof that he trusted would be absolutely conclusive on the subject.

Mr Cockburn next spoke at length, detailing the history of the foal dropped by the mare Mab, having been got by The Saddler, from the time of his birth on 11 May 1841 up to the time of the objection raised by the Duke of Rutland at the Second October Meeting at Newmarket in 1843.

He continued that a public investigation had taken place before the stewards of the Jockey Club. It had been conducted in a fair and impartial manner and had decided that the colt had been a two-year-old, and not a three-year-old, thus rejecting the claim of the Duke of Rutland. It was a painful position that the plaintiff now found himself placed in, afterwards to be told, not withstanding the public investigation, that the objection was to be revived and submitted to another tribunal. It may well have been that Mr Goodman was not a man of high reputation, but what on earth had that to do with Mr Wood? Why should he be the loser because Mr Goodman was a man whose habits and transactions with the Turf may be said to be unfavourable, and because certain noblemen and gentlemen, having bet thousands and thousands of pounds against the horse, in the knowledge that if the horse was beaten their bets were safe, and if he should win, they would revive the objection and refuse to pay? That was the honour of British noblemen of the Turf. He did not hold Colonel Peel party to this dirty transaction, but there were members of the Jockey Club who had large bets against the horse, and a large stake on the case, who ventured to put themselves into the witness box, and whom he promised he would turn inside out.

Mr Cockburn continued that he was at a loss to know what case would be raised by the defendant. Allegations had been made that the plaintiff's horse had been substituted, but how, when or where they had not said, being content on throwing out vague insinuations for the purpose of perplexing the plaintiff, for prejudicing public opinion and for bringing the tribunal, which will have to decide the question, with a prejudiced and biased mind. They had acted on the advice and direction of that excellent advocate Lord George Bentinck, who had played the part of attorney, interested party and even policeman, but he reiterated that before his learned friend's witnesses had been done with, Lord George Bentinck may have wished to take his (Mr Cockburn's) earlier advice and gone out of court. He would steer clear of Mr Goodman. If they were to insinuate that Mr Goodman had been guilty of any malpractices, it would be for them to prove them, but he would be most singularly mistaken if it could be shown that Mr Goodman had been guilty of the slightest misconduct with reference to the horse that was now the matter of the court's consideration.

The first witness called by Mr Cockburn was Thomas Lofthouse, who had worked for Dr Cobb and who confirmed that he had taken Mab to Squire Osbaldeston's on 5 June 1840 to be mated with The Saddler. He had not been present at the colt's birth, but he had seen him a few days later, in a loose box at Dr Cobb's and later at John King's, at Grove House.

Thomas Lofthouse was followed into the witness box by John Kitchen, who as a 17-year-old had been present at the birth of the colt and generally had care of him. When Stebbings had bought the colt he (Kitchen) had taken him, with Robert Stanton, to John King's at Grove House, a short distance from Sutton House. Mr Cockburn then moved on to the time that Kitchen had travelled down to Newmarket to attend the inquiry, after Running Rein had won the Fifty Pound Plate at the Second October Meeting in 1843. To Baron Alderson's question of identity, Kitchen confirmed that it was the same colt that he had attended at Dr Cobb's and had seen at Epsom for the Derby. When asked whether, when he went to see the colt at Newmarket, he at any time had communication with Mr Goodman, or anybody on Mr Goodman's behalf, he replied, "No".

Kitchen was an unconvincing witness. He could not recollect whether a veterinary surgeon by the name of Barrow had been present at the Newmarket inquiry, whether Goodman had been in the stables, or whether Lord Stradbroke had requested Goodman to allow Barrow, or the person that went with him, to examine the horse's mouth.

Kitchen had not been in employment since the Derby, and had been living with Mr Gill, Wood's attorney, although to the judge's annoyance he was seemingly unable to remember how long he had been there. From Mr Gill's he had gone to Glenn's house, Eagle Lodge, at Queens Elms. The judge wanted to know if Mr Gill had promised Kitchen anything by way of a place, or money - anything for his trouble should he win the trial, but he replied that he had no expectation of being promised anything.

Baron Alderson asked Kitchen if he had heard the questions that had been put to him, and he answered in the affirmative. He then handed Kitchen a letter and asked him to confirm whether it was his (Kitchen's) handwriting, to which Kitchen replied that it was. It was a letter that Kitchen had written to his father, and Baron

Alderson asked Kitchen to read it. Now it became obvious to the court why the judge had put the questions relating to payment, as the letter had alluded to a promise by Mr Gill to get Kitchen a place in London.

The judge questioned Kitchen again on the matter, but Kitchen maintained that Mr Gill had not promised him anything. The judge persisted, asking again if Kitchen had read the letter and whether, if he won the trial, he would expect to be paid for his trouble. After continual questioning by the judge Kitchen finally confessed that he had written the letter to pacify his father, who had been anxious as to where he was, and that he had not been promised anything he had put in the letter.

Henry Stebbings was next into the witness box. He had been at Newmarket when the objection to Running Rein had been raised, but he was uncertain that it was the horse he had bought for Goodman as he had not seen him since he was a foal. When cross-examined by the solicitor general Stebbings stated that he had received no specific instructions from Goodman, either verbally or in writing, as to the sort of colt he wanted, and that Goodman had simply told him to buy a foal or two if he (Stebbings) saw any that suited him and they were cheap.

Next, William Wilds, a servant to Stebbings, testified that he had gone to Dr Cobb's to pay for the foal and had directed it to be sent to John King's.

Baron Alderson intervened at this point, stating that if the jury wished to see the horse it could be brought into court, to which the solicitor general replied that, under an order of his lordship to inspect the horse, permission had been refused. This was the first indication to the court that there might be a question mark as to the whereabouts of the horse, and the judge expressed surprise at the refusal as he had signed the order.

Mr Cockburn explained that they had refused to allow the examination of the horse because the manner in which it was demanded was improper, facetiously remarking that they had taken half of London.

The solicitor general countered that there was no impropriety in the mode used for the order and that they had given the plaintiff notice of their intention to come.

Baron Alderson commented that he did not care whether the order had been used properly or not and that, whatever the grounds for rejecting the order, that was no reason for refusing to allow the horse to be seen by proper persons, and that the jury were thus entitled to see it. He would only excuse their previous refusal to show the horse if it was brought up now. Mr Cockburn said he had not the least objection to the jury seeing it.

Robert Stanton, who had been in the service of John King, when examined by Mr Cockburn confirmed that in December 1841 he had gone to Dr Cobb's and, with the assistance of Kitchen, had taken the colt to Mr King's.

Next into the witness box was Henry Stebbings's brother, James, who had taken The Saddler colt from York to London, and who had seen it at Goodman's stables in Foley Place the next day and at Newmarket in October 1843, although, like his brother Henry, he could not give an opinion as to whether it was the same as the foal he had delivered to Goodman.

Daniel White, examined by Mr James, stated that he was employed at Mr Joseph's (Goodman's brother-in-law) livery stables in Foley Place. He had gone to Euston Square station to collect The Saddler colt and take it to Goodman's stables in Chapel Mews, Foley Place, where it was kept for two days and a night. He had then taken it to James Pearl's in Milton Street, Dorset Square. He *claimed* that he had next seen the colt at Bean's at Finchley in September of the same year, when he had gone to collect it, accompanied by George White, and take it first to Goodman's house in Foley Place and then on to Haines's livery stables in Langham Place.

The solicitor general, knowing from his own witnesses that the colt had remained at Bean's until the following February, during cross-examination enquired:

"What makes you say it was September?"
"I know it was September."
"What makes you say so – how do you know it?"
Obviously well briefed, or well rehearsed, White replied:
"Just after Doncaster races."

James Pearl testified that he had kept a record in his book, which had been seen by Lord George Bentinck, that the colt had been at his livery stables at Milton Street, Dorset Square, between 20 and 30 January 1842, when it was fetched away by William Bean. He had seen the colt a number of times at Bean's, and at Epsom, and to the best of his belief it was the same horse.

So far, none of the witnesses for the plaintiff was particularly convincing, and some of their evidence was contradictory. For instance, Kitchen, a fairly inexperienced youth, was adamant that the colt he had care of at Dr Cobb's was the same he had seen at Newmarket two years later and at Epsom the following year, whereas Stebbings, who had worked with horses all his life, was not convinced that it was the same horse.

And the next witness, William Bean, examined by Mr James, was even less convincing.

He corroborated Pearl's statement that he collected the colt on 30 January 1842 and took it to his premises at Finchley. When asked how long the colt had remained on his premises, Bean replied: "'Until the 24th of September.'" He then produced a letter that was brought by Daniel White, requesting delivery of the colt, which the solicitor general asked to see.

Questioned by Baron Alderson, Bean testified that after the colt had left his premises the next time he had seen him was at Newmarket. He could not say that he recognised the horse, but to the best of his belief it was the same colt. "'No doubt about that?'" asked the judge. "'Oh, not the least about *that*,'" the solicitor general cut in.

Bean continued that when he received the order to deliver the colt he had asked one of his men to carry it out; he was unable to do so himself as he was off to town, and on his return the colt had gone. "'No doubt about that?'" the judge again asked. "'Oh yes there is,'" the solicitor general angrily cut in, knowing that Bean was perjuring himself.

When cross-examined by the solicitor general Bean continued to discredit himself. He confirmed that his business of 30 years as a horse dealer had by no means been successful and he had, in fact, been twice bankrupt and twice insolvent. However, when asked by the judge whether a dividend had been paid to his creditors, and what it had been, Bean did not know; he was unable to say whether they had actually received a single farthing, or what sum they might have received if they were paid anything.

Bean was now beginning to annoy the judge. He either had no recollection of the circumstances, or was suffering from complete memory loss when repeatedly interrogated by the judge regarding one of his creditors, a Mr Hammond, whom he had cheated of £75. When asked by the judge if he would swear that it did not happen, expecting that he should be able to confirm it one way or another – either it did or it did not, Bean would only say that he could safely swear that he had no recollection of it. This in no way satisfied the judge and he demanded a distinct answer, but Bean maintained that he had no recollection of the kind.

It was clear that Baron Alderson was becoming exceedingly frustrated by Bean's answers. He questioned whether Bean was so much in the habit of committing fraud that when it was put to his memory he could not remember anything of the kind. Bean gave no answer.

The judge brought laughter to the court when continuing, "'I am astonished a man should not know that one way or the other; if he did not do it he would remember. I suppose I might venture to ask you whether you have committed murder?'" Bean again failed to answer.

When cross-examined by the solicitor general Bean was equally evasive when answering questions concerning the period of service of Fanny Fage, a maidservant to Mrs Bean. He could not confirm that she was there on 24 September 1842, when Daniel White and George White had supposedly collected the Saddler colt; whether she was there in February 1843, when the colt was actually taken away; or whether she was there whatever the date the colt was taken away.

The next witnesses called were John Derby, who worked for James Pearl; James Love, the landlord of The Queen's Head, Finchley; and William Marshall, a cow-keeper from Finchley, who delivered milk to Bean's and who described the colt as a sort of a rusty dark colour. None of them could recollect seeing the colt after August 1842.

George Rayner, in the service of Edmund Haines, a livery-stable keeper at Langham Place testified that, on reference to the books, a colt was brought in on 24 September 1842 and remained until 27 September. The man who brought the colt was someone he had never seen before; it was neither George White, whom he knew as a servant of Goodman's, nor the witness, Daniel White, who had already been examined. Neither did he know who had taken it away. He also did not know William Drewett. He recollected Goodman bringing a bright bay colt – he thought in February 1844

– which remained there for four nights, but it was impossible for him to say whether it was the same colt that was brought to their stables a year or more earlier.

William Drewett, when examined, stated that he had fetched a bay colt from Haines's stables and taken it to William Smith's at Epsom. He had seen the colt at Epsom, when George Hitchcock was breaking it, and also at Newmarket, when he had beaten the Duke of Rutland's Crenoline, in October 1843.

When cross-examined by the solicitor general Drewett confirmed that he was at the Epsom Spring Meeting in 1843 and remembered seeing a horse *called* Maccabeus, which he had never seen before, beaten by Captain Flathooker.

And George Hitchcock, who was next into the witness box, testified that the colt he had broken at Smith's was the same horse that had won the Derby.

Little of the evidence so far produced by the counsel for the plaintiff seemed relevant to the identity of the colt.

The first indication that there may have been a substitution for the genuine Maccabeus was when William Smith, the Epsom trainer, was cross-examined by the solicitor general.

When asked if he had attended the Spring Meeting at Epsom in 1843 and had seen Maccabeus run, Smith brought laughter from the court when he answered, "'I saw a horse that was called Maccabeus.'" "'Aye, exactly, you are quite right.'" the solicitor general replied.

Smith testified that, at the request of William Sadler, the horse *called* Maccabeus had been in his stables prior to the race. He claimed that he had not seen the horse before. But the solicitor general expressed dissatisfaction with his response, requesting that he carefully reconsider his answer.

Smith stated that Goodman had shown him a horse he had for the Derby, in London, but he could not swear that it was the same horse that had run at the Epsom Spring Meeting. When pressed by the solicitor general and the judge he explained that he could not be certain, as the horse he had seen run at the Epsom Spring Meeting had a "much shorter tail" than the one that Goodman had shown him in London.

The jury must have detected Baron Alderson's cynicism that Smith, despite his considerable skill and experience, and putting the tail aside, could not be positive that it was the same horse. It was also surprising that Smith, at the request of Goodman, and on the understanding of an order from Mr Wood, had sent Running Rein to Goodman's to be tried.

It was at this stage of the proceedings that the court had an inkling that there may be a question mark as to the whereabouts of the horse, when Mr Cockburn asked Smith if the horse was now in his possession. His response was that it was not; it had been taken away on the previous Wednesday by Francis Ignatius Coyle (an associate of Goodman's, and a frequenter of the bankruptcy courts) on a verbal order from Mr Wood, and he was unaware of its whereabouts. Mr Cockburn continued:

"And what Mr.Ignatius Coyle did with the horse you have no notion?"
Witness: "No."
Mr.Cockburn: "Not the least idea?"
Witness: "No; I delivered the horse up out of my possession; I begged Mr.Wood to get the horse out of my yard."
Mr.Baron Alderson, interrupted: "For what?"
Witness: "I was in fear. There has been from one man to six or seven around my house for the last fortnight. I was in fear they would take the horse away."
Mr.Baron Alderson: "The more afraid you were, the more certain you should have been to have a written order?"
Witness: "There were persons round the horse; I could not tell who they were."
Mr.Baron Alderson: "How did you know he was not one of them?"
Witness: "This man I had seen before."
Mr.Baron Alderson: "So then you had seen these people?"
Witness: "Not before they came."
Mr.Baron Alderson: "You should be cautious, because nobody can believe that."
Witness: "Not believe me!"
Mr.Baron Alderson: "Not that you delivered it to a third person, without knowing who he was."
Witness: "If I had not known the man before, I would not."
Mr.Baron Alderson: "It was the day before I ordered the horse to be shown, Sir! That was what you were afraid of. You had better be a little more cautious, or we shall have you up in the court next term if you do not mind. Do not be contemptuous to the orders of the court; take good care of what you are about. I can assure you I will not be satisfied again

with any such story."

Witness: "I beg pardon if I am telling a story."

Mr. Baron Alderson: "Giving it up to a person without any order, because you saw him go to Mr. Wood's house without knowing who he was. Pooh!"

Witness: "I had seen the same man before."

Mr. Baron Alderson: "You said just now you had not."

Witness: "I had seen him the night before."

Mr. Baron Alderson: "Did Mr. Wood give you authority to deliver it to this man the night before?"

Witness: "He did not."

Examined by The Solicitor General: "You either do not know him, or you do. Do you know him?"

Witness: "I have seen him repeatedly before, but I could not pronounce his name."

The Solicitor General: "What was he, do you know?"

Witness: "I have no idea what profession the man has."

Mr. Baron Alderson, interrupting, again: "What do you mean by delivering a valuable animal of this kind to a person you don't know? Have you seen Mr. Coyle here?"

Witness: "Yes I saw him here this morning."

The Solicitor General: "Now attend to this. Was not the order of his lordship read to you?"

Witness: "Yes."

The Solicitor General: "Did you tell the person who read it, or any other person, at that time, that the horse had been taken away?"

Witness: "That was not asked of me."

The Solicitor General: "Did you not say that you would go down to Wood to get an order for showing the horse?"

Witness: "I said if they required it I would."

The Solicitor General: "Did you not go down to Mr. Wood?"

Witness: "Yes."

The Solicitor General: "And did you not come back and say, 'Mr. Wood was not at home?'"

Witness: "Yes."

Mr. Baron Alderson: "Why, the horse had been sent away the day before!"

The Solicitor General: "Yes, my lord."

Mr. Baron Alderson: "Why did you not tell the people so?"

Witness: "I was not asked the question."

128

Mr.Baron Alderson: "Pooh! Pooh!"

The Solicitor General: "Now just attend to this. You have sworn you were not asked; I ask you whether it was not distinctly asked."

Mr.Baron Alderson: "A gross fraud!"

The Solicitor General: "I ask you whether it distinctly was not put to you whether the horse was or was not there, and whether you did not say they had no right to ask that?"

Witness: "I said they had no right to ask the question."

The Solicitor General: "Then what did you mean by swearing a moment ago they did not ask if the horse was there, and that was the reason for you not telling them. Answer that?"

The witness failed to answer.

The Solicitor General: "You stated about a minute ago that you did not tell them that the horse was gone because they did not ask you. You have now told me that they did ask you?"

Witness: "I said they asked me whether the horse was there, and I said I should not answer that question. That was the answer I made to Mr.Johnson."

The Solicitor General: "Have you not told me, and that not five minutes ago, that you did not tell them the horse was gone because they did not ask you whether it was there?"

Witness: "Well, if I did, I beg your pardon."

Baron Alderson: "It is quite clear there has been an attempt to keep the horse out of the way to avoid its being seen; it is a gross fraud; to act the lie is quite as bad as to tell it, and to pretend to go to ask for leave to show a horse which everybody must have understood to lie in the stable at the time; when it had been taken away the day before! Nobody can doubt it was for the purpose that my order might not be complied with; it seems to me to be very gross fraud and very improper conduct, and for which this gentleman will have to answer next term. You had better take care.

"All this can be easily set right by producing the horse now; that is the best answer to the whole."

Mr.Cockburn: "My lord, I am perfectly ready to produce the horse for the inspection of your lordship and the jury."

Mr.Baron Alderson: "I shall be quite satisfied with that, but give me leave to say I shall permit other persons to see it."

The Solicitor General: "My friend seems to be qualifying this a little. I hope if the horse is produced veterinary surgeons will be permitted to examine it."

129

Mr.Cockburn: "As far as I have been concerned, I have found the strongest evidence of the fallibility of that testimony."

Mr.Baron Alderson: "You may give that too. Why shut it out?"

Mr.Cockburn: "For this reason; we are perfectly assured that a body of veterinary surgeons will be produced. I have had experience what takes place myself."

Mr.Baron Alderson: "Truth is always best ascertained by openness; if it be a fallible criterion, the better way will be to let it be shown, and then prove it to be a fallible criterion. I suppose there is something peculiar about this horse's mouth. I do not know any other reason why it should not be shown. If it is a fallible criterion, I do not mean for one moment to say it ought not to be laid before the jury as a fallible criterion. The honest way of deciding a question is never to conceal the truth, but let it be seen and examined. I can tell you one criterion I myself should like to know very much."

Mr James – Mr Cockburn's junior – was adamant that the witnesses had distinctly proved the horse's identity: they had seen it run at Newmarket.

However, the judge was not satisfied with their apparent intention of concealment: either the mouth was, or was not, a fallible criterion. He wanted the advantage of seeing it and wanted those persons who were skilful in this matter to have the opportunity to see it, so that it could be fairly tested.

Mr James facetiously regretted that if it made so great an impression on his lordship's mind he could not resist the horse's mouth being examined.

The judge rebuffed Mr James, countering that what made an impression on his mind was his (Mr James's) anxiety to conceal it. He demanded that the horse be produced. Then, if it were proven to be a fallible criterion, he would instruct the jury to disregard it.

Mr Cockburn, still trying to convince the judge of the unwarranted need for veterinary surgeons, doubted that they would admit to it being a fallible criterion. But the judge would not be swayed, questioning Mr Cockburn as to why the jury should not be permitted to look at the horse: if there were a dead body, would one say that it is useless for surgeons to examine the body to see what the man died of? There were questions of identity, and these demanded that the horse should be produced.

The solicitor general intended to prove that the horse that ran at

Newmarket and in the last Derby was the Gladiator colt. Mr Cockburn was quite willing to produce the horse for the court after the defendant's witnesses had given their description of the Gladiator colt, to see how far it resembled the testimony of the plaintiff's witnesses, but objected to showing him to the witnesses first, in order that they may describe the Gladiator colt.

The judge likened the case to that of a witness being called to examine the handwriting on a bill of exchange, to save much time and useless evidence and questioned what was the slightest difference in examining the horse.

Mr Cockburn replied:

"The difference is this, my Lord – they say, 'this is another colt, which all these witnesses, whom they are about to call, must have seen and have seen.' The question is whether this be the Gladiator colt or Running Rein. If they have seen the Gladiator colt, and know what were the appearances of the Gladiator colt, they can describe them without seeing this horse, and then it will be seen whether or not what they point out as the appearances of the Gladiator colt tally and correspond with the appearance of this horse. If they are to see this horse first, knowing as I do what the character of testimony is, we know perfectly well that a number of witnesses may be got to come into this court and give a description of the Gladiator colt which shall exactly correspond with the winner of the Derby race."

There was great applause from a section of the court following Mr Cockburn's remarks, which the judge considered to be in contempt.

With considerable warmth his lordship rose and requested the ushers to clear the court:

"Let them be turned out – every one of them. Out you shall go, gentlemen, depend on that.
"At the same time if anybody will be so good as to inform me who the persons were who did it I will be perfectly contented, for I shall only commit them for the contempt. Bring me the persons who did it. If you choose to tell me who it was, well and good; I give you fair warning.
[There was a pause, the rioters as dumb as flounders.]
I pass it over this time, and remember I expect order, and for persons to applaud anything whatever that passes in a court of justice is a very

great contempt and a very great impropriety, and persons who do
anything of that description shall be punished, if it is in my power to
punish them, and it is in my power, provided I can find out who they
are."

The solicitor general remarked that the age of the Gladiator colt was four years old, whereas if the plaintiff was right in saying that it was the Saddler colt it would only be three years old. It therefore appeared to the solicitor general that it was very important that the horse was produced in order that the question could be settled. Mr Martin suggested that the horse that had won the Derby should be placed in the hands of the veterinary surgeons to let them draw their own conclusions.

In further cross-examination by the solicitor general, William Smith claimed that he had made an application to Mr Wood to take the horse away on account of the number of men being round his house. He stressed that he had no other motive and that he had no idea that the judge was going to send an order to have the horse examined until Lord George Bentinck came to his house.

The penultimate witness for the plaintiff was Thomas Breedon, a blacksmith, who shoed Smith's horses. He recollected shoeing Running Rein in December 1842, when he was being broken by George Hitchcock, and also when it returned in December 1843 up until the present time. He confirmed that there were some slight cracks in his heels, and that the horse had the appearance of a yearling when he had first seen him.

The final witness for the plaintiff was Baron de Tessier, who, with Sir Gilbert Heathcote, had been a steward at the Epsom Derby Meeting. On being asked by the solicitor general if he took an interest in matters connected with horse racing, he replied, "'I have had quite enough of it if you ask me the question.'"

He confirmed that the protest was brought to him by Lord George Bentinck, John Bowes and John Scott and called on Mr Wood to produce a certificate of the breeder, or such documents that would establish the qualifications of the horse. He had been furnished with certain declarations that had been considered reasonable evidence to enable the horse to start, subject to Mr Wood being prepared for further examination afterwards, in a public court. These were shown to the solicitor general. In addition to the declarations of the persons examined on the foregoing trial, which were submitted to the stewards at Epsom, and on the faith of which they permitted Running Rein to start, subject to further investigation, were the following:

I, *ABRAHAM LEVY GOODMAN, late of Foley Place, but now of Portland Street, in the county of Middlesex, gentlemen do solemnly and sincerely declare that towards the latter end of the year one thousand eight hundred and forty-one I requested Mr.Henry Stebbing, of Hambleton, training groom, to purchase for me a foal or two that looked like racing: that in the month of December one thousand eight hundred and forty-one I received a letter from the said Henry Stebbings informing me that he had purchased for me from Mr.Cobb of New Malton, in the county of York, surgeon, a bay colt foal got by The Saddler, out of Mab, and that he had ordered the said foal to be sent to the stables of Mr.John King of Norton, near New Malton aforesaid, training groom, to be there kept until an opportunity occurred of sending the said foal to me in London aforesaid; and that the said foal was brought to London in the month of January one thousand eight hundred and forty-two by James Stebbings, the brother of the said Henry Stebbings, and was delivered by him to me at the London and Birmingham Railway station in Euston Square, and from thence taken to my stables in Foley Place aforesaid, and on the following day I sent the said foal to the stables of Mr.James Wilson Pearl, of Malton Street, Dorset Square, in the said county of Middlesex, livery stable keeper and horse dealer, with directions to deliver the said foal to Mr.William Bean, of Finchley, in the said county of Middlesex, horse dealer, with whom I had made arrangements for the keep of the said foal in his stables and paddocks at Finchley, aforesaid; that the said foal was delivered by the said Mr.Pearl to Mr.Bean, who sent the same to Finchley, aforesaid; that between the months of January and September in the year one thousand eight hundred and forty-two, I frequently went to the said Mr.Bean's, at Finchley, aforesaid, and there saw the said foal; that about the month of August one thousand eight hundred and forty-two, Mr.William Sadler, of Stockbridge, in the county of Southampton, training groom, accompanied me to see the said foal; that the said colt left Mr.Bean's at Finchley aforesaid, in the month of September one thousand eight hundred and forty-two, for the stables of Mr.Haines, of Langham Place, Regent Street, livery stable keeper, where it remained for two or three days, and was then sent for by Mr.Smith, of Epsom, in the county of Surrey, training groom, for the purpose of breaking the said colt and*

133

making him ready for training; that on the suggestion and at the request of the said Henry Stebbings, I named the said colt Running Rein, and entered him under such name in all his engagements; that the said colt remained with Mr.Smith at Epsom, aforesaid, until the month of February one thousand eight hundred and forty-three, when I removed him to my stables at Sutton, near Epsom, aforesaid, under the care of my private trainer; and I further solemnly and sincerely declare that the said colt Running Rein which ran at the October meeting at Newmarket last year, and which is engaged in a Sweepstakes of 50 sovereigns each on the Monday in the First Spring Meeting, and also in the Two Thousand Guineas Stakes at Newmarket, in the county of Suffolk, one thousand eight hundred and forty-four, and also in the Derby Stakes at Epsom aforesaid, one thousand eight hundred and forty-four, and the St.Leger Stakes at Doncaster, in the said county of York, one thousand eight hundred and forty-four, is the same colt as was purchased by the said Henry Stebbings when a foal, in the year one thousand eight hundred and forty-one, from the said Mr.Cobb aforesaid, and delivered to me by the said James Stebbings and subsequently sent to the stables of the said Messrs.Pearl, Bean, Haines, and Smith, as aforesaid. And I make this solemn declaration conscientiously.

A.L.Goodman.

Declared at the Public-Office, Southampton Buildings, Chancery Lane, this twenty-seventh day of March, one thousand eight hundred and forty-four, before me. – G.Rose.

I WILLIAM SADLER, of Stockbridge, in the county of Southampton, training groom, do solemnly and sincerely declare, that about the month of August, one thousand eight hundred and forty-two, I went with Mr.Goodman to Mr.William Bean, at Finchley, in the county of Middlesex, to see a colt there, then his property; that the said colt was a bay yearling colt; that I was present at the October Meeting at Newmarket, in the county of Suffolk, in the year one thousand eight hundred and forty-three, and there saw run at the same meeting a colt called Running Rein. And I further solemnly and sincerely declare that the said colt called Running Rein was and is the same colt as I saw, when a yearling, at Mr.William Bean's at Finchley aforesaid, in or about the month of August, one thousand eight hundred and forty-two; that I testified to the facts before stated before the Stewards of the Jockey Club at Newmarket aforesaid when they decided on the objected of the said colt. And I make this solemn declaration conscientiously.

134

William Sadler.
Declared at Stockbridge, in the county of Southampton, this seventeenth
day of March, one thousand eight hundred and forty-four, before me. –
Wm.Bersigin, a Master Extraordinary in Chancery.

There can be no doubt that the stewards had no other option than to permit the horse to start.

Mr Baron Alderson did not believe that this in any way proved the identity of the horse. There was no question that there was a colt of the proper age got by The Saddler out of Mab; the question was whether the winner of the Derby was that horse.

Sir Frederick Thesiger then rose to open the case for the defendant, Colonel Peel. He expressed astonishment at the abrupt termination of the plaintiff's case without clearly establishing beyond all possibility of doubt the case he had set out to prove. It was his intention to establish that a gross and scandalous fraud had been committed by the plaintiff, or by those to whom the plaintiff had entrusted the horse in question. He was anxious that if a fraud had been committed they should be able to expose it, because if practices such as those alleged to have been carried out were allowed to pass with impunity there was a considerable danger that the sport of horse racing would be destroyed. He condemned Mr Cockburn's complete lack of common courtesy towards Lord George Bentinck, regarding the disparaging remarks made against him. In his opinion Lord George Bentinck was desirous that frauds of this description should be detected and defeated and, acting under that impulse, Lord George Bentinck was ready to declare that he had taken part in the investigation. But his learned friend was insinuating that there had been something unfair in Lord George's conduct, which was that frauds of this kind should not be permitted to pass with impunity, and he defied his learned friend to prove anything to the contrary.

The solicitor general explained to the jury that his learned friend had complained about the position in which the plaintiff had found himself placed, but that had been his choice; Colonel Peel had been quite ready to take the initiative and appear before the *jury first,* and to have stated and proved his case. As a consequence, Colonel Peel had been at a disadvantage arising from innumerable technical difficulties that bound him by strict legal evidence, whilst out of court he would have been able to introduce facts of the most important nature into his case, which had now to be omitted. However, notwithstanding that difficulty, he was confident that the evidence he would place before the jury would be so perfectly clear that no reasonable doubt would exist in their minds.

He then detailed why Mr Cockburn had endeavoured to dispose altogether of Mr Goodman, and for very good reason, for if Mr Goodman had been a witness in the case it would have been found that he was aware of the whole event from beginning to end, and had he been subject to examination he would have been well aware that he would have had to answer some very awkward questions. Mr Goodman had been quite prepared to join with others who made formal declarations in favour of the plaintiff. But when he knew that the inquiry must necessarily become public he thought it more prudent not to appear in public before the jury, and his learned friend, with great dexterity, had endeavoured to cast Mr Goodman aside. His learned friend's case was that this was not a fraud, that it was all perfectly honest and that the horse that had won at Newmarket and had won the Derby was the identical Saddler colt that was bought from Mr Cobb. Yet, if this was an honest and fair transaction, then surely Mr Goodman could have come forward and corroborated it, for that is all that was required. Was it not a most remarkable thing that Mr Goodman should not have been called to establish it, and did it not make the case extremely suspicious indeed? Then, with respect to the conveyance of The Saddler colt to Bean's at Finchley and from Bean's to Smith's at Epsom, one would have thought they would have called before the jury all the witnesses who had knowledge of the transfer from one place to another. It was very odd that Daniel White was the only witness called for proving the transfer of the horse from Bean's at Finchley. He had been accompanied by George White, who had been seen within the last two months, and who was the person who had received the horse at Bean's. It was George White who should have been called before the jury, but his learned friend had failed to call him.

The solicitor general then proceeded at some length to comment on whom he considered to be the most important witnesses for the plaintiff: Kitchen, Bean and Daniel White. With respect to Kitchen, he had been secured as a witness by Mr Gill, the plaintiff's attorney, kept under his control and influenced by tempting offers in order that the claim of the plaintiff could be established. He had been present at The Saddler colt's birth, and he had ventured to say that having been taken down to Newmarket in October of 1843, never having seen the colt for such a considerable time, that he recognised The Saddler colt. He had stated to the stewards of the Jockey Club his firm conviction that it was the same colt he had under his care when he had been in the service of Mr Cobb. But when the very next witness, Henry Stebbings, was called, who had been accustomed to horses all his life and who had seen the horse at Newmarket, as Kitchen had done, and was asked whether it was the same horse he had bought from Mr Cobb, he said, "'It is quite impossible for me to say,'" which led the solicitor general to infer that it was quite impossible for anyone, who had only known the horse as a foal, to say that they would recognise it after a considerable period of time.

He then came to Mr Bean, whom his learned friend had introduced as a gentleman of undoubted respectability and of high station and eminence in his business (had it been a modern TV courtroom drama, one could almost imagine the solicitor general shaking his head and smiling in his absolute disbelief): of such respectability that he was compelled to confess that he had been *twice* bankrupt, and *twice* insolvent, who had never paid a farthing to any of his creditors, and furthermore "'did *not recollect*'" whether anything of that kind took place.

He departed from Mr Bean to make a short mention of Daniel White, who was hardly a person on whom one could rely with any great confidence, and it would be proved that he would be distinctly contradicted by evidence of facts that would leave no doubt in the minds of the jury. He would return to Daniel White later, with some further observations.

He then turned to the simple question of identification. The case on the part of the plaintiff was that the horse that beat the Duke of Rutland's Crenoline at Newmarket in October 1843 and won the last Derby was the colt got by The Saddler out of Mab, the property originally of Mr Cobb; whereas the case for the defendant, Colonel Peel, was that it was not Running Rein but a colt by Gladiator, belonging originally to Sir Charles Ibbetson, which had the name of Running Rein imposed on it, having originally been named Maccabeus, and having been entered for several stakes in that name. To avoid any confusion he would refer to them as The Saddler colt and the Gladiator colt. Putting aside the plaintiff, what he meant to allege was that Goodman and Mr Henry Higgins, and perhaps some other person, were engaged in a concert of conspiracy for the purpose of running horses above the proper age, and in pursuance of that concert between them, it would be proved that Goodman purchased the Gladiator colt at Doncaster in September 1841.

Before the colt had been purchased, with its engagements, by Mr Goodman it had been entered for the Derby of 1843, as 'a bay colt by Gladiator, dam foaled in 1823, by Capsicum out of Acklam Lass', in the name of a Mr Watson (a pseudonym used by Sir Charles Ibbetson).

The solicitor general then turned to the history of the Gladiator colt, from its time of purchase by Goodman to its time at George Worley's farm at Sywell, and its journey with Richard Watson from Northampton to Haines's livery stables in Langham Place, where it remained from 24 September to 27 September 1842, when it was taken by William Drewett to Smith's stables at Epsom. He had hoped that Richard Watson could have been produced, as he would have been able to establish if the horse he had brought from Northampton was the same horse that had won the Derby. He had been subpoenaed, but where he was now was as much a mystery as the location of the horse, since it was removed by Mr Ignatius Coyle. He would, however, be able to show Watson's course, from leaving Northampton on 21 September and arriving at Haines's livery stables on 24 September. What he intended to establish was that it was here that the fraud began, with the attempt to palm off the Gladiator colt as Running Rein; that it was the Gladiator colt that remained at Haines's from 24 to 27 September; and that this was the colt taken by Drewett to Smith's at Epsom. The case of the plaintiff was that The Saddler colt was brought to London in the month of January 1842; it was sent to Mr Bean's at Finchley; it remained at Mr Bean's at Finchley until 24 September; that *he* was the colt who was then brought up to Haines's and remained there until 27 September; and that he was the colt who was taken by Drewett to Smith's. The question was: although it was not in dispute that a colt had been sent, which was that colt? Bean had sworn that it was The Saddler colt that had been collected from his premises on 24 September, knowing it to be false. It was fortunate that there had been only one colt at Bean's; had Mr Bean been more ingenious and claimed that he had two colts, it would have been difficult for the defendant to prove his case. As Bean had admitted he had only one colt, the solicitor general would prove, by a number of witnesses, that the colt was in fact at Bean's at Finchley until the month of February 1843. One such witness was a female servant of Bean's, who had no reason to tell an untruth and who would prove that The Saddler colt was at Bean's in February 1843 and that it was taken away by George White. Then there was Mrs Bean, who had offered George White something to drink; she had not been produced by the plaintiff. There was also Mr Meeson, who was a neighbour of Bean's, and others, who had no interest in the matter and who would confirm that the colt was at Bean's until February 1843.

The solicitor general then returned to the evidence given by George Rayner with respect to the identity of the person who brought the colt to Haines's livery stables on 24 September 1842. According to Bean, this gentleman of unquestionable respectability, it was George White who had collected it; it would therefore have been George White who delivered it to Haines's stables. Rayner knew George White, and he had Daniel White pointed out to him in court, but he stated that it was neither of these who had brought the colt. It was therefore impossible to reconcile Bean's evidence with the fact that neither of the Whites had brought the colt to Haines's in the month of September, according to the testimony of Rayner.

There was a further observation, partly with regard to Daniel White's testimony, concerning the letter he had delivered to Bean, requesting that Bean deliver the colt to the bearer. It struck the solicitor general that a person who could substitute one horse for another could easily make a document of this kind. And it further appeared to him a little extraordinary that such a valuable document as that should have been preserved with such extreme care by Mr Bean, a man who kept no book and yet considered the order to be of such importance that from the month of September it had been preserved, beautifully clean for a horse dealer, by him among his repositories.

There was one further very remarkable thing that the solicitor general wished to draw to the court's attention: in the short distance between Bean's at Finchley and Haines's at Langham Place the colt appeared to have changed its colour. The cowkeeper, William Marshall, had described it as a rusty dark colt, but on its arrival at Haines's Rayner had described it as a bright bay. That had been a wonderful metamorphosis – not quite as wonderful as the transformation of the Gladiator colt into Running Rein, and not enough, he supposed, to convince the jury that the colt that was brought to Haines's on 24 September was not the Gladiator colt, which was a bright bay but, as the plaintiff alleged, Running Rein, a scrubby dark bay.

He asserted that while the colt had been at Worley's it had been called Maccabeus, but when it arrived at Smith's at Epsom on 27 September it there assumed the name of Running Rein. He continued with the deception that Maccabeus had played at Newmarket in October of 1843, and the subsequent inquiry at which Goodman had repeatedly refused to allow the horse's mouth to be examined. His learned friend claimed it was a 'fallible test'. The solicitor general admitted that it was not an infallible test, but nevertheless it was a test in the transaction of horses and, even if it was fallible, there was no good reason for Mr Goodman not to permit the investigation.

Having detailed the history of the Gladiator colt, Maccabeus, up until October 1843, in order to establish fully the practices of Mr Goodman he then introduced the part that Thomas Ferguson's horse, Goneaway, had played in impersonating Maccabeus.

Lord George's detective work was now put to good use by the solicitor general: first, he produced the memorandum of agreement between Goodman and Ferguson for the hire of Goneaway: "'I have it in the handwriting of Goodman,'" he confidently stated. And then there was the dye produced by the hairdresser Rossi to Goodman's requirement: "'He purchased a *dye* – he dyed this *white pastern* black. This is handed to me as the mixture which was used,'" he said, holding the bottle of metamorphosing elixir to the court, "'which was bought of a person of the name of *Rossi*.'" He stated that Goneaway was a four-year-old, but that was not important; the important fact was that there had been a substitution of one horse for another, which was a fraud, intimately connected with the inquiry.

The judge did not think that the part Goodman played was evidence, and to introduce it was exciting prejudice. He agreed that the solicitor general had a perfect right to show that the horse called Maccabeus was Goneaway, but whether the substitution was done by Goodman or another person was not material to the case.

He wanted to keep clear of Mr Goodman, as this was the case of Mr Wood.

The solicitor general countered that the matter did involve Mr Goodman up to November 1843, as he was still the owner at that time and the events took place in the spring of 1843, although the judge did not believe that it should extend to Mr Goodman's declarations at that time.

Mr Cockburn asked the judge to take note that he objected, declaring that what Goodman did with regard to the horse that ran as Maccabeus at the Epsom Spring Meeting of 1843 was not a matter that should be gone into, otherwise they might as well have gone into any fraudulent transaction on the part of Mr Goodman. The judge said that it was quite clear that the solicitor general was at liberty to show that the horse that ran as Maccabeus was not the correct Maccabeus, but he doubted whether he had any right to go into any fraudulent conduct on the part of Mr Goodman simply because Mr Goodman was at the time the owner of Maccabeus, when the fraudulent conduct may have applied to another horse.

The solicitor general believed that he was at liberty to give the acts and declarations of Mr Goodman up to the month of November 1843, in the same way as if he (Goodman) had been the plaintiff. He addressed the judge, emphasising the importance of showing that Mr Goodman had not performed the engagements of the Gladiator colt, which was part of the purchase from Sir Charles Ibbetson, by reason of having substituted Goneaway for the Gladiator colt. From the dread of discovery, when Mr Ferguson had unearthed his intentions, in order to elude inquiry he had declared that Maccabeus was dead. That may have deluded the jury, believing that the Gladiator colt was in fact dead. But far from Maccabeus being dead, the horse that had run in the name of Maccabeus at the Epsom Spring Meeting was not, in fact, the Gladiator colt, but the Irish horse, Goneaway, and that was the horse that had died, not Maccabeus.

The judge agreed that the solicitor general could show that the horse that ran at the Epsom Spring Meeting was not the Gladiator colt and that the horse called Goneaway had died, but beyond that he could not go, as he wanted to try the case without prejudice. The solicitor general hoped that he was incapable of introducing any prejudice: he only ventured to think that it was very important evidence, but he would abide by his lordship's instruction.

Following this minor altercation with the judge the solicitor general turned to address the jury. He stressed that it was Goneaway – who had run as Maccabeus at the Epsom Spring Meeting – that had died; and that it was utterly untrue, as alleged by Mr Goodman, that Maccabeus – who was full of life and had run at the October Newmarket Meeting and also at the Derby – had died. He would further produce evidence that Messrs Worley and Odell, who had seen the alleged Running Rein win the Derby, would swear that they had not the slightest doubt that it was the same Gladiator colt that Mr Worley had kept in his paddock; and he would trace the colt step by step, proving that it was George White who had taken The Saddler colt to Goodman's in February 1843, and not Daniel White on 24 of September 1842, as alleged by the plaintiff. He would prove those facts to the satisfaction of the jury, such that not a particle of doubt would be left in their minds that a gross fraud had been committed, whereby a substitution of one colt for another had been made, concluding that he hoped that there would be no question whatever that the defendant would be entitled to the verdict. And if the facts related by Mr Worley and Mr Odell and other witnesses were not true, he challenged his learned friend, as he had done so with Mr Goodman and other witnesses, to call Mr Henry Higgins to contradict them, as he considered that his learned friend, who alleged he had an honest and true case, was duty bound to have thrown all necessary light on the investigation that he thought the jury was entitled to demand. That was the case that he was prepared to lay before the jury, but he thought that the court – when dealing with an individual who was alleged by his learned friend to be wholly free from suspicion, not connected in any degree with the fraud that would be proved to be practised – would have expected from him a fair opportunity for investigating the case, as was there entitlement and which justice demanded. If the horse that ran as Running Rein was really The Saddler colt, born in the year 1841, it was qualified in every respect to run for the Derby of 1844, and there was no ground for imputing the smallest impropriety. But if Mr Wood had been the fair and respectable man that was alleged by his learned friend, surely he would have been cooperative in terms of dispelling any suspicion of an alleged fraud? What better mode of cooperation could there have been than to submit the horse to a proper inspection, which had been authorised by the learned judge? Yet, on the very day before the order was to be carried out, it was found that the horse had been removed by Mr Ignatius Coyle, hardly, he contended, without any authority. Mr Wood had allowed the horse to be removed at the very moment the judge had intended it to be submitted for examination, and from that time they had been denied any means of identifying it.

He asked the jury to consider if Mr Wood's case had been a just one when he had refused to allow an inquiry, which the judge thought was just and reasonable. He concluded by expressing a hope that he would make out such a case that a fraud had been practised, and, by the verdict that he hoped the jury would pronounce, it would read a salutary lesson to persons of the station of Mr Goodman, thereby clearing the Turf of similar miscreants and averting the destruction of horse racing, which had been threatened by the recent exposures.

The first witness called for the defendant was Lord Stradbroke. When questioned by Mr Wortley he confirmed the objection made by the Duke of Rutland. He then entered into the detail of the inquiry during the Newmarket Houghton Meeting in respect of the identification of Kitchen and the refusal by Mr Goodman – which his lordship was led to understand he would resist by force – to permit the horse's mouth to be examined.

The next witnesses called were George Hayward, Isaac Grey, Edward Messenger and George Wharton, who had all been employees of Sir Charles Henry Ibbetson. George Hayward stated that he had been the land agent for Sir Charles Ibbetson in 1840 and had arranged for the Gladiator colt to be sold at the Doncaster sales, and Isaac Grey confirmed that he had taken the Capsicum mare to York to be mated with Physician. Edward Messenger stated that he had been the stud groom and had given directions to Weatherbys to enter the Gladiator colt for the Derby of 1843 in the name of Mr Watson; with George Wharton he had delivered the colt to Goodman at the Doncaster Arms stables, and the latter had taken the colt, at Goodman's request, to Masborough station to be delivered to London. When questioned by Baron Alderson, Messenger said that, if he was allowed to see the horse again, he was in no doubt that he could identify him.

Charles Weatherby, examined by Mr Martin, produced the entry for the Gladiator colt for the Derby at Epsom in 1843: it was in the hand of his clerk, Robert K. Smart, entered in the name of Watson.

He confirmed that the colt was later entered, as Maccabeus, for the Liverpool Cup of 1843 by Mr Goodman, against a forfeit of five pounds, paid for by a Mr Maughan in the presence of Goodman.

Clerk for the stewards at Epsom, Joseph Farrell, proved that on 27 March Goodman entered Maccabeus (Goneaway), as a three-year-old, for the sweepstakes of five sovereigns each, with fifty sovereigns added by Sir Gilbert Heathcote, to be held at the Epsom Spring Meeting, where he was beaten by Captain Flathooker. When questioned by Mr Cockburn as to whether he was the means for 'hooking the flats', he did not know.

Mr Weatherby was called again and was asked by Mr Martin to give the entries of Running Rein, which proved that he had been entered for a sweepstakes of fifty sovereigns each for foals of 1841, to run at the Newmarket First Spring Meeting of 1844, the next entry being the Derby of 1844; he was also entered for the Clearwell Stakes at the Second Newmarket October Meeting of 1843, and for the Two Thousand Guineas in the spring of 1844.

By now it was past 7 o'clock, and the court was adjourned for the day.

In spite of the unfavourable state of the weather on the following day, the court was again thronged at an early hour, the disclosures of the previous day having served to whet rather than dampen the anxiety of those concerned in this exciting proceeding, as well as the curiosity of those who merely looked on it as an interesting trial.

Just before the learned judge took his seat a great sensation was created by the hurried entry of Baron de Tessier, who beckoned Colonel Peel and Lord George Bentinck out of court. A short and earnest consultation took place between these parties, during which the plaintiff joined the group, and it appeared that some proposition was made to the Colonel, as he decidedly shook his head before retracing his steps to his seat near his counsel.

Shortly afterwards the plaintiff descended to the floor of the court and, approaching Colonel Peel, again entered into conversation with him and showed him a letter, which he held open in his hand. Just at this moment the learned judge came in. He called on the solicitor general to proceed with his evidence and asked who his next witness was.

The solicitor general replied that it was George Worley, at which point Mr Cockburn suddenly interrupted, requesting his lordship to hear the circumstances in which he and the plaintiff had been placed.

Both he and the plaintiff had considered it their bounden duty to produce the horse. He had Mr Wood's assurance that the horse had been taken away without his sanction or knowledge and he did not know where it had gone. As a result of enquiries that Mr Wood had made the previous day regarding the horse's whereabouts, he had gone to a place where he had been informed the horse had been taken,[8] only to discover that it had again been moved on.

His lordship asked why Mr Wood had not gone to the police to pursue these felons, as it was obvious that they were guilty of horse stealing, stating that if he were to try them he would for certain transport them for life.

He wondered what was then to be done, as it was clear that the horse could not be produced if it had been stolen. Mr Cockburn claimed that it would be in vain to struggle on without production of the horse and he was in the hands of his lordship. The judge stated it was not for him – it was a matter for the jury.

He quoted an ancient case to the court, in which a poor boy had found a diamond and had taken it to a diamond merchant to ascertain its value. The merchant detained the diamond, and when an action was brought against him the jury was directed to presume against the merchant, on the basis that, as the merchant could not produce the jewel, it was of the greatest possible value. This example illustrated that failing to produce the horse would surely warrant the jury in any presumption against Mr Wood.

His lordship continued, stating that the nub of the case revolved around the horse that had been delivered to Haines's livery stables. There had been no doubt that the colt that went to Bean's was the colt bred by Dr Cobb, and there was no doubt that the colt that went from Haines's became Running Rein. The question was: did Dr Cobb's colt go from Bean's to Haines's? On that question there was only the testament of Daniel White.

Being unable to produce the horse, Mr Cockburn found himself in a difficult predicament. The judge appreciated his position and offered him the option of proceeding in any way he wished. The solicitor general agreed that his learned friend should pursue whatever course he pleased. He was prepared to go on with the case and to prove the defendant's case distinctly.

George Worley was finally called and examined by Mr Wortley. He testified that he farmed at Sywell in Northamptonshire, and that at the 1841 Doncaster St Leger Meeting Henry Higgins had said he would send him a colt, which was delivered to him on 20 September. The judge asked Worley to describe the colt, and then whether he would know the horse if he were to see him again. Worley responded positively that he certainly had seen him – at the Derby at Epsom, and had not the least shadow of doubt that the horse named Running Rein was the horse that he had kept in his paddock; in fact he had expressed that opinion on the course.

On further questioning by the judge, Worley confirmed the injury to the colt's near foreleg and the naming of the colt at his house. He told the judge that Prizefighter was thought a suitable name for a colt got by Gladiator, but they could not use that name because Lord Chesterfield had it already, and so they called him Spartacus. Mr Higgins had looked in a book and had found the name, but it was afterwards changed to Maccabeus.

The judge facetiously asked, "'He did not say he found *that* in a book?'" Worley replied in the negative. "'At least not in any book *he* was likely to read,'" responded the judge.

George Odell, when examined by Mr Martin, testified that he was a horse dealer at Northampton and knew both Henry Higgins and George Worley. He described the horse and confirmed that he had seen it almost every day that he went to Worley's house, and at Vigo Cottage, where he had seen it led about by Higgins's man, Jaques,[9] whom he believed had since died. He confirmed the second accident that the horse had suffered at Markham's paddock and, like Worley, he said that he had not the least doubt that the horse Running Rein that he had seen at Epsom was the same colt that had been at Northampton.

The judge asked Odell if he had seen the scars on the horse's leg. Odell confirmed there were two.

"'Now if we could see the horse,'" said the judge, "'that would decide the question in a moment. I make the order the horse shall be seen on Thursday, and on Wednesday he has vanished out of the place. You must take us for geese!'"

Mr Cockburn, who had been engaged in close conversation with his team and Mr Wood during the examination of Mr Odell, responded that indeed they certainly did not. He had the veterinary surgeon in court that had attended the colt after the accident, and he would confirm that there was only one scar, although he admitted that there had been two accidents.

Mr Cockburn then explained to his lordship that he had only just learned from his client what had taken place between him and Colonel Peel before he (Mr Cockburn) had entered the court, and he had only now been acquainted with the contents of the letter that his client had written, stating that he himself had been deceived, and he did not intend to go on with the case. After that he (Mr Cockburn) could only carry out that intention by submitting to a verdict for the defendant, but he could not do so without expressing on behalf of Mr Wood that if any tricks had been played he had been the victim.

The judge agreed that there was nothing to show that he had anything to do with it, as he had bought the horse with his engagements.

Mr Cockburn then addressed the court, stating that his client had instructed him to withdraw from the cause and consent to a verdict for the defendant, to which his lordship agreed. Mr Cockburn then continued:

Will your lordship allow me to avert for a moment to another matter which is immediately connected with this case and in what I am about to say, I trust I shall give offence to no one, and possibly may remove it. My lord, I have received a communication from my Lord George Bentinck, couched, I must say, in terms of perfect courtesy to myself, and perfectly unexceptionable in every point of view, in which his lordship complains of my having made a charge against him yesterday, with respect to his conduct in the matters connected with the case, and that I have not put him into the witness box, or called witnesses to prove that charge. My lord, I will just explain in a moment the position in which I stand; my instructions were clear, specific, positive and unqualified as to this *– that my Lord George Bentinck had (for I can use no milder term) tampered with the plaintiff's witnesses; that he had held out threats to them, and where threats had failed, had held out promises to them to induce them to withhold their evidence. That he had procured by the greatest exertions, and by the use of his personal influence, witnesses to appear for the defendant; that he had to a certain degree associated with those witnesses; that he had them at Harcourt House, his new place of residence, that he had fed them, that he had clothed them, that his valet had been seen to take one of them to a tailor's to fit him out with clothes, and that his lordship had helped out to another a pecuniary promise – had actually given money, and had held out a* *pecuniary promise. I was instructed, my lord, that from his lordship, if he was called as a witness for the defendant, I should be enabled to extract these matters. I was instructed, that from the defendant's witnesses, when called, I should be enabled to elicit these facts; and I was instructed, that with regard to one of them, especially one to whom it was alleged a promise had been made, that I should be enabled if he denied the fact, or denied his admission of the fact, that I should be enabled to call a body of witnesses to whom he had made such admission. Under these circumstances, my lord, it being a fact in the cause, if Lord George Bentinck was not a party in the cause, still he had been the great mover in it, which is not denied by my learned friend the Solicitor-General. I thought it better at once to open these matters, in order that my learned friend, the Solicitor-General, might know the course I should adopt when the witnesses for the defence were to be put into the box; that the observations that I might think myself called upon afterwards to make on my Lord George Bentinck, might not be made by me when there should be no opportunity of replying on me. That was the reason I adopted that course.*

With regard to examining my witnesses to that fact, my learned friend would be aware, although Lord George Bentinck could not, that I could not ask them as to what Lord George Bentinck had done or said with them until my lord was put into the box. With regard to the others I could ask no question until they were called by my friends. Lord George was subpœnaed as a witness on our side, because we understood there was a person of the name of Carlon [sic], with whom there had been transactions with his lordship, and that Carlon [sic] would be called on the other side, and it would be essential for me to call Lord George to contradict Carlon [sic]. I have had no opportunity of doing that which his lordship complains I have not done – put him into the box as a witness, or examined any one witness as to the matters I have charged against Lord George.

I have made this statement for the purpose of setting myself right so far with my Lord George Bentinck, and also at the same time to take the opportunity of telling him clearly and explicitly what was the matter as to which my instructions went against him, and gave him this opportunity, or any other of which he may think proper to avail himself of giving any denial to that charge which his lordship should think most consistent.

I am bound to say, as far as regards my Lord George Bentinck, that he does not in the slightest degree complain of that; on the contrary, he has expressed his high sense of value of the privileges of the English bar.

Mr Baron Alderson commented that nothing had been done improperly by Mr Cockburn, nor had there been any impropriety on the part of Lord George Bentinck. He had done that which was perfectly right – he had traced out the truth, and the truth had come out.

Mr Wortley requested to say on behalf of Lord George Bentinck that not only did they not complain of the course that Mr Cockburn took, but neither did Lord George Bentinck. As he had expressed in his letter to Mr Cockburn, he would have been most anxious to have had the opportunity to meet those charges, and he would have courted the utmost investigation into the truth of those instructions of Mr Cockburn.

The abrupt termination of the case had prevented the possibility of investigating the truth. William Carlin would have been called, and those instructions provided to Mr Cockburn would have been entirely refuted and contradicted by a full investigation of the circumstances.

The letter from Lord George to which Mr Cockburn referred read as follows:

Harcourt House, July 1, 1844.
Monday Night.
Sir, - I am too fully cognizant of your duty as well as privilege as a counsel, and much too highly appreciate the value and usefulness of such a privilege, for a moment to question the propriety of the remarks which you felt it right, I doubt not, in obedience to your instructions, to pass upon my conduct this morning.
I am quite aware that an honest counsel is professionally bound to assume as true all that is stated in his brief, and would betray his trust if he were to spare the feelings of any one against whose integrity and uprightness he either had, or might be misled by his instructions to believe he had, any facts, proof, or evidence to adduce.
Conceiving the latter to be your position this morning, I admired the manliness and honesty with which you made your attack, though I myself was the victim of it, perfectly content on my own account patiently to abide my time, when I confidently anticipated you would put me in the witness-box, and thereby at once prove your words to be true, or

convince yourself and all the world besides, that grave charges were never made with less foundation against mortal man, than those you hurled at me.

As in duty bound, I was in court under your client's subpœna, and had brought with me all the documents in my power to bring, in faithful and honest obedience to the wide scope of your duce tecum subpœna: bound by my oath, I should have had no choice to answer freely every question you had thought proper to put to me; but more than that, I pledge you my word as a man of honour and as a gentleman, that if you had put me in the witness-box, or will still do so, where your instructions or your own acuteness had fallen, or may fall, short in directing your examination, I would have freely and frankly supply, the want, and will fully disclose every act of mine connected with this transaction.

Having said this much, I appeal to you, not in the way of a threat (for I have none to make, and have none in thought or reservation) but I, as a supplicant, appeal to you as a man of honour, honesty and truth, to afford me that redress to which I have pointed, without which your opening speech cannot be justified. I appeal to you either to make good your charges, or in open court as publicly and as loudly as they were made to acknowledge and to proclaim that they have no foundation save in your false instructions.

Lastly, I appeal to you, for the sake of the English bar, which scarcely prides itself more for its unrivalled ability and talent, than for its exalted sense of honour and integrity, not in your person, who ought to be one of its brightest ornaments, to dim its lustre by degrading it into the base instrument of the wanton, wilful, wicked, and revengeful calumnies of detected and defeated fraud.

I have the honour to be, Sir,
Your obedient humble servant,
G.Bentinck.
To A.E. Cockburn, Esq., Queens Counsel.

In summing up the case, Baron Alderson said:

Gentlemen, the only remaining matter, it being now admitted that the verdict must be for the defendant, will be for you to proceed to give your verdict. Give me leave to say that this case has produced a very great degree of sorrow and disgust in my mind. I have seen the opening out of a most atrocious fraud which has been practised, and I have seen with great regret gentlemen associating with persons of infinitely lower rank

150

than themselves, which is the cause of it all. If gentlemen would only race with gentlemen there would not be any difficulty in the matter; but if they condescend to race with blackguards they must condescend to expect to be cheated.[10]

Thus ended the great Derby fraud.

14
After the Trial

The result of the trial flew like wildfire to all parts of the town, and the friends of Orlando were in a state of euphoria. On the news reaching Newmarket the exultation was extraordinary; all the bells were ringing, bands of music paraded about the streets, and the place was in a perfect uproar of delight.[1]

It was relief, indeed, for the backers of Orlando: at the start of the trial it looked certain that Running Rein would keep the race, odds of 2 to 1 being laid on him; but by the end of the first day, with the plaintiff unable to respond to Judge Alderson's demand to produce the horse, and Goodman making himself scarce, the betting market changed in favour of Orlando.

Arising from this fiasco is one of those intriguing stories that so enriches the history of the great game. Patrick Osborne, a young soldier, who hunted with the Crick in Northamptonshire, found himself on the wrong side of credit. His only expectation of extricating himself from his plight was by betting. Here, the stories vary as to his route to salvation: some say he backed Orlando for all the money he could lay his hands on, and, seeing it beaten into second place by Running Rein, he held out little hope that the resulting objection would be reversed; others say that that he backed Running Rein and feared that the objection would be upheld, again ruin staring him in the face. Whichever way, his downfall seemed inevitable.

On the morning after the race he was walking down Bond Street when a young man thrust a piece of paper into his hand (why the young man happened to be in Bond Street at the same time as Captain Osborne does not appear to be recorded – probably indicating an element of fabrication in the story). Captain Osborne read the profoundly illiterate communiqué:[2]

Honnerd Sur, – You did me and my missus a good turn, and I want to do you the same. Running Rein is a himposter, and he won't get the

*race. I noes all. Buy all the bets you can on Orlando, and you'll make
a fourtin, but no more at present, from your humble servant,
A.Simmons, formerly your helper at Crick.*

The Captain's memory had not failed him. He did, indeed, recall
the young man whom he had tided over with the gift of a fiver.

Acting on the information, he hastened to Tattersalls and bought
up all the bets on Orlando that he could get hold of, many
speculators being only too keen to part with them for a song. And
when Orlando secured the jury's verdict Captain Osborne collected
a cool £28,000.

Not so fortunate was the diminutive Squire Osbaldeston. He had
bet several thousand pounds on Running Rein. He knew the
Running Rein party, and on the advice of Thomas Gill, Mr Wood's
solicitor, who assured the Squire that theirs was a '"plain
unvarnished tale"'[3] and it was impossible to upset it, he did not
hedge a shilling.

The trial was not the end of matters: a just result may have been
achieved. Heigh-ho for Colonel Peel; the Members of the Jockey
Club were, however, not satisfied. They felt that there was sufficient
evidence to prosecute the miscreants. Goodman, Higgins, William
Sadler, William Smith and Alexander Wood had conspired to cheat
or obtain money under false pretences, and Bean and Daniel White
had relentlessly perjured themselves.[4]

The evidence of Benyon Drage regarding Goneaway certainly
appeared to be ample enough to condemn Higgins. He had
attended the Epsom Spring Meeting in 1843 with Higgins, who
had taken him to Smith's stables to see the horse that was to run as
Maccabeus. Higgins had previously told him that this horse's leg
had been stained, and after the race he had confessed that the
horse was Mr Ferguson's Goneaway.

They then turned to the Gladiator colt at Newmarket in October
1843, where Goodman alone appeared as the owner in the
subsequent inquiry following the Duke of Rutland's objection. The
evidence of Benyon Drage, however, showed that Higgins was still
taking advantage of the fraud.

After the Newmarket races the evidence showed that the colt
returned to Goodman's at Sutton until the following November,
when it was removed to William Smith's, and except for a few days
when it was sent to London it remained there until after the Derby.

At about this time Mr Wood became the owner, although the

entry of 'Running Rein' for the Derby had been made by Goodman. The stake had been paid by parties unknown to Mr Weatherby and his clerk Mr Smart.

Although ownership of Running Rein had passed to Mr Wood, according to the evidence of Messrs Worley, Odell and Drage both Goodman and Higgins were still participating in the fraud,

Mr Wood's case at the trial was that the colt that was delivered to Haines's livery stables on 24 September 1842 was the colt by The Saddler out of Mab, and one witness, Daniel White, had sworn to the fact that he had accompanied Goodman's servant, George White, to fetch the colt from Bean's at Finchley, afterwards delivering it at Haines's.

Rayner, however, on being cross-examined, proved that the colt delivered on 24 September 1842 was not brought to the stables either by George White or Daniel White.

The declarations of Goodman and Higgins, however, independently of the evidence of the colt that had been stabled at Bean's at Finchley until February 1843, precluded such a defence being again attempted.

With respect to Wood and William Smith, the case against them rested solely on the evidence of Mr Bartlett and, giving it credit, it showed that they both knew the colt to be four years old. There was not, however, any evidence to suggest that either Wood or Smith knew that the colt was not the colt by The Saddler.

The part that William Sadler took in the fraud was training Goneaway to run as Maccabeus at the Epsom Spring Meeting. There was no evidence that William Sadler knew that the horse he had in training was not Maccabeus, although there was no doubt that he knew that the horse was more than three years old, and the fact that the horse's tail had been pulled by John Day, on Goodman's orders, must have induced him to suspect that a trick of some kind had been intended. The evidence however, was far from conclusive.

It was additionally proposed to indict witnesses Bean and Daniel White for perjury. The false statement made by Bean was that on 24 September 1842 he received an order from Goodman for the delivery of the colt that he had been caring for on his behalf, and that he ordered the colt to be delivered accordingly, finding on his return to his premises that same evening that the colt was not there.

Bean admitted in his evidence that he only ever had one colt at his premises at Finchley, and there were numerous witnesses to prove that the colt remained at Bean's until February 1843.

The false statement made by Daniel White was that he accompanied Goodman's servant, George White, to Finchley in September 1842; that he delivered the note to Bean and afterwards joined George White, who had the colt, in the lane; and that he took the colt to Goodman's house first and then on the same day delivered it at Haines's stables.

During the court prosecution proceedings numerous attempts were made to tamper with the witnesses for the defence, and in the case of Watson it had succeeded. It had almost succeeded with William Carlin, who resisted the persuasions of Goodman, Glenn and Anderson to keep out of the way.

There were a number of issues here that Mr Peacock, attorney for the Jockey Club, was requested to investigate:[5]

1. Based on the evidence prepared for the defence, had any offence been committed by Goodman, Higgins, Wood, Smith or Sadler and, if so, what? What would be the proper mode of proceeding against them? And, on the evidence, was the probability of a conviction such that it would render a prosecution advisable?
2. Would any objection to an indictment arise from the stakes for the different races not having been paid at the time of the contract for the race being entered into?
3. Could perjury be assigned, on the evidence given by Bean and White? And, on the evidence of the different witnesses set forth in the proofs, would the probability of convicting both or either be such as to render a prosecution expedient?
4. What would be the proper mode of proceeding against these parties? And, on Carlin's evidence, some particulars of which would be confirmed by his wife, would the likelihood of a conviction for either of the parties be reasonable enough to make it advisable to prosecute them?
5. On the statement of John Watson, could any proceedings be taken against Mr Gill and, if so, what?

Mr Peacock's opinion was that there was insufficient evidence to convict Wood, Smith or Sadler of any indictable offence. However, he believed that there was sufficient evidence, provided that the jury believed all the witnesses, to prove that Goodman and Higgins were guilty of a conspiracy to substitute the Gladiator colt for Running Rein in order that he might win the plate at the Newmarket meeting, and that there was a reasonable probability of convicting them of that offence and also of the similar offence with respect to the Derby in 1844.

In regard to the stakes, he was of the opinion that no objection to the indictment should arise as a result of their not having been paid at the time of the contracts for the races being entered into. As the entry of Running Rein for the Derby took place at Newmarket on Mr Weatherby's evidence, he thought an indictment might be preferred for the two offences.

Concerning Bean and White, his view was that perjury might be assigned on the evidence given by them and that of the different witnesses, with a reasonable probability of convicting them.

As for the tampering of witnesses, he was of the opinion that the proper course of proceeding against Goodman, Glenn and Anderson would be by indictment for a conspiracy and misdemeanour, but he thought that a jury would scarcely be induced to convict any of them, on the evidence of Carlin and his wife. Likewise, the statement of Watson was not sufficient to justify proceedings against Mr Gill.

Having considered all the circumstances of this extraordinary case, the character and conduct of many of the witnesses that it would be necessary to call in order to procure a conviction, and having in mind that there were some witnesses whose evidence would be materially damaging, if not entirely broken down on cross-examination, Mr Peacock did not believe that the probability of obtaining a conviction was sufficient enough to render it expedient for the Jockey Club to prosecute any of the parties, and after the successful termination of the case of Wood versus Peel and several other cases in which members of the Jockey Club had been lately concerned he thought the most prudent and desirable course was to let this matter end and not to institute any further proceedings.

15
The Ratan Affair

The trial was over. Running Rein – or rather the poor creature that ran in his name – was proved to be a fraudulent winner of the Derby. He had been whisked away by Francis Ignatius Coyle, firstly to The Lord Nelson[1] at Cheam, eventually ending up in John Peck's stables at Beverley.[2] Leander was also proved to be a four-year-old. There was also the issue of Ratan (who had barely raised a gallop) and The Ugly Buck. Old Crocky, not long for this world, when delivered the news of Ratan's defeat, knew that the robbers had beaten him. If he was able to show a glimmer of smugness, it was that his old enemy, Gully, had also probably suffered at the hands of the robbers.

His almost dying words were: "'I've been done. Depend on it that was not Ratan's true form.'"[3]

The robbery was probably contrived at an early period, possibly as early as after Ratan's victory in the Criterion Stakes at the 1843 Houghton Meeting, and a constant fusillade of bets against him was kept up until his easy victory at the Newmarket Craven Meeting, when Sam Rogers, who was up to his neck in it with his 'friend' Bream, made a partial confession of his misdeeds to Mr Crockford's son, who passed them on to Lord George Bentinck.

Despite Rogers spending the night in the adjoining stall, and a doubling of the guard, there was little doubt that Ratan had been 'made safe'; whether he had been nobbled during the night by Rogers – or the guards, if they had been bribed – and/or pulled by Rogers was debatable. In hindsight, it does not appear that adequate precautions were taken to protect Ratan. After Sam's confession, Lord George probably trusted his integrity and considered locking him in the adjoining stall with a doubling of the guard, adequate security. But he should have been a trifle more aware. He had been backing Ratan throughout the winter, more than likely through his commissioner, Harry Hill, who was a good friend of Gully and also had horses at Danebury: is it not conceivable that he would have suggested to Lord George to exercise some caution in backing Ratan?

Crockford was too ill to take any preventative action, although he must have had an inkling that Gully and some of the other 'legs' were out to get Ratan; and it could not even have entered Joe Rogers's mind that his own son would stoop so low as to cheat his father.

Sylvanus tells us of Ratan on the very evening before the Derby:

We saw him grinding his last supper previous to the race, with a skin like satin, and muscles of iron. We saw the jockey, Sam Rogers, locked up with him, his bed being made up in the adjoining stall; and we saw Ratan hardly more than twelve hours afterwards, unable to make a gallop, with his coat blue and shivery, and standing in fright, and finally beaten by wretches he could have distanced, had not villainy marked him for her own.[4]

In another version, Thormanby writes:

Every conceivable precaution was taken, and there seemed no possibility of foul play. When the key was turned on Ratan he was in glorious health, with a skin like satin and muscles of steel. When he showed on the downs the next morning his coat was standing 'like quills upon the fretful porcupine,' his eyes were dilated, and he shivered like a man with the ague.[5]

These portrayals of Ratan's condition may be somewhat embellished as a result of his poor showing in the race, for Bell's Life had reported him 'extremely blooming',[6] and starting second favourite would not have reflected such a poor condition.

Was Sam a party to the robbery? He seemed to have convinced Lord George of his innocence. There was a plot, no doubt, and he knew well of it, but, his conscience troubled, he told Lord George that he intended, if possible, to 'drop his seducers into a hole', by winning if he could; also, he did not intend to pocket a single guinea of the 'shamefully offered money'.[7]

It did not appear that he was true to his word. Try or not, Sam was easily beaten, and some time after Lord George ascertained that Sam had departed somewhat from the truth, especially in respect of not receiving any money, for it turned out that he had received £1,660.[8] This fact, with other suspicious matters, induced Lord George – who had more that a pecuniary interest – and Captain Rous to request the Jockey Club to investigate the matter, and the stewards discussed the case at the Second October Meeting, when, after a searching inquiry, it was finally brought to a close at the Houghton Meeting. After due deliberation, they framed their Report and submitted it to the Jockey Club. It was in the following terms:

The Stewards of the Jockey Club, assisted by the Duke of Beaufort and Colonel Peel, having investigated the charges brought forward against S.Rogers and J.Braham, and heard their statements, as well as the evidence of various witnesses, and the account given by Mr.Crommelin and Mr.Ives of their share in the transaction of betting for Rogers and Braham against Ratan for the late Derby race, are of opinion that the transaction originated in an agreement between S.Rogers and J.Braham to bet both ways about Ratan, under the impression that the parties whom they might commission to bet for them against the horse would be influenced by their representations of the impossibility of his winning, to lay such sums of money against him as to prevent their appearing on the settling day. S.Rogers and J.Braham confess that they received a large portion of the money won by laying against Ratan, although it was not their intention to pay if the horse had won. Their conduct during the whole proceeding was of such a nature as to merit the severest punishment in the power of the Jockey Club to inflict. The committee has further to observe, that although the conspiracy to bet large sums against Ratan originated with Rogers and Braham, and that no inducement was held out to them by any party to prevent the horse from winning, yet it would have been difficult for them to have carried their plan into execution, unless persons of influence had been found to execute their commissions.
The committee cannot express too strongly their opinion of the impropriety of gentlemen betting large sums of money for jockeys or for parties entrusted with the care of racehorses.
The committee recommend that S.Rogers and J.Braham be warned off all of the property over which the Jockey Club has any control, and that S.Rogers be prevented from training horses or riding at Newmarket, or at any other place where the rules of the Jockey Club are in force; and that the Stewards of all other races be apprised of this resolution, in

order that they may adopt a similar course.
Stradbroke, chairman.[9]

Sam had maliciously insinuated that Mr Crommelin and Mr Ives – both respected commissioners – had gone to him to "'offer a bribe to induce him to prevent the horse from winning'".[10] Nothing could have been further from the truth, as it was proved. Sam had, indeed, pursued both of these gentlemen at separate times – Ives in February, and Crommelin at the Chester meeting – in order to hedge his money, and both had been given the same story: namely, that Rogers had backed Ratan to win a large stake but that, his impression being that the horse could not win, he was anxious to hedge his bets so that he might win either way.

At the inquiry it was stated that Sam Rogers stood to win £5,562 if Ratan won and £362 if he lost.[11]

Bream had continually laid against Ratan, never hedging a penny, and had then signed a contract – with whom, it was never divulged – which brought him in three sovereigns a week, with a chaise and horse, in return for making himself scarce until the inquiry had blown over.

Well, no honour among thieves then, as far as Bream was concerned. He took his leave, all right – just a month's pleasure – before reneging on his contract and returning to Newmarket, where it was publicly stated on the Friday morning of the Houghton Meeting that he had won large sums of money on two of Lord Lonsdale's horses: the Turquoise colt in the Criterion Stakes and brother to Chummy in a Fifty Pound Subscription Plate. As both these colts were trained by Joe Rogers, against whom there had not been the slightest suspicion, there was obviously someone in his stable who continued to give the right office.

The accusation Rogers and Bream had concocted against Crommelin and Ives - that these gentlemen were connected with the robbery - had left them under an implied cloud of distrust for having executed the commissions of these scoundrels, but the inquiry completely exonerated them of any wrongdoing. The fact was that Mr Crommelin and Mr Ives had done no more than execute what they had considered to be Rogers's bona fide commissions, and what had been for aeons a recognised practice.

In fact the chairman of the inquiry, Lord Stradbroke, whose character was beyond reproach, had adopted the very same procedure as Rogers in respect of his own horse Evenus, the winner of the Cambridgeshire. He had hedged upwards of £600 against him, from a belief that he could not beat Foig-a-Ballagh. It could have been inferred from this that the noble Lord did not intend his horse to win. The reverse was, of course, true. Evenus did win, and thus Lord Stradbroke lost a large proportion of the stakes that he would have won had he not hedged his money.

What was not revealed by Rogers and Bream at the inquiry was the complicity of Hargreaves, a sinister and somewhat mysterious character who operated on the edge of the Danebury confederacy. Hargreaves was the type of person who would have probably laid his grandmother's life against a Derby favourite had he been certain of a profit. Had he lived in a later age he would have probably worn flashy suits, smoked the choicest Havana cigars and carried a Smith & Wesson 38 for comfort. He was a crook all right, but very little is known of him.

Sylvanus came across him at the White Bear in Piccadilly and asked the infamous 'leg' Crutch Robinson who was the lucky, screaming gentleman with the large face and pink eyes. The uncouth old cripple pursed up the left corner of his mouth, half closed one eye and, with an air of sneering lordliness, simply replied: "'Who is he? Why, four years ago he had na four shilling. That's who he is.'"

This was a surprise to our scribe, who wondered how he could have accrued such an amount of money as the Ring now gave him credit for, if he had nothing to commence with.

"'How did he get it?" retorted the old cripple; "Why, by nobbling Ratan; that's how he done it: he was put in by his pal, Sam.'"[12]

Hargreaves certainly made a considerable fortune out of the Derby: possibly by being bribed by Gully to make Ratan safe, and for good measure fixing The Ugly Buck, too.

The punishment inflicted on Sam Rogers was lifted after three years, partly, it must be said, owing to the generosity of Lord George, who was now the senior steward of the Jockey Club and believed that Sam had conducted himself well since his admonishment. The stewards condescended to remit the sentence passed on Sam, sincerely hoping that the punishment he had received would be a warning he would never forget, and that his conduct thereafter would justify the leniency extended to him. The relinquishment of this penalty did not, however, apply to Bream, who continued to be warned off.

It would appear that Sam took good notice of the stewards' advice. Four years later, with all recollection of Ratan's year and of other transgressions obliterated from the public mind, he was praised for his riding in winning the Cambridgeshire, on Mr Stirling Crawford's The Cur,[13] trained by his father.

16
Lord George

The routing of Goodman and his gang of thieves was recognised as the crowning accolade of Lord George's career on the Turf. His triumph did not go unrecognised. Two days after the trial the following notice appeared in *The Times*:

> *The noblemen and gentlemen of the Jockey Club, several proprietors of racehorses and others interested in the honour and prosperity of the Turf intend to present to Lord George Bentinck with a piece of plate to mark their sense of immense service he has rendered to the racing community by detecting and defeating the attempt at fraud exposed in the late trial in the Court of Exchequer. The subscription is to be confined to £25 and from the number of names already down at Messrs Weatherbys, comprising some of the highest on the Turf, it will no doubt be a very large one.*

And at a meeting of the Jockey Club on 6 July a resolution was passed:

> *That the thanks of the Jockey Club are eminently due and are hereby offered to Lord George Bentinck for the energy, perseverance and skill which he has displayed in detecting, exposing and defeating the atrocious frauds which have been brought to light during the recent trial respecting the Derby Stakes.[1]*

He gained the greatest acclaim in all quarters by his conduct throughout this affair, contrary to the scant praise he received five years earlier, when he had endeavoured to get Bloomsbury disqualified on similar grounds to Running Rein, namely that he was not the horse he was claimed to be.

The subscription raised to honour his exertions amounted to around £2,000, but Lord George was not persuaded to accept anything for himself. Instead, he wished the money to be applied towards the establishment of a fund, with a view to securing in perpetuity, for children of deserving trainers and jockeys, support and education from infancy until they arrived at an age to seek their own living. Thus The Bentinck Testimonial Fund was duly established. As one scribe sardonically put it, 'It was doubtful whether there were many qualified recipients in the year of 1844.'[2]

Lord George was a paradoxical character. He was portrayed as a great Turf reformer, but many of his reforms were embedded in the way money could be made. For all the acclaim bestowed on him, his honour was, at times, questionable. His estranged cousin, Charles Greville, who at one time had been his racing partner, poured scorn on some of his actions, considering them dishonest and disgraceful. He invariably seized on any opportunity that would benefit his financial standing, as illustrated by the story of his wonderful filly Crucifix (bay filly 1837 Priam-Octaviana).

Before Crucifix ran for the Criterion Stakes at Newmarket she injured her leg while turning in her box. After the race her leg swelled considerably, causing Lord George great concern. He immediately sent for Mr Barrow, the veterinary surgeon who was to participate at the inquiry into the Duke of Rutland's objection to Running Rein. Mr Barrow, who was not informed of the cause of the injury, opined that it was a serious case, that it was unlikely she would stand training and, furthermore, that it should be blistered, fired and rested for a long time. Imagine Lord George's concern: he had backed Crucifix for a large sum in the Oaks. His only option was to lay against her by way of hedging, which, of course, was perfectly legitimate.

On her return to Danebury, young John Day, who was himself a veterinary surgeon, diagnosed that the injury was not as serious as Mr Barrow had maintained and claimed that it would be healed in ten days. On this news, Lord George hatched a plan to recover all that he had laid against Crucifix and as much on top of that as he could. His plan was simple enough, although ingenious. He needed to convince everybody that Crucifix was lame and would never run again. He requested Mr Barrow to put his diagnosis in writing. Once obtained, he made a copy of the letter and sent it to John Day, instructing him to find any pretext to show it to all and sundry. At the same time, while discussing other matters, he would as if by accident show the original letter to other parties, complaining of his ill luck and advising them to hedge, while taking care to plant somebody to take the odds when the unfortunate hedger laid them. His plan worked to perfection: Crucifix duly obliged, winning Lord George a great sum of money on both Guineas and the Oaks.[3]

Lord George's pursuit of Goodman and his gang over Running Rein was probably brought about by the *Qui Tam* menace a year earlier – an obscure state of affairs in which, under an Act of Parliament (9 Anne cap. 14), an informer could obtain a reward amounting to the sum won and three times the amount as a penalty by wagering on all other games, other than small sums on cards and dice. The *Qui Tam* gang took their name from the statute: '*qui tam pro domino rege quam pro se ipso in hac parte sequitur*' – who sues in this matter for the king as well as for himself.

Warned off, this coterie of bankrupts and defaulters felt that they had been cheated by persons withdrawing their horses – a practice to which Lord George was not averse if he could not obtain favourable odds. This, it was argued, had been their reason for defaulting; and, led by a low-life solicitor by the name of Russell, they sought to use the law to recover their gambling losses. Russell, with prima facie the law on his side, pursued Lord George for a bet of £12,000 to £3,000 that he had with John Day. Had Russell been succesful, it could have been disasterous for racing. Fortunately, the witnesses had an opportune loss of memory; the plaintiff failed to prove that the defendant had made the bet with Day, which brought a worthy end to Mr Russell and his *Qui Tam* actions.

Despite their reasons, Lord George was intolerant of this objectionable class, referred to as Levanters. One who suffered the consequences of defaulting was Adam Glenn, the Regent Street biscuit maker – a close associate of Goodman in the Running Rein affair. Glenn had lost £2,000 to Lord George. When Lord George called to claim his bet Glenn offered to pay him half straight away and the rest as soon as possible. But Lord George was not prepared to compromise, insisting that the bet be settled immediately; otherwise he would denounce Glenn as a defaulter. He knew that Glenn had a good reputation in Tattersalls and a good business, and that to be a defaulter in the one, or to lose the other, would be his ruin. Thus, rather than face the prospect of either disastrous event, he was sure that Glenn would in some way or other find the money and pay the debt. But Glenn could not pay. Lord George lost his money and declared Glenn a defaulter.[4] There was no doubt that Glenn was a villain, but was it necessary to expose him in this way? Had Lord George not persisted in his high-handed principles, he would have collected his money and Glenn's reputation (for the time being) would have remained intact.

Rather than holding Lord George in high regard for his intense loathing of the dishonesty and trickery that had discredited the Turf, there were many who saw Lord George in a completely different, more cynical light. Writing shortly after the trial, Greville fired off a stinging salvo in his diary:

What a humbug it all is, and if everybody knew all that I know of his tricks and artifices what a rogue he would be thought! And yet strange to say, I am persuaded he would not commit for anything on earth a clear, undoubted act of dishonesty. He has made for himself a peculiar code of morality and honour, and what he has done, he thinks he has a right to do, that the game at which he plays warrants deceit and falsehood to a certain extent and in a certain manner. He cannot but know that if all the circumstances relating to Crucifix, by which he won so much money, were revealed, they would be considered disgraceful and dishonest, but he no doubt justifies them to himself. Then about betting against horses; nobody has ever been more unscrupulous than he in making money in this way. In short, while he is thundering away against poor low-lived rogues for the villainies they have committed, he has himself been doing the same things.[5]

A year after the Running Rein affair, Lord George surprisingly turned his back on the Turf and threw himself into politics. He sold his horses with the indifference of a gypsy selling his worn-out pony to the knacker's yard, from Bay Middleton to the great Crucifix, her yearling son, Surplice and Loadstone, considered the two best yearlings he had ever owned. He offered George Payne the lot for £10,000 at a Goodwood house party.

Against a deposit of £300, George Payne said he would give his answer in the morning. And at breakfast, without a word, he handed Lord George the £300, whereupon Edward Mostyn, after conferring with his cousin, Cynric Lloyd, took up the offer. The bargain – and what a bargain for Mr Mostyn – was struck, and Lord George was divested of his stud for a trifling £10,000. The magnitude of the bargain was emphasised when shortly after the sale Mr Mostyn was offered £7,000 for Crucifix, Surplice and

Loadstone, and a further £5,000 for two two-year-olds, Planet and Slander.

For Lord George it must have been a fate almost comparable to death when, two years later, Surplice (bay colt Touchstone-Crucifix), in the colours of Lord Clifden, won the Derby and thus denied him his lifelong ambition. Even Disraeli could not console him. All his life he had tried for this – and for what had he sacrificed it?

He lived long enough to see Surplice win the St Leger and The Flying Dutchman, the finest son of his great Bay Middleton, win the Champagne Stakes. On his return from Doncaster, much as he needed rest, he immersed himself in the intensity of overwork and abstinence, in the mistaken belief that he could not do himself justice should he take unnecessary sustenance. A week after his return from Doncaster he spent the morning occupying himself in correspondence to the Duke of Richmond, Lord Enfield and a seven-page missive to Disraeli. Then, late in the afternoon, he set out on the three-mile hike to Thoresby Park, the home of Lord Manvers, where he was to spend a few days. When there was no sign of his guest, a message was relayed to Welbeck. The search party found his cold and lifeless body near the gate leading to the water meadow, less than a mile from Welbeck: a spasm of the heart had killed him, unconsciously brought about by a state of near starvation.

Irrespective of his dubious morality, Lord George was rightly called 'Lord Paramount of the Turf' by Disraeli. He lived in an era that would have been unrecognisable today: an era of sharp-practising individuals, nobblers and fraudsters seeking every opportunity to enrich themselves at the expense of others. He was resolute in his pursuit of skulduggery on the Turf, on occasions bending the law to achieve his aims. His untiring quest to compile the evidence against the perpetrators of the Running Rein fraud earned him celebrity unsurpassed by racing men. It was the zenith of a glittering career on the Turf; and yet even in death Greville did not spare him: 'The world will and must form a very incorrect estimate of his character; more of what was good than of what was bad in it was known to the public; he had the credit of virtues which he did not possess.'[6]

17
Zanoni

The thoroughbred that had just arrived at John Peck's stables in Beverley was no ordinary racehorse. Peck casts his eye over him. He is certainly a magnificent specimen. One can imagine his thoughts, as he stands back to admire him. He has probably never trained such a horse – a horse who had galloped into history on 22 May 1844.

This was Maccabeus – winner of the Derby, but not a Derby winner. He had been taken from Smith's stables in Epsom prior to the trial – first to The Lord Nelson at Cheam, before mysteriously becoming the property of the veterinary surgeon, Owen Henry Parry,[1] who had officiated at the 'Bloodstone' case. His path to Beverley was unknown. Certainly no record would appear to exist as to how he arrived, or how he came into Mr Parry's ownership.

The first knowledge of his whereabouts appeared in the 10 November 1844 issue of *Bell's Life*: a north-country correspondent informed them that Running Rein was now in training at John Peck's, at Beverley, and that the colt by The Saddler out of Mab had stood there until disappearing before the trial. Running Rein, the writer added, would probably be seen in the Chester Cup.

A week later John Peck called at their offices, mischievously denying that the colt by The Saddler out of Mab was ever in his stable or under his care; Running Rein, namely the horse that came in first for the Derby was, however, under his charge.[2]

Maccabeus, or Running Rein, or whatever one liked to call him, had indeed been entered for the Chester Cup, under his new name of Zanoni. However, an objection was raised, to the effect that he had not been properly described in the entry, or rather for an alleged want of proof of his being the horse described by his owner. Mr Parry had honestly entered him as 'a horse who came in first for the Derby, pedigree unknown,' against which description no objection could be taken. This seemed reasonable enough, but it was overruled by Weatherbys.

Who was the main progenitor behind this objection? Why, none other than the noble Lord George, who had openly declared his determination to call for proof of the horse's identity on every occasion of his starting, with a view to the punishment of the Running Rein conspiracy.[3]

To bring the question to issue, the objectors turned to a rule established at a meeting of the Jockey Club in October 1838, when it was resolved:

> ... *that no horse, though coming in first, shall hereafter be deemed the winner of any plate, match, or sweepstake, whether handicap or not, who shall be proved to have run under a false description, and such disqualification shall remain in force until his proper pedigree be ascertained and recorded.*[4]

For the betting public this rule had a double blow: it disqualified the horse, yet it did not render bets void, for no reference was made to bets being cancelled, so those bets on Zanoni were assumed to remain, which was contrary to another rule that said 'that where there exists no possibility of winning there can be no loss'.

The question arose as to the identity of the real objectors and the reason for their objection: what benefit would the objectors reap from Zanoni's exclusion? Leading people on the Turf denied any hostility towards Zanoni, declaring their satisfaction with his identity. The only ostensible objector was Colonel Peel, but a letter from Mr Parry's counsel, requesting to know the proof required about the horse, only brought a response that Colonel Peel simply desired to have him identified as the horse he was represented to be. This looked simple enough: quoting from Colonel Peel's own counsel and applying his own evidence, all difficulty would seem to vanish, as the horse in question was exactly as described by the solicitor general during the trial.

Even *Bell's Life* sided with the objectors, comparing their cause to the objection made to Bloodstone. They did not consider that, just because the horse had got into honest hands, this should at all interfere with the principle on which the regulations of the Jockey Club were founded, continuing that the penalty could not be too stringent against attempts at fraud, and when it was known that they would be enforced it must operate as an additional punishment to the wrongdoers, by rendering the instruments of their intended fraud of less value and deterring those who might be free from suspicion from being the purchasers.[5]

What this would appear to imply is that Zanoni, being an instrument of fraud, was forever tarnished and that Mr Parry, or anyone else for that matter, however honest they may be, should not be associated with him.

Mr Parry, who officiated in the Bloodstone case, had not owned racehorses until 1845, when, in addition to Zanoni, he became the owner of Adonis (bay colt 1842 Gladiator), who ran unsuccessfully in the Derby, and Sally Brown (bay filly 1842 Master of the Rolls), who incidentally was out of the same mare as Zanoni.

The case was brought before the stewards of the Jockey Club in the last week of April 1845. On the part of Mr Parry, Isaac Grey (Sir Charles Ibbetson's groom) and George Wharton (the lad who had taken the colt to Masborough station, after being purchased by Goodman at the Doncaster sales in September 1841) confirmed his identity, as did the veterinary surgeon Mr Barrow, who pronounced him the same horse that ran as Running Rein for the Fifty Pound Plate at Newmarket. One link in the chain, however, was missing: Higgins was not present at the meeting to prove that the colt was the same one that he had delivered to Mr Worley at Sywell. The stewards, on the grounds that it was possible that the colt may have been changed, gave an opinion that Mr Parry had not sufficiently proved his pedigree to qualify him to start for any race, and consequently he was withdrawn from the Chester Cup.

The case came again before the stewards on 15 May, this time with Higgins in attendance. Having proved that he and Goodman had received the same colt from Wharton and had delivered it to Mr Worley, the stewards gave the following verdict:

We are of the opinion, that the horse called Zanoni was bred by Sir Charles Ibbetson in 1840, and that he was got by Gladiator, dam foaled in 1823 by Capsicum out of Acklam Lass; and that he is the same horse that ran for the Derby 1844 under the name of Running Rein.[6]

Unfortunately, this admission came too late, as the Chester Cup had already been run.

The objections behind him, Zanoni was allowed to run in the Ascot Gold Vase. His reputation promoted him to second favourite, behind Mr Hill's Sweetmeat (bay colt 1841 Gladiator), and his appearance in the saddling enclosure excited a good deal of curiosity. Observers noted him to be a fine, powerful animal, but some were struck that his preparation for such a race had not been sufficient. Nevertheless, he found numerous backers. His mouth, like that of Bloodstone (aptly renamed Perkin Warbeck) in the preceding race for the Ascot Stakes, underwent examination, but it was all too obvious that it had been subjected to painful operations to disguise his age. Attempts had been made to extract his teeth, which were broken and jagged and discoloured by the application of caustic. The race was won by Sweetmeat, with his stable mate, The Libel, close at his heels; Zanoni was unplaced.

The Sporting Magazine joined with the earlier objectors, rejoicing in poor Zanoni's defeat. They reported that his party was daily becoming less and that the sooner a split came among them the better for the right-minded betting gentry.[7] Were they really suggesting that Mr Parry was associated with the malefactors?

Zanoni next ran in The County Cup at York, but was unplaced to Mid Lothian, in a field of only five. It was somewhat surprising that a horse that had finished first in the Derby, even though being a four-year-old, could perform so badly; not so much against Sweetmeat, who was a really good horse, but Mid Lothian was only a moderate handicapper.

And that was very nearly the last of Zanoni: he passed from the racecourse through an apparently inglorious period in the breeding shed in England – where, according to the *General Stud Book*, he sired only two offspring,[8] before being purchased by the Polish Count Branicki, in 1847, to serve as a stallion in Russia.

For some time the Russians had sought some of the best English sires: the St Leger winners Memnon and Birmingham; Middleton and Coronation, both Derby winners; and the grand sprinter, Jereed. But few had been liked as much as Zanoni, who was considered a horse of very great style and beauty (does this sound anything like the genuine Running Rein?) He retained a memento of his old Derby days in the broken tusk, on the near side; and he was so shy about his mouth that to give him physic became an almost physical impossibility.[9]

Zanoni died in 1854 but left one reminder of his short time in Russia: Mr Lubomirski's bay colt, Manifik, out of Mary, a 21-year-old mare, by Waterloo. Manifik found few to beat him, his victories including an Emperor's Prize at Carskoje Sielo in 1853.[10]

18
Epilogue

The events that took place in the Derby of 1844 were almost beyond the realms of coincidence: the winning horse being a four-year-old; another, who met a tragic end in the race, also being a four-year-old, possibly even older; the second favourite, almost certainly nobbled and probably the same of the favourite - making the event the most infamous in the annals of the great race. However, as scandalous as this event was, perhaps we should, in some way, be grateful to Abraham Levi Goodman, the anti-hero of this astonishing comedy, for providing us with one of the great parodies in the history of the great game.

The historian must ask the question: how did Goodman and his clique believe that their scheme, despite its apparent intricate planning, could possibly succeed?

There is little doubt that Goodman was an intelligent operator. He realised that if a horse's pedigree could be falsified it could be possible to pass off a four-year-old as a three-year-old. He had a pedigree for the genuine Running Rein – what matter that it was appended to another horse? On request of proof, all Goodman would have required to answer would be: "Of course, Gentlemen; here is the bill of sale from Dr Cobb, and here is the pedigree." In those far-off days there were not the means of identification available today. So maybe he thought he had a reasonable chance of getting away with it.

Dishonesty on the Turf during this period, whilst perhaps not rife, was certainly open to question. St Giles in 1832, Dangerous in 1833 (owned and trained by William Sadler) and Little Wonder in 1840 all had been suspected of being old 'uns; and others, like Bloomsbury in 1839, were thought not to be the horses they were claimed to be. However, no action had ever been taken – another point in Goodman's favour.

By the skin of his teeth, and through the naivety of the stewards, Goodman had successfully evaded any action against himself following the Duke of Rutland's objection at the previous year's Houghton Meeting, which must have bolstered his confidence to pursue his goal to the end. It was probably reinforced by the presence of Litchwald's Leander: there was no evidence that Litchwald was in league with Goodman, but, given their shared Jewish roots and their previous history at the 1840 Houghton Meeting, it would have been a contentious issue. Had there been an alliance, it would not have mattered had either won: neither owner would have objected to the other - had they done so, any subsequent inquiry would have proved the owner of the second to be as guilty as the owner of the winner.

The facetious remarks in the racing press concerning Running Rein's maturity were a puzzling factor. On one occasion Goodman even played along with them, referring to his 'four-year-old'. One would have assumed that this might have given Goodman second thoughts. However, having gone so far, he must have thought it worth the risk to carry on.

What was significant was that the Jockey Club made no attempt to examine and disqualify the horse before the race. Would it be too presumptuous to suggest that their reluctance may have been due to some of the honorable members having backed Running Rein, thus wanting to see him win even if he was a four-year-old?

Once it came to court, it was almost certain that Judge Alderson would demand production of the horse, at which point Goodman would have realised that the game was up. He probably ordered the removal of the horse, and Francis Ignatius Coyle, described by John Corlett, editor of the *Sporting Times*, as 'probably the most unutterable of all unutterable scoundrels who ever disgraced the Turf', had brazenly ridden Maccabeus out of Smith's Yard without the knowledge or consent of Mr Wood. This was rather a risky act on the part of Coyle; had he been caught, it is likely that he would have spent the remainder of his life on Norfolk Island.

Mr Wood demanded that Goodman return the horse henceforth. Goodman replied that Wood would never see the horse again, but might have a quarter of him should he liquidate it in a fortnight. Rumour circulated that the poor horse (although it is not clear which one is being referred to) had been made the sacrifice of this abominable conspiracy and had actually been killed, boiled and his head burnt.[1]

This, of course, was one of the many imaginative stories emerging from this fascinating comedy concerning not only Maccabeus but also The Saddler colt – the genuine Running Rein.

William Carlin, who had been Goodman's groom at Hallmead Farm, tells us that The Saddler colt was taken away by one of Goodman's boys, called Fiddler, in November 1843, shortly after Running Rein (Maccabeus) had returned from Newmarket. He may have been taken to Smith's. Goodman had told Ferguson that he was going to be his Derby horse for 1845. Even though he had been castrated, he still would have been eligible for the Derby, as geldings were permitted up until 1906. As to his outcome, it can only be surmised. He was unknown by name to Carlin, and Goodman had not named him to Ferguson, although he had, in passing, mentioned to Ferguson that he was by The Saddler.

If The Saddler colt was to have been Goodman's Derby horse for the following year, it is unlikely, as has been opined, that Goodman would have substituted him for Running Rein (Maccabeus) at the Houghton inquiry.

A similar speculation was made that, during the trial, Lord George suddenly saw the loophole through which Goodman could escape, by removing the four-year-old that had masqueraded as Running Rein and finally producing the genuine Running Rein, which Judge Alderson had demanded. A veterinary surgeon would have confirmed him to be a three-year-old, and the jury, who may not have been present at the Derby to witness whether it was the same horse, would have been hard-pressed to give a verdict other than in Mr Wood's favour.

The postulation continues that Lord George, realising the loophole, sought to trump Goodman by arranging for the genuine Running Rein to be stolen, believing that Goodman would not possibly dare to produce Maccabeus. This, however, would appear to be a highly unlikely scenario. Would Lord George really have known the genuine Running Rein? It was, as Carlin had stated, a horse with no name. And even if Lord George had some knowledge of him, it would have been pointless to produce him at the trial, as it would have soon become apparent that this shabby brown horse was not the magnificent specimen that had passed the winning post first on Derby day.

It is not surprising in a case such as this, with so many twists and turns, that the stories abounding about Running Rein that have travelled down through the ages, fascinating as they are, have become cradled in legend. Some say that Maccabeus had his leg stained to look like Running Rein, whereas it was Goneaway's leg that was stained to assume the appearance of Maccabeus; others that Maccabeus ended his life on the Northamptonshire farm, where it is said his ghost still haunts the lane that passes the farm – in one variation he is even pulling a cart in ignominy with his head held in shame; and the Sywell legend of Running Rein being buried in Pond Close, at the back of the church, and on being exhumed found to be headless – presumably an adaptation of the exhumation of Leander.

The two horses were not the only ones to disappear. When the trial began to turn in Orlando's favour, Goodman beat a hasty retreat to Boulogne, not only to escape the law but also his creditors. One of these was Mr Wood – poor, innocent Mr Wood – not actually a creditor but out of pocket to the tune of £1,500, being the costs he paid to Colonel Peel for apparently being duped by Goodman. In the absence of Goodman, Mr Wood sought to recover these costs from Adam Glenn, one of Goodman's closest associates in the fraud, and against which costs Glenn had given Mr Wood a bond of indemnity that Running Rein was the horse that Goodman had claimed him to be, which, not surprisingly, transpired to have been fraudulently obtained. Glenn's counsel, Mr Chapman made an application for a commission to examine Goodman in Boulogne, and to stay the proceedings until the return of the commission, probably in the hope that admissions could be extracted from Goodman that he was also party to the indemnity. For this indulgence Baron Rolfe compelled Glenn to pay £1,500 into court, as security to Mr Wood. Mr James, counsel for Mr Wood, scoffed that this was merely delaying tactics and doubted if any jury would believe the evidence of Mr Goodman.

In a simultaneous cross-action, Glenn filed a bill in chancery against Wood, as he believed that Wood was party to the fraud. Mr Wood, however, managed to provide affidavits and had sworn in chancery that he had had no communication whatsoever with Goodman, and until the first day of the trial he claimed that he had no suspicion of the fraud practised on him. In addition to this, Goodman had made a solemn declaration that the horse was of the correct pedigree. Mr Wood's memory was obviously failing him, conveniently forgetting the meetings with veterinary surgeon John Bartlett, and his offer to Bartlett of standing him £100 to nothing on Running Rein.

The case of Wood versus Glenn, which was to have been tried at the Surrey Assizes, was suddenly terminated by Mr Glenn, who, instead of proceeding to examine Goodman under the commission, drew up a judge's order to stay the proceedings on payment to Mr Wood of the amount for which the action was brought plus costs, the £1,500 being paid out of court to Mr Wood's attorney in part discharge of the amount. Unfortunately for Glenn, for Mr Wood's answer in chancery he also incurred a further cost of £68 1s. 10d.

Mr Wood collected his costs, despite his partial guilt in knowing that Running Rein was a four-year-old. But this was not the end of the Running Rein affair, which in one way or another kept rumbling on.

Almost a year had passed by before a meeting of the Jockey Club was called in consequence of the accusations made against Sir Gilbert Heathcote and Baron de Tessier in their handling of the protest against Running Rein and Leander prior to the Derby, and their refusal to allow Colonel Peel's solicitor to see the declarations provided by Mr Wood. Baron de Tessier made a lengthy explanation of his conduct, which resulted in the following resolution by the members:

> That in the investigation which took place as to the qualification of Running Rein before the race at Epsom, the Baron de Tessier took an erroneous view of his duty as a Steward and ought not to have given a decision by which the horse was allowed to start on the ex-parte statements of Mr. Wood and in the absence of the objectors to the qualification of Running Rein. That he was equally wrong in refusing to give to the solicitors of Colonel Peel, while the action was pending of Wood v. Peel, copies of the affidavits on the strength of which his previous decisions had been made.
>
> That this meeting acquits Baron de Tessier of any corrupt or dishonest motive but censures him chargeable with great want of discretion in the exercise of his official functions.[2]

It was understandable that this resolution did not humour Baron de Tessier, a generally honorable man, who shortly after resigned his stewardship at Epsom and his membership of the Jockey Club.

At a further meeting of noblemen and gentlemen interested in the Wood versus Peel trial held at Mr Weatherby's office, it was agreed that an appeal should be made to all those who had benefited by the defeat of the Running Rein fraud, either in the shape of winnings on Orlando or by being saved of loss from the establishment of Running Rein's protestations, to contribute a percentage on their bets, sweepstakes or lotteries towards the legal costs of the case, which were estimated at £3,065.

Did this prick the conscience of at least one involved in the fraud? One William Sadler, perhaps, who wrote to Messrs Weatherby at Old Burlington Street as follows:

High Street Buildings
Doncaster, June 29th 1845
Gentlemen,
Having seen in Bell's Life the revelations which the Gentlemen have come to respecting the Trial of Orlando, I beg to hand you this amount of any small winnings having drawn Orlando in a sweepstake which is £22.
I remain yours etc.,
William Sadler[3]

The impact of the Running Rein fraud was far less significant than credited to it by the Turf writers. The anger caused by this disgraceful affair created a widespread impression that the authorities would launch an energetic agenda of moral improvements. In fact Sylvanus tells us that the Jockey Club, having dismissed the convicted parties from the racecourses within their jurisdiction, soon admitted them again, whitewashed and laughing in their sleeves.[4] Most of the reforms introduced by Lord George were simply a facade and did not have their anticipated effect, as the Jockey Club seemed reluctant to implement any major tenor towards Turf ethics.

In fact, barely a fortnight after Running Rein's victory in the Derby the stewards were confronted with yet another fraud, when the winner of the New Stakes at Ascot, Bloodstone, was objected to by John Day, owner and trainer of the second horse, Old England, on the grounds that he was a three-year-old. The case was held at Guildford Assizes to decide whether Mr Herbert, the owner of Bloodstone, or Mr Day was entitled to the stakes.

Mr Herbert, the owner of Bloodstone, vigorously denied that his horse was a three-year-old. His evidence rested on the claim that Bloodstone was got by Bubastes out of Romaike, foaled in 1842, and was therefore only a two-year-old. But John Day claimed that the horse was in fact by Beiram and was at Romaike's foot when she was put to Bubastes. Despite several witnesses for Mr Herbert swearing that the first colt by Beiram died, John Day was able to prove that it was, in fact, the colt by Bubastes that had died, and that Richard Newman, who was then the owner of Romaike, requested Mr Hicks, the owner of Bubastes, to provide him with a receipt, stating that the mare had been covered in 1841. Mr Hicks, suspecting that Newman had the intention of using this receipt to claim a horse was a year younger than it really was, refused to oblige.

Furthermore, Henry Bell, who rode Bloodstone, claimed that Richard Newman's brother, John, who had sold Bloodstone to Mr Herbert, had told him to ride the horse a quarter of a mile and then pull him up, but on no account to win the race. This was obviously to avoid attention as to his real age when running for future two-year-old races. Bell, however, not being tarnished with dishonesty, communicated his orders to Captain Rous, who advised that he should win if he could, which, as expected for a three-year-old in a two-year-old race, he did in a canter.

Several other witnesses swore positively that the colt that won the race was not the colt by Bubastes, and others believed it to be the Beiram colt. Two eminent veterinary surgeons – Mr Field of Oxford Street and Mr Owen Parry of Reading – were of the opinion that Bloodstone was a three-year-old and gave certificates at Ascot to that effect.

The jury did not hesitate in concluding that the colt by Bubastes had died and that the Beiram colt had been substituted, but they gave their opinion that Mr Herbert, the current owner of Bloodstone, might have honestly bought the horse, with his engagements, believing him to be a two-year-old, and that he was not aware of the fraud perpetrated by the Newman brothers.

As our story reaches its close, what of the real hero of the day – old Orlando, a Derby winner denied being first past the winning post? He showed on that notorious day in May 1844, when he felt the sting of Nat's whip as he galloped to victory over Epsom's asphodel, that the form had not been all wrong. And when he died at Hampton Court in 1868, at the age of 27, his legacy was to have been champion sire three times: in 1851, 1854 and 1858. He was the sire of the Derby winner Teddington (chestnut colt 1848); the Two Thousand Guineas winners Fazzoletto (bay colt 1853), Fitz Roland (chestnut colt 1855) and Diophantes (chestnut colt 1858); and the One Thousand Guineas and St Leger winner Imperieuse (bay filly 1854). Probably the finest of all Turf writers, The Druid, gave him this accolade in the St Martin's summer of his life:

We could never tire of looking at him, as he stood at ease in his box, resting his near hind foot, and showing the rich folds of that beautiful muscular neck, as he turned his high-bred forehead round, and looked with that fine, but now dim eye at his visitors.[5]

Ah, yes, Orlando – maybe not the most convincing of Derby winners, but certainly one that deserved to be remembered.

By the end of the decade almost all recollections of Running Rein's Derby had been erased from the racing public's mind: Sam had redeemed himself; Lord George and old Crocky had departed this earth; Levi Goodman had returned, although it was likely that only a few knew of this, or cared, only for him to be embroiled in yet another scandal, albeit not of his making, when his daughter Rose was abducted on the promise of marriage by one Captain Erlam; and that unutterable rogue, Francis Ignatius Coyle, continued to frequent the bankruptcy courts, even experiencing a period in Dover gaol.

There was just one subtle – maybe even facetious – reminder of that notorious year. At Writtle in Essex and Beccles in Suffolk a brown filly was winning low-class handicaps; at Beccles she ran in five races, each of two heats, in successive days, winning two of these and finishing second in the other three.[6] She was the result of a union between The Saddler and Dr Cobb's old mare Mab, thus being a full sister to Running Rein. Her name ... Genuine.

Appendix 1
An Exchequer Epic

Here's a regular no-mistake Bell's Life report
Of the Match just come off in the Westminster Court.
On each side of the Bench sat the Jockey Club band,
Known to Newmarket pumps and the Doncaster Stand.
In slap up condition a little below
Were some Gentlemen six, fit and ready to go,
Sporting black, out of compliment I should suppose,
To Lord Stanley, or perhaps, Mr.Cotherstone Bowes.
With his eyes beaming horseflesh, all game for a lark,
Baron A_____ took the Chair as the proxy for Clark;
With horselaw in his head, and his thoughts in a cunning vein,
To ferret out each transmigration of Running Rein.
No Bentinck acuteness one needs to descry
A right comical leer in that comical eye;
Aye, I'll take two to one, "on its arrowy track,
Borne on wings of the blast, flew his memory back"
(As that sweet poet Wakley* remarks in his lays)
To his old Senior Wrangler and Medallist days.
       Then conics and statics,
        In Caius College Attics,
Or perhaps an occasional spurt of aquatics,
He thought well in their way, but still sadly beneath
An eleven mile ride to the Newmarket Heath.
Often there, as the Legends of M.A.'s relate,
In the year of Our Lord eighteen hundred and eight,
Mounted on very remarkable flesh,
To eternity warranted "terrible fresh,"
Unblest with tract, or a pulpit appeal
Of twenty horse power, from Close or Mac-Neale,
"Like a Heathen Ojibbeway laden with sin,"
Young Mr.Alderson sported his tin.
       So I'm right in surmising,

'Twas not so surprising
If Balfe's "Light of past days" in his heart was arising.
Aye he bravely determined to shew each man there
That he still thought of Cambridge, and reverenced "the square,"
With a fervour that nothing could crush.

"Gentlemen of the Jury!"..........."Now silence" – for Lush
Is making the running for Cockburn........Hush!
> *"The facts of this case require careful digestion,*
> *I'll be brief, and not give you much gab;*
> *The plain issue is this – Is the bay colt in question*
> *By The Saddler out of Queen Mab?"*

"Now just take a pull Lush; that's all we shall need,"
Whispered Cockburn, "and I'll rattle on with the lead."

Now the Bench and the Bar are all ready to say
Mr.Cockburn is very polite in his way;
But like other Q.C.'s if he don't take care of them.
Odd expressions escape him before he's aware of them.
No matter:- 'tis certain, sans physical force,
One Lord he was wishful to warn off the course.
When he found that "no go," he shewed awful ferocity
In viewing his valet's Newmarket atrocity.
> Vide *"Bread-and cheese gorge –*
> *Paid for by Lord George,*
> *To make Kitchen's wits vig'rous, and ready to forge*
> *Some new Malton Legend; or letting that story be,*
> *To be seized 'awful sudden' with 'lapsus memoriæ.'"*

But stop, while our Cockburn
Is clearing his throat,
Apropos to the subject,
Some Shakespeare I'll quote,
Heigho! – "Gentlemen all, your attention turn,
To thoughts that breathe, and to words that *burn*."

"Odd Facts I can prove – let Lord George then beware,
> *And be mindful what he is about;*
Or I'll just make him stand up in the witness-box there,

And I'll just turn him inside out.
I'll examine him well about bran new clothes,
Which a young fellow Carlon,** wears;
And queer things my Solicitor swears that he knows
'Bout his snug little turf affairs.
To Calummy's tales I am perfectly deaf,
Yet some individuals I feel,
Could not come in a trial of virtue, A.F.,
Within lengths of the good Colonel Peel.
Humble indeed are my efforts to-day,
But I'll bring lots of grooms to confirm what I say."

Very good, Mr.C.; but you know it is true
Some Barons ain't always so easy to do;
But, putting; both silk gowns and stuff on the shelves,
Take the part of the Barristers on to themselves.
'Twas so in this case: there was no legal barrier,
So the Knight of the Ermine turned amateur farrier.
"Mr.C., where's the colt Baron Alderson cried,
The fair tide of your case, Sir, is ebbing:
I will see his mouth, and I won't be denied –
What care I for Bean, Pearl or Stebbing!
As for you Mr Lofthouse,*** how durst you do so,
You outrager of filial piety?
If young men 'are out,' and their fathers don't know,
Why they naturally feel some anxiety.
Did you lay to your soul then this £100 unction?"

"It was feer'd, Zur, my father would larn
I'd no Place." – "Stop! – I'll give you a moral injunction,
Never write to your father a yarn."

Lofthouse shuffled down with an old swimming head,
Convincing Baron A. was a silly bore;
And Hitchcock then mounted the box in his stead,
To talk of the colt and "one Phillimore."

Once at Epsom, Hitchcock say,
On a fine October day,
Did you not in accents bold

Talk about a "four-year-old?"
On your oath declare the pith
Of your interview with Smith.
Did he not, Sir, make you smart
On a vulnerable part?
Like a man of pluck you swore
You would stand such work no more;
Since to *break* your back he'd fain,
You'd ne'er break his colts again.

"Usher call William Smith!" – Then with might and with main
  The Baron's at work with his questions again.
        "William Smith, and can it be
        No memory remains to thee?
        Goodman's dockings make, I find,
        No impression on your mind.
        'Don't remembers' won't avail, Sir;
        Mark'd you not the altered tail, Sir?
        'Bout that colt's removal too?
         I won't believe it, Sir – Pooh! Pooh!!
        Mind, such stories are the germ
         Of a case for us next term:
        Epsom trainers must be taught
        Proper deference to my Court
        Don't try then my plans to foil,
        Who is F.Ignatius Coyle?"
"Why really, my Lord, it is hard I should fear
        His identity for me to fix;
His features are red and remarkably queer,
        And in height he is five feet six;
And he seemed most uncommonly wishful to bolt,
But where I don't know, with the Derby colt.
If I laughed at your order, my Lord, humbly crave I,
Like Mr.John Day, to exclaim, *'perquavi!'"*

William Smith he sat down looking fearfully bored:
Cockburn bowed, and said, "That is our case, my Lord."

Then Thesiger rose – then Thesiger smiled,
And the Legend commenced of

"The Saddler's Child"

Very odd things occur in this very odd earth,
But especially so at New Malton;
For there a Queen Mab to a colt gave birth,
Which was neither a "lame or a halt-'un."

So said Goodman to Stanton, "If you want a job,
Go and buy me this colt from that Sawbones Cobb."
    This colt he was torn from his fatherland
    And his sweet bracing Yorkshire air;
    And then, by some process I don't understand,
    He vanished, Old Nick knows where:
But I *rather* think he and his friend Maccabeus
Were fused into one like the twin Siamese.
    Of Maccabeus' "premature death" to each groom
    Mr.G. told a sorrowful tale
    (As lately was *told for himself* by Lord B------m);
    But first he sped off by "the rail,"
And at Liverpool hired Tom Ferguson's "brown"
For a small I.O.U. and £400 down.

Goneaway soon arrived, and suspicion to case
    His "long tail" sent in resignation;
    But his "white leg" remained, and the real Maccabeus
    Required a close imitation.
Then said Goodman, "My troubles I'll end like a saint,
From the children of Israel I'll purchase some paint."

    The paint it was bought, 'twas a delicate brown,
    Compounded by one Mr.Rossi;
    Then Abraham he went on his marrow-bones down,
    And shaded the leg nice and glossy.
For Herring and Cooper he cared not a rush,
None like him among horseflesh can handle the brush.

    Poor Goneaway's pluck by the paint was unnerved,
    He turned stale and declined of his feed;
    But the real Maccabeus was but lately observed

184

On the Derby day holding the lead
Round Tattenham Corner:- while "catch me who can,"
Was stamped on the features of Samuel Mann.

But yet not his winning Derby debarred
This gallant brown colt from rude slaughter;
Miles' boy (so they say) lately viewed in a yard
Some men with a gun and hot water;
Saw the colt then arrive, and "this *mortal coil*
Shuffle off" from his back – killed – and set to boil.

Abraham, mount on some old blood weed;
Abraham, off to the Wilderness speed:
Or perhaps it were better your course should be bent
To some tropical cocoa-nut continent:
Be off where the red-ochred savages dwell,
Paint yourself into a South-Sea "swell:"
Take along with you the lovely and gracious
Second edition of Saint Ignatius:
Mind, don't think of your station beneath
To barter for breadfruit the "knocked-out teeth;"
Mount on top of the rude wigwam
And lecture the Natives on the rules of "Qui Tam."

If you'll take my advice,
Just continue there,
Feast on roots and rice,
And enjoy the air,
While for true Sportsmen's weal I'll compose a short prayer:-
May the Russell gang's pockets *ne'er* find extra pence in them!
May we see Milner Gibson convinced it's a pity
To commune with rogues while he sits on Committee!
May Levanters and Black Legs the sting ever feel
Of Doe. dem. "A.Wood *versus* Jonathan Peel!"

* "I can write verses like Wordsworth by the mile." – Wakley, House of Commons, 1843.

** It was Carlin – not Carlon.

*** The judge was referring to Kitchen – not Lofthouse.

The Sporting Magazine, August 1844.

Appendix 2

Tybalt (GB) br c 1817 Family 17-a					
Thunderbolt (GB) bl 1806 18	Sorcerer (GB) bl 1796 6-a1	Trumpator (GB) bl 1782 14	Conductor (GB) ch 1767 12-b	Match`em b 1748	4
				Snap Mare 1762	12-b
			Brunette (GB) br 1771 14	Squirrel b 1754	4
				Dove b 1764	14
		Young Giantess (GB) b 1790 6-a1	Diomed (GB) ch 1777 6-b	Florizel b 1768	5
				Juno [Sister] b 1763	6-b
			Giantess (GB) b 1769 6-a1	Match`em b 1748	4
				Molly Long Legs b 1753	6-a1
	Wowski (GB) bl 1797 18	Mentor (GB) br 1784 15	Justice (GB) br 1774 3-a	King Herod b 1758	26
				Curiosity br 1760	3-a
			Shakespeare Mare (GB) 1763 15	Shakespeare ch 1745	15
				Miss Meredith 1751	15
		Maria (GB) b 1777 18	King Herod (GB) b 1758 26	Tartar ch 1743	48
				Cypron b 1750	26
			Lisette (GB) b 1772 18	Snap bl 1750	1
				Miss Windsor b 1754	18
Meteora (GB) b 1802 17-a	Meteor (GB) ch 1783 7	Eclipse (GB) ch 1764 12	Marske (GB) br 1750 8	Squirt ch 1732	11
				Ruby Mare 1740c	8
			Spilletta (GB) b 1749 12	Regulus b 1739	11
				Mother Western 1731	12
		Merlin Mare (GB) ch 1765 7	Merlin (GB) b 1748 15	Second br 1732	9-a
				Blank [Sister] b 1739	15
			Mother Pratt (GB) b 1748 7	Marksman b 1741	21
				Brother To Mixbury Mare 1731c	7
	Maid of all Work (GB) b 1786 17-a	Highflyer (GB) b 1774 13	King Herod (GB) b 1758 26	Tartar ch 1743	48
				Cypron b 1750	26
			Rachel (GB) b 1763 13	Blank b 1740	15
				South [Sister] 1751	13
		Tandem [Sister] (GB) b 1771 17	Syphon (GB) ch 1750 9-c	Squirt ch 1732	11
				Syphon`s Dam 1740c	9-c
			Regulus Mare (GB) 1762c 17	Regulus b 1739	11
				Judgment [Sister 2] 1758	17

Pedigree of Tybalt, alias Tom Paine, who won many races confined to half-breds. He ran under a false pedigree by Prime Minister out of a mare by True Blue. In his true identity, Tybalt had won a Royal Plate at Guildford, in June 1821, only two months before the start of his trail of deception under his pseudonym.

Appendix 3

Maccabeus (GB) b c 1840-1854 Family 17-d					
Gladiator (GB) ch 1833 22	Partisan (GB) b 1811 1-e	Walton (GB) b 1799 7	Sir Peter Teazle (GB) br 1784 3	Highflyer b 1774	13
				Papillon br 1769	3
			Arethusa (GB) ch 1792 7	Dungannon b 1780	33
				Termagant [Sister] gr 1777	7
		Parasol (GB) b 1800 1-e	Potooooooooo (GB) ch 1773 38	Eclipse ch 1764	12
				Sportsmistress ch 1765	38
			Prunella (GB) b 1788 1-e	Highflyer b 1774	13
				Promise br 1768	1-d
	Pauline (GB) b 1826 22	Moses (GB) b 1819 5-b	Seymour (GB) b 1807 3-a	Delpini gr 1781	30
				Bay Javelin b 1793	3-a
			Castanea [Sister] (GB) b 1807 5-b	Gohanna b 1790	24
				Grey Skim gr 1793	5-b
		Quadrille (GB) b 1815 22	Selim (GB) ch 1802 2-n	Buzzard ch 1787	3-a
				Alexander Mare b 1790	2-n
			Canary Bird (GB) br 1806 22	Sorcerer bl 1796	6-a
				Canary b 1797	22
Capsicum Mare (GB) br 1823 17-d	Capsicum (GB) br 1805 8-a	Sir Peter Teazle (GB) br 1784 3	Highflyer (GB) b 1774 13	King Herod b 1758	26
				Rachel b 1763	13
			Papillon (GB) br 1769 3	Snap bl 1750	1
				Miss Cleveland 1758	3
		Evelina (GB) br 1791 8-a	Highflyer (GB) b 1774 13	King Herod b 1758	26
				Rachel b 1763	13
			Termagant (GB) 1772 8-a	Tantrum b 1760	21
				Cantatrice 1767	8-a
	Acklam Lass (GB) b 1819 17-d	Prime Minister (GB) br 1810 12-g	Sancho (GB) b 1801 17	Don Quixote ch 1784	13
				Cowslip [Sister 2] b 1789	17
			Miss Hornpipe Teazle (GB) br 1802 12-g	Sir Peter Teazle br 1784	3
				Hornpipe b 1793	12-g
		Young Harriet (GB) b 1812 17-d	Camillus (GB) gr 1803 2-c	Hambletonian b 1792	1
				Faith gr 1779	2-c
			Harriet (GB) b 1804 17-d	Precipitate ch 1787	24
				Young Rachel b 1799	17-d

The correct pedigree of the Gladiator colt (Maccabeus), illegal winner of the 1844 Derby. He was disqualified following the trial at the Court of Exchequer, when it was proven he was a four-year-old. He ran without success in 1845, as a genuine five-year-old and was eventually exported to Russia, where he served as a stallion until his death in 1854.

Appendix 4

Goneaway (IRE) b c 1839 Family 2					
Economist (GB) b 1825 36	Whisker (GB) b 1812 1-o	Waxy (GB) b 1790 18	Potooooooooo (GB) ch 1773 38	Eclipse ch 1764	12
				Sportsmistress ch 1765	38
			Maria (GB) b 1777 18	King Herod b 1758	26
				Lisette b 1772	18
		Penelope (GB) b 1798 1-o	Trumpator (GB) bl 1782 14	Conductor ch 1767	12-b
				Brunette br 1771	14
			Prunella (GB) b 1788 1-e	Highflyer b 1774	13
				Promise br 1768	1-d
	Floranthe (GB) b 1818 36	Octavian (GB) ch 1807 8	Stripling (GB) ch 1795 2	Phoenomenon ch 1780	2-m
				Laura b 1778	2
			Oberon Mare (GB) 1795c 8	Oberon b 1790	9-b
				Sharper [Sister 2] ch 1779	8
		Caprice (GB) b 1797 36	Anvil (GB) b 1777 9-a	King Herod b 1758	26
				Quill [Sister] br 1761	9-a
			Madcap (GB) b 1774 36	Eclipse ch 1764	12
				Sappho br 1763	36
Fanny Dawson (IRE) ch 1823 2	Nabocklish (IRE) ch 1810 4	Rugantino (IRE) ch 1803 57	Commodore (IRE) ch 1793 21	Tom Tug b 1777	1
				Smallhopes 1785c	21
			Moll In The Wad (GB) b 1791 57	Highflyer b 1774	13
				Shift ch 1779	57
		Butterfly (IRE) b 1804 4	Master Bagot (IRE) ch 1787 9	Bagot b 1780	41
				Harmony b 1776	9
			Bagot Mare (IRE) 1785c 4	Bagot b 1780	41
				Mother Brown b 1771	4
	Miss Tooley (IRE) b 1808 2	Teddy the Grinder (GB) b 1798 5	Asparagus (GB) ch 1787 15	Potooooooooo ch 1773	38
				Justice Mare b 1781	15
			Stargazer (GB) br 1782 5	Highflyer b 1774	13
				Miss West ch 1777	5
		Lady Jane (GB) b 1796 2	Sir Peter Teazle (GB) br 1784 3	Highflyer b 1774	13
				Papillon br 1769	3
			Paulina (GB) b 1778 2	Florizel b 1768	5
				Captive b 1771	2

Pedigree of Goneaway, who was hired from Thomas Ferguson, by Levi Goodman, to impersonate Maccabeus. Goneaway was believed to have been sired by Economist, which would have made him a full-brother to Harkaway; but possibly sired by Barkston. When Ferguson discovered what Goodman intended to do with his horse he took him back to Ireland, but the unfortunate horse lost his life owing to a rough crossing of the Irish Sea.

Appendix 5

Captain Flathooker (GB) b c 1839 Family 23-b					
Muley Moloch (GB) br 1830 9-c	Muley (GB) b 1810 6-a	Orville (GB) b 1799 8-a	Beningbrough (GB) b 1791 7	King Fergus ch 1775	6
				Herod Mare [Fenwick's] b 1780	7
			Evelina (GB) br 1791 8-a	Highflyer b 1774	13
				Termagant 1772	8-a
		Eleanor (GB) b 1798 6-a	Whiskey (GB) b 1789 2-a	Saltram br 1780	7
				Calash b 1775	2-a
			Young Giantess (GB) b 1790 6-a	Diomed ch 1777	6-b
				Giantess b 1769	6-a
	Nancy (GB) b 1813 9-c	Dick Andrews (GB) b 1797 9	Joe Andrews (GB) b 1778 4-b	Eclipse ch 1764	12
				Amaranda 1771	4-b
			Highflyer Mare (GB) b 1790 9	Highflyer b 1774	13
				Cardinal Puff Mare 1777	9
		Spitfire (GB) b 1800 9-c	Beningbrough (GB) b 1791 7	King Fergus ch 1775	6
				Herod Mare [Fenwick's] b 1780	7
			Milfield Mare (GB) 1790c 9-c	Milfield b 1780	15
					9
Smolensko Mare (GB) b 1818 23-b	Smolensko (GB) bl 1810 18	Sorcerer (GB) bl 1796 6-a	Trumpator (GB) bl 1782 14	Conductor ch 1767	12-b
				Brunette br 1771	14
			Young Giantess (GB) b 1790 6-a	Diomed ch 1777	6-b
				Giantess b 1769	6-a
		Wowski (GB) bl 1797 18	Mentor (GB) br 1784 15	Justice br 1774	3-a
				Shakespeare Mare 1763	15
			Maria (GB) b 1777 18	King Herod b 1758	26
				Lisette b 1772	18
	Miss Cannon (GB) b 1811 23-b	Orville (GB) b 1799 8-a	Beningbrough (GB) b 1791 7	King Fergus ch 1775	6
				Herod Mare [Fenwick's] b 1780	7
			Evelina (GB) br 1791 8-a	Highflyer b 1774	13
				Termagant 1772	8-a
		Let's-Be-Jogging [Sister] (GB) b 1796 23-b	Weathercock (GB) gr 1785 23	Highflyer b 1774	13
				Trinket gr 1767	23
			Cora (GB) ro 1777 23-b	Match'em b 1748	4
				Turk Mare 1770c	23-b

Pedigree of Captain Flathooker, who gave two-stone and defeated Goneaway (impersonating Maccabeus) at the 1843 Epsom Spring Meeting. Captain Flathooker was considered to be of limited ability and not worth backing for a shilling.

Appendix 6

Running Rein (GB) b c 1841 Family 5					
				Potooooooooo ch 1773	38
		Whalebone (GB) br 1807 1-o	Waxy (GB) b 1790 18	Maria b 1777	18
			Penelope (GB) b 1798 1-o	Trumpator bl 1782	14
	Waverley (GB) br 1817 2-a			Prunella b 1788	1-e
			Sir Peter Teazle (GB) br 1784 3	Highflyer b 1774	13
		Margaretta (GB) br 1802 2-a		Papillon br 1769	3
The Saddler (GB) br 1828 3-h			Cracker [Sister 2] (GB) b 1792 2-a	Highflyer b 1774	13
				Nutcracker b 1767	2-a
			Buzzard (GB) ch 1787 3-a	Woodpecker ch 1773	1
		Castrel (GB) ch 1801 2-n		Misfortune br 1775	3-a
			Alexander Mare (GB) b 1790 2-n	Alexander ch 1782	13
	Castrellina (GB) br 1823 3-h			Highflyer Mare 1780	2-m
			Waxy (GB) b 1790 18	Potooooooooo ch 1773	38
		Waxy Mare (GB) b 1815 3-h		Maria b 1777	18
			Bizarre (GB) b 1811 3-h	Peruvian b 1806	27
				Violante b 1802	3-h
			Remembrancer (GB) b 1800 9-b	Pipator b 1786	14
		Trissy (GB) b 1810 2-m		Queen Mab ch 1785	9-b
			L'Orient Mare (GB) 1805 2-m	L'Orient b 1799	1-a
	Duncan Gray (GB) gr 1821 19-b			Constitution Mare 1795c	2-m
			Beningbrough (GB) b 1791 7	King Fergus ch 1775	6-x+
		Albuera (GB) gr 1808 19-b		Herod Mare [Fenwick's] b 1780	7
Mab (GB) b 1833 5			Constantia (GB) gr 1796 19-b	Walnut b 1786	24
				Contessina gr 1787	19-a
			Sorcerer (GB) bl 1796 6-a1	Trumpator bl 1782	14
		Macbeth (GB) br 1811 12-b		Young Giantess b 1790	6-a1
			Precipitate Mare (GB) 1795 12-b	Precipitate ch 1787	24
	Macbeth Mare (GB) b 1819 5			Lady Harriet b 1783	12-b
			Hambletonian (GB) b 1792 1	King Fergus ch 1775	6-x+
		Margaret (GB) ch 1808 5		Grey Highflyer gr 1782	1
			Rosamond (GB) ch 1798 5	Buzzard ch 1787	3-a
				Roseberry ch 1792	5

Pedigree of the genuine Running Rein, bred by Dr Charles Cobb at Sutton House, Norton, nr Malton. This is also the pedigree of his full-sister, facetiously named Genuine, who won low-class handicaps at Beccles and Writtle.

Appendix 7

Croton Oil (GB) c 1841 Family 17-d					
Physician (GB) b 1829 21	Brutandorf (GB) b 1821 11-g	Blacklock (GB) b 1814 2-t	Whitelock (GB) b 1803 2-l	Hambletonian b 1792	1
				Rosalind ch 1788	2-l
			Coriander Mare (GB) b 1799 2-t	Coriander b 1786	4
				Wildgoose br 1792	2-t
		Mandane (GB) ch 1800 11-g	Potooooooooo (GB) ch 1773 38	Eclipse ch 1764	12
				Sportsmistress ch 1765	38
			Young Camilla (GB) b 1787 11-b	Woodpecker ch 1773	1
				Camilla b 1778	11
	Primette (GB) b 1820 21	Prime Minister (GB) br 1810 12-g	Sancho (GB) b 1801 17	Don Quixote ch 1784	13
				Cowslip [Sister 2] b 1789	17
			Miss Hornpipe Teazle (GB) br 1802 12-g	Sir Peter Teazle br 1784	3
				Hornpipe b 1793	12-g
		Miss Paul (GB) b 1811 21	Sir Paul (GB) b 1802 8-a	Sir Peter Teazle br 1784	3
				Pewett b 1786	8-a
			Miss Dunnington (GB) b 1807 21	Shuttle b 1793	21
				Miss Grimstone b 1796	21
Capsicum Mare (GB) br 1823 17-d	Capsicum (GB) br 1805 8-a	Sir Peter Teazle (GB) br 1784 3	Highflyer (GB) b 1774 13	King Herod b 1758	26
				Rachel b 1763	13
			Papillon (GB) br 1769 3	Snap bl 1750	1
				Miss Cleveland 1758	3
		Evelina (GB) br 1791 8-a	Highflyer (GB) b 1774 13	King Herod b 1758	26
				Rachel b 1763	13
			Termagant (GB) 1772 8-a	Tantrum b 1760	21
				Cantatrice 1767	8-a
	Acklam Lass (GB) b 1819 17-d	Prime Minister (GB) br 1810 12-g	Sancho (GB) b 1801 17	Don Quixote ch 1784	13
				Cowslip [Sister 2] b 1789	17
			Miss Hornpipe Teazle (GB) br 1802 12-g	Sir Peter Teazle br 1784	3
				Hornpipe b 1793	12-g
		Young Harriet (GB) b 1812 17-d	Camillus (GB) gr 1803 2-c	Hambletonian b 1792	1
				Faith gr 1779	2-c
			Harriet (GB) b 1804 17-d	Precipitate ch 1787	24
				Young Rachel b 1799	17-d

Pedigree of Croton Oil, bred by Sir Charles Henry Ibbetson and owned by Lord George Bentinck. Croton Oil, the younger half-brother to Maccabeus, ran unplaced in the 1844 Derby. This is probably the only incident of half-brothers running in the same Derby.

Appendix 8

Leander b c 1840-1844 Family 32					
Scamander ch 1834 2-f	Priam (GB) b 1827 6-a	Emilius (GB) b 1820 28	Orville (GB) b 1799 8-a	Beningbrough b 1791	7
				Evelina br 1791	8-a
			Emily (GB) ch 1810 28	Stamford br 1794	30
				Froth [Sister] ch 1799	28
		Cressida (GB) b 1807 6-a	Whiskey (GB) b 1789 2-a	Saltram br 1780	7
				Calash b 1775	2-a
			Young Giantess (GB) b 1790 6-a	Diomed ch 1777	6-b
				Giantess b 1769	6-a
	Arachne (GB) br 1822 2-f	Filho da Puta (GB) br 1812 12-a	Haphazard (GB) br 1797 35	Sir Peter Teazle br 1784	3
				Miss Hervey ch 1775	35
			Mrs. Barnet (GB) b 1806 12-a	Waxy b 1790	18
				Woodpecker Mare b 1788	12-a
		Treasure (GB) 1810 2-f	Camillus (GB) gr 1803 2-c	Hambletonian b 1792	1
				Faith gr 1779	2-c
			Hyacinthus Mare (GB) ch 1804 2-f	Hyacinthus ch 1797	2-I
				Flora ch 1789	2-c
Sister to Mussulman br 1836 32	Muley (GB) b 1810 6-a	Orville (GB) b 1799 8-a	Beningbrough (GB) b 1791 7	King Fergus ch 1775	6
				Herod Mare [Fenwick's] b 1780	7
			Evelina (GB) br 1791 8-a	Highflyer b 1774	13
				Termagant 1772	8-a
		Eleanor (GB) b 1798 6-a	Whiskey (GB) b 1789 2-a	Saltram br 1780	7
				Calash b 1775	2-a
			Young Giantess (GB) b 1790 6-a	Diomed ch 1777	6-b
				Giantess b 1769	6-a
	Sister To Troubadour 32	Dick Andrews (GB) b 1797 9	Joe Andrews (GB) b 1778 4-b	Eclipse ch 1764	12
				Amaranda 1771	4-b
			Highflyer Mare (GB) b 1790 9	Highflyer b 1774	13
				Cardinal Puff Mare 1777	9
		Donna Clara (GB) b 1807 32	Cesario (GB) br 1800 3-b	John Bull ch 1789	13
				Olivia ch 1786	3-b
			Nimble (GB) b 1784 32	Florizel b 1768	5
				Rantipole ch 1769	32

There is no official pedigree of Leander, as his dam, Sister to Mussulman, was never registered in the General Stud Book, only appearing amongst the produce of her dam. As Leander was proved to be at least four years old, it cannot be certain that this pedigree is a true representation of the horse that ran in the name of Leander in the Derby.

Appendix 9

Orlando (GB) b c 1841 Family 13-a					
Touchstone (GB) br 1831 14-a	Camel (GB) br 1822 24	Whalebone (GB) br 1807 1-o	Waxy (GB) b 1790 18	Potooooooooo ch 1773	38
				Maria b 1777	18
			Penelope (GB) b 1798 1-o	Trumpator bl 1782	14
				Prunella b 1788	1-e
		Selim Mare (GB) b 1812 24	Selim (GB) ch 1802 2-n	Buzzard ch 1787	3-a
				Alexander Mare b 1790	2-n
			Maiden (GB) b 1801 24	Sir Peter Teazle br 1784	3
				Phoenomenon Mare ch 1788	24
	Banter (GB) br 1826 14-a	Master Henry (GB) b 1815 3-b	Orville (GB) b 1799 8-a	Beningbrough b 1791	7
				Evelina br 1791	8-a
			Miss Sophia (GB) b 1805 3-b	Stamford br 1794	30
				Sophia b 1798	3-b
		Boadicea (GB) b 1807 14	Alexander (GB) ch 1782 13	Eclipse ch 1764	12
				Grecian Princess ch 1770	13
			Brunette (GB) 1790c 14	Amaranthus b 1766	4
				Mayfly b 1771	14
Vulture (GB) ch 1833 13-a	Langar (GB) ch 1817 6-a	Selim (GB) ch 1802 2-n	Buzzard (GB) ch 1787 3-a	Woodpecker ch 1773	1
				Misfortune br 1775	3-a
			Alexander Mare (GB) b 1790 2-n	Alexander ch 1782	13
				Highflyer Mare 1780	2-m
		Walton Mare (GB) ch 1808 6-a	Walton (GB) b 1799 7	Sir Peter Teazle br 1784	3
				Arethusa ch 1792	7
			Young Giantess (GB) b 1790 6-a	Diomed ch 1777	6-b
				Giantess b 1769	6-a
	Kite (GB) b 1821 13-a	Bustard (GB) b 1813 35	Castrel (GB) ch 1801 2-n	Buzzard ch 1787	3-a
				Alexander Mare b 1790	2-n
			Miss Hap (GB) b 1806 35	Shuttle b 1793	21
				Haphazard [Sister] b 1798	35
		Olympia (GB) b 1815 13-a	Sir Oliver (GB) b 1800 13	Sir Peter Teazle br 1784	3
				Fanny ch 1790	13
			Scotilla (GB) b 1795 13-a	Anvil b 1777	9-a
				Scota b 1783	13-a

Pedigree of Colonel Jonathan Peel's Orlando, the eventual winner of the 1844 Derby.

The Ugly Buck (GB) b c 1841 Family 4-l					
Venison (GB) br 1833 11-c	Partisan (GB) b 1811 1-e	Walton (GB) b 1799 7	Sir Peter Teazle (GB) br 1784 3	Highflyer b 1774	13
				Papillon br 1769	3
			Arethusa (GB) ch 1792 7	Dungannon b 1780	33
				Termagant [Sister] gr 1777	7
		Parasol (GB) ch 1800 1-e	Potoooooooo (GB) ch 1773 38	Eclipse ch 1764	12
				Sportsmistress ch 1765	38
			Prunella (GB) b 1788 1-e	Highflyer b 1774	13
				Promise br 1768	1-d
	Fawn (GB) br 1823 11-c	Smolensko (GB) bl 1810 18	Sorcerer (GB) bl 1796 6-a1	Trumpator bl 1782	14
				Young Giantess b 1790	6-a1
			Wowski (GB) bl 1797 18	Mentor br 1784	15
				Maria b 1777	18
		Jerboa (GB) b 1803 11-c	Gohanna (GB) b 1790 24	Mercury ch 1778	9-b
				Challenger [Sister] b 1779	24
			Camilla (GB) b 1778 11	Trentham b 1766	5
				Coquette b 1765	11
Monstrosity (GB) ch 1838 4-l	Plenipotentiary (GB) ch 1831 6-b	Emilius (GB) b 1820 28	Orville (GB) b 1799 8-a	Beningbrough b 1791	7
				Evelina br 1791	8-a
			Emily (GB) ch 1810 28	Stamford br 1794	30
				Froth [Sister] ch 1799	28
		Harriet (GB) bl 1819 6-b	Pericles (GB) br 1809 17	Evander gr 1801	2-c
				Precipitate Mare 1803	17
			Selim Mare (GB) ch 1812 6-b	Selim ch 1802	2-n
				Pipylina br 1803	6-b
	Puce (GB) ch 1834 4-l	Rowton (GB) ch 1826 29	Oiseau (GB) b 1809 42	Camillus gr 1803	2-c
				Rosa [Sister] ch 1797	42
			Katherina (GB) b 1817 29	Woful b 1809	1-o
				Landscape b 1813	29
		Pucelle (GB) ch 1821 4-l	Muley (GB) b 1810 6-a1	Orville b 1799	8-a
				Eleanor b 1798	6-a1
			Medora (GB) ch 1811 4-l	Selim ch 1802	2-n
				Sir Harry Mare 1803	4-l

Pedigree of the Ugly Buck, winner of the Two Thousand Guineas in 1844 and favourite for the Derby. Lord Chesterfield described The Ugly Buck as the finest horse he had ever seen; and Isaac Day likened him to just the size he would choose for a racehorse – in fact, like his sire Venison, on a larger scale. His poor showing in the Derby indicated that he may have been nobbled, probably by an unscrupulous commissioner named Hargreaves.

Ratan (GB) ch c 1841 Family 9-b

Buzzard (GB) b 1821 8-k	Blacklock (GB) b 1814 2-t	Whitelock (GB) b 1803 2-l	Hambletonian (GB) b 1792 1	King Fergus ch 1775	6-x+
				Grey Highflyer gr 1782	1
			Rosalind (GB) ch 1788 2-l	Phoenomenon ch 1780	2-m
				Atalanta ch 1769	2-c
		Coriander Mare (GB) b 1799 2-t	Coriander (GB) b 1786 4	Potoooooooo ch 1773	38
				Lavender b 1778	4
			Wildgoose (GB) br 1792 2-t	Highflyer b 1774	13
				Co-Heiress ch 1786	2-t
	Miss Newton (GB) gr 1804 8-k	Delpini (GB) gr 1781 30	Highflyer (GB) b 1774 13	King Herod b 1758	26
				Rachel b 1763	13
			Countess (GB) gr 1760 30	Blank b 1740	15
				Rib Mare gr 1745c	30
		Tipple Cyder (GB) ch 1788 8-k	King Fergus (GB) ch 1775 6-x+	Eclipse ch 1764	12
				Creeping Polly [Tuting's] ch 1756	6-x+
			Sylvia (GB) ch 1783 8	Young Marske b 1771	12-c
				Ferret b 1765	8
Picton Mare (GB) b 1831 9-b	Picton (GB) br 1819 6-a1	Smolensko (GB) bl 1810 18	Sorcerer (GB) bl 1796 6-a1	Trumpator bl 1782	14
				Young Giantess b 1790	6-a1
			Wowski (GB) bl 1797 18	Mentor br 1784	15
				Maria b 1777	18
		Dick Andrews Mare (GB) b 1814 6-a1	Dick Andrews (GB) b 1797 9	Joe Andrews b 1778	4-b
				Highflyer Mare b 1790	9
			Eleanor (GB) b 1798 6-a1	Whiskey b 1789	2-a
				Young Giantess b 1790	6-a1
	Selim Mare (GB) ch 1824 9-b	Selim (GB) ch 1802 2-n	Buzzard (GB) ch 1787 3-a	Woodpecker ch 1773	1
				Misfortune br 1775	3-a
			Alexander Mare (GB) b 1790 2-n	Alexander b 1782	13
				Highflyer Mare 1780	2-m
		Remembrancer [Sister] (GB) b 1804 9-b	Pipator (GB) b 1786 14	Imperator br 1776	28
				Brunette br 1771	14
			Queen Mab (GB) ch 1785 9-b	Eclipse ch 1764	12
				Tartar Mare ch 1757c	9-b

Pedigree of William Crockford's Ratan, who was unbeaten before the Derby and started second favourite. He was nobbled and could only finish seventh. He never won another race, and, as his pedigree would suggest, he was not a success as a stallion.

Appendix 12

Manifik (RUS) b c 1849 Family 31				
Zanoni (GB) b 1840 17-d	Gladiator (GB) ch 1833 22	Partisan (GB) b 1811 1-e	Walton (GB) b 1799 7	Sir Peter Teazle br 1784 — 3
				Arethusa ch 1792 — 7
			Parasol (GB) b 1800 1-e	Potooooooooo ch 1773 — 38
				Prunella b 1788 — 1-e
		Pauline (GB) b 1826 22	Moses (GB) b 1819 5-b	Whalebone br 1807 — 1-o
				Castanea [Sister] b 1807 — 5-b
			Quadrille (GB) b 1815 22	Selim ch 1802 — 2-n
				Canary Bird br 1806 — 22
	Capsicum Mare (GB) br 1823 17-d	Capsicum (GB) br 1805 8-a	Sir Peter Teazle (GB) br 1784 3	Highflyer b 1774 — 13
				Papillon br 1769 — 3
			Evelina (GB) br 1791 8-a	Highflyer b 1774 — 13
				Termagant 1772 — 8-a
		Acklam Lass (GB) b 1819 17-d	Prime Minister (GB) br 1810 12-g	Sancho b 1801 — 17
				Miss Hornpipe Teazle br 1802 — 12-g
			Young Harriet (GB) b 1812 17-d	Camillus gr 1803 — 2-c
				Harriet b 1804 — 17-d
Mary (GB) bl 1828 31	Waterloo (GB) b 1814 1-o	Walton (GB) b 1799 7	Sir Peter Teazle (GB) br 1784 3	Highflyer b 1774 — 13
				Papillon br 1769 — 3
			Arethusa (GB) ch 1792 7	Dungannon b 1780 — 33
				Termagant [Sister] gr 1777 — 7
		Penelope (GB) b 1798 1-o	Trumpator (GB) bl 1782 14	Conductor ch 1767 — 12-b
				Brunette br 1771 — 14
			Prunella (GB) b 1788 1-e	Highflyer b 1774 — 13
				Promise br 1768 — 1-d
	Chaldea (GB) b 1810 31	Sorcerer (GB) bl 1796 6-a1	Trumpator (GB) bl 1782 14	Conductor ch 1767 — 12-b
				Brunette br 1771 — 14
			Young Giantess (GB) b 1790 6-a1	Diomed ch 1777 — 6-b
				Giantess b 1769 — 6-a1
		Orangeade (GB) b 1803 31	Whiskey (GB) b 1789 2-a	Saltram br 1780 — 7
				Calash b 1775 — 2-a
			Orange Bud (GB) b 1788 31	Highflyer b 1774 — 13
				Orange Girl b 1777 — 31

Pedigree of Mr Lubomirski's, Manifik, probably Zanoni's most successful son, winning the Emperor's Cup at Carskoje Sielo in 1853.

Appendix 13

Zoto (POL) br c 1853 Family 2-b						
Zanoni (GB) b 1840 17-d	Gladiator (GB) ch 1833 22	Partisan (GB) b 1811 1-e	Walton (GB) b 1799 7	Sir Peter Teazle br 1784		3
				Arethusa ch 1792		7
			Parasol (GB) b 1800 1-e	Potooooooo ch 1773		38
				Prunella b 1788		1-e
		Pauline (GB) b 1826 22	Moses (GB) b 1819 5-b	Whalebone br 1807		1-o
				Castanea [Sister] b 1807		5-b
			Quadrille (GB) b 1815 22	Selim ch 1802		2-n
				Canary Bird br 1806		22
	Capsicum Mare (GB) br 1823 17-d	Capsicum (GB) br 1805 8-a	Sir Peter Teazle (GB) br 1784 3	Highflyer b 1774		13
				Papillon br 1769		3
			Evelina (GB) br 1791 8-a	Highflyer b 1774		13
				Termagant 1772		8-a
		Acklam Lass (GB) b 1819 17-d	Prime Minister (GB) br 1810 12-g	Sancho b 1801		17
				Miss Hompipe Teazle br 1802		12-g
			Young Harriet (GB) b 1812 17-d	Camillus gr 1803		2-c
				Harriet b 1804		17-d
Ebony (GB) bl 1840 2-b	Muley Moloch (GB) br 1830 9-c+	Muley (GB) b 1810 6-a1	Orville (GB) b 1799 8-a	Beningbrough b 1791		7
				Evelina br 1791		8-a
			Eleanor (GB) b 1798 6-a1	Whiskey b 1789		2-a
				Young Giantess b 1790		6-a1
		Nancy (GB) b 1813 9-c+	Dick Andrews (GB) b 1797 9	Joe Andrews b 1778		4-b
				Highflyer Mare b 1790		9
			Spitfire (GB) b 1800 9-c+	Beningbrough b 1791		7
				Milfield Mare 1790c		9-c+
	Miss Iris (GB) br 1824 2-b	Blucher (GB) b 1811 4-b	Waxy (GB) b 1790 18	Potooooooo ch 1773		38
				Maria b 1777		18
			Pantina (GB) b 1804 4-b	Buzzard ch 1787		3-a
				Trentham Mare b 1789		4-b
		Iris (GB) br 1802 2-b	Sir Peter Teazle (GB) br 1784 3	Highflyer b 1774		13
				Papillon br 1769		3
			Isabella (GB) b 1783 2-b	Eclipse ch 1764		12
				Squirrel Mare 1775		2-b

Pedigree of Zoto, whose racing record is unknown, although he probably met with some success, as a number of his progeny appear in the Russian and Polish Stud Books.

Appendix 14
Diary of Running Rein

• March/April 1840: Isaac Grey, groom to Sir Charles Ibbetson, took the mare by Capsicum out of Acklam Lass from Denton Park to York to be put to Physician. A few days after the mare arrived at York, on 14 April 1840, she dropped a colt foal by Gladiator. After being put to Physician she returned to Denton Park.

• 5 June 1840: Mab is covered by The Saddler.

• 12 June 1840–October 1842: Edward Messenger is stud groom to Sir Charles Ibbetson.

• October/November 1840: George Hayward, land agent to Sir Charles Ibbetson, repeatedly saw the colt by Gladiator, out of Capsicum mare, out of Acklam Lass, by Prime Minister.

• 11 May 1841: Mab dropped her foal by The Saddler.

• Before 8 July 1841: Robert Smart, clerk at Weatherbys, received a letter from Edward Messenger to enter the Gladiator colt for the Derby in 1843, as the nomination of Mr C. Watson.

• 6 August 1841: Letter from Lord George Bentinck to Sir William Gregory regarding his visit to Thomas Ferguson.

• September 1841: George Hayward gave directions that the Gladiator colt was to be sold. George Wharton, in service to Sir Charles Ibbetson, took the colt, with Edward Messenger, to the Doncaster sales.

• 16 September 1841: Colt sold at Doncaster Tattersalls sales. Abraham Levi Goodman bid £52; knocked down to him. Sold with his engagement for the Derby Stakes. On the same day Goodman bought a black colt by Voltaire-Saltarella; a chestnut colt by Langar, dam by Cervantes; and a brown filly, by Muley Muloch out of Melody. Edward Messenger delivered the colt to Goodman and Higgins at the stables of the Doncaster Arms on Thursday evening, the day of the sale. George Wharton, who had accompanied Messenger to Doncaster, then took the colt to Masborough Station, nr Rotherham. At this meeting George Worley, who farmed 500 acres of land at Sywell near Northampton, met Abraham Levi Goodman and Henry Higgins, a coachmaker of Northampton. Higgins told him that he and Goodman were going to buy a couple of colts, and that he intended to send one to run in Worley's paddock. Higgins requested Worley to look in, but he did not and left Doncaster after the races.

• 19 September 1841: Higgins called on Worley (a Sunday) to say that he had got the colt over from Weedon to Northampton, and that he was at The George Hotel.   Higgins told him that the colt was by Gladiator dam by Capsicum out of Acklam Lass by Prime Minister. The next day Worley drove to Northampton with his man, Pinney. On arriving at Northampton Worley sent Pinney to The George Inn, which was kept by two cousins of Higgins, to take the colt back. The colt remained at Worley's until the latter end of January 1842. During his time at Worley's he tried to jump a wall and cut his near foreleg badly.   .

• 21 September 1841: Goodman paid for the horses in London. The Gladiator colt was sold with his Derby engagement.

• About 26 September 1841: Higgins informed Worley that the Gladiator colt was named Spartacus.

• October 1841: Stebbings entered into negotiations with Dr Cobb for the Saddler colt, eventually purchasing it for £28.

• 7 December 1841–17 January 1842: The Saddler colt was kept at John King's after being purchased by Stebbings.

• On or before 1 January 1842: Weatherbys received instructions from Goodman to enter the bay colt Running Rein by The Saddler out of Mab, by Duncan Grey, for Sweepstakes of 50 sovereigns each, for foals of 1841 out of mares that had never bred a winner, at the Newmarket First Spring Meeting in 1844.

• 17 January 1842: The Saddler colt is taken away from King's at Malton by John Watson (William King's evidence).
• 20 January 1842: Daniel White took the Saddler colt to Pearl's at Milton Street.

• January 1842: Goodman showed the Saddler colt to Thomas Coleman.

• 30 January 1842: The Saddler colt left Pearl's for Bean's at Finchley (taken by Henry Sanders).

• End of January 1842: The Gladiator colt left Worley's for The George at Northampton.

• February 1842: Odell next saw the Gladiator colt at Vigo Cottage.

• Spring 1842: Thomas Field and Amos Simmons took the Gladiator colt to Davis's, the coachmaker.

• 13 May 1842: Maccabeus was in Mr Markham's paddock (taken by Thomas Field, a groom employed by Higgins).

• May 1842: Higgins took Mr Odell to see the Gladiator colt in Markham's paddock.

• About 25 June 1842: The Gladiator colt jumped a wall at Mr Markham's paddock and cut himself again, in the same place as at Worley's. Afterwards he was taken to the Rose and Crown at Northampton, where he remained a full week. When the wound had repaired he was taken back to the paddock and remained there for three or four months. During this period Richard Watson, who had been hired by Higgins, began to break him and had him in hand seven or eight weeks altogether

• June 1842: Higgins took Benyon Drage to the Rose and Crown to see Running Rein (Maccabeus).

• On or before 9 July 1842: Weatherbys received instructions from

201

Mr Goodman at Newmarket to enter his Running Rein for the Derby in May 1844.

• 15 July 1842: Goodman met Thomas Ferguson at Liverpool races to discuss the hire of Ferguson's horse Goneaway.

• 21 September 1842: Richard Watson left Northampton to take the Gladiator colt to London.

• 24 September 1842: Richard Watson delivered the Gladiator colt to Edmund Haines's stables in Foley Place, London, where he remained until 27 September.

• 24 September 1842: Running Rein was also taken from Bean's to Haines's stables in Foley Place. (This was according to Bean, but it cannot be correct as George White collected the Saddler colt from Bean's in February 1843 and delivered him to Hallmead Farm [See Carlin's evidence]. There were several witnesses claiming that Running Rein was at Bean's until February 1843.)

• 27 September 1842: William Drewett took the Gladiator colt away from Haines's and delivered him to Smith at Epsom.

• October 1842: William Smith employed George Hitchcock to break the Gladiator colt.

• On or before 29 October 1842: Mr Goodman personally gave instructions to James Manning (Weatherbys clerk) to enter the bay colt Running Rein for the 2000 Guineas at the First Newmarket Spring Meeting in 1844. He also entered the bay colt Running Rein for the Clearwell Stakes at the Second October Meeting at Newmarket in 1843.

• First week of November 1842: William Webb became head lad to William Smith.

• December 1842: Carlin saw the Gladiator colt at Smith's.

• Christmas 1842/early January 1843: Higgins told Odell that the horse was named Maccabeus.

• On or before 2 January 1843: Weatherbys (Robert King Smart) received orders from Goodman to enter the Gladiator colt for the Tradesman's Cup at the Liverpool July Meeting 1843. He also entered Running Rein for the St Leger.

• 2 January 1843: William Carlin joined Goodman as head groom.

• January 1843: Goodman signed the agreement with Thomas Ferguson for the hire of Goneaway.

• 6 January 1843: Ferguson delivered Goneaway to Goodman at Liverpool.

• 10 January 1843: Goneaway arrived at Hallmead Farm, Sutton.

• Approx. 13–16 January 1843: Carlin took Goneaway to Kingston station with William Sadler.

• January 1843: John Day junior saw Goneaway at Sadler's.

• February 1843: The genuine Running Rein left Bean's at Finchley, collected by George White, and arrived at Goodman's at Sutton (according to Carlin). Goodman stated that he was a half-bred yearling. Carlin stated that it was never called by any name.

• 7 February 1843: Running Rein (Maccabeus) left Smith's for Goodman's stables at Sutton, following a dispute over bills with Goodman.

• March 1843: Higgins, while out hunting with Worley, told the latter to stand in with Maccabeus.

• April 1843: Higgins took Benyon Drage to Smith's house. Goodman and William Sadler were there. Drage, Higgins, Goodman and Sadler went to the stables to see the horse that was to run for Maccabeus in the £50 Sweepstakes. Higgins had told Drage previously that it was a four-year-old and that his leg and foot had been stained. Drage was quite certain that it was not the horse that Higgins had at Northampton. Drage was not shown the real Maccabeus. Drage later saw the horse run at the Epsom Spring Meeting and that he came second in the £50 Sweepstakes.

• 7 April 1843: Goneaway, substituting for Maccabeus, was surprisingly beaten by Captain Flathooker in a £50 Sweepstakes at the Epsom Spring Meeting. Drage saw this. Some time later Higgins told Drage that it was Mr Ferguson's horse, Goneaway, and that the horse was dead.

• Spring 1843: Higgins, Worley and Odell dined at the Kings Arms, Northampton. Higgins told them that Maccabeus was dead.

• April 1843: Carlin stated that the Saddler colt was castrated by Mr Coleman of Cheam.

• May 1843: Goodman showed Ferguson the genuine Maccabeus at Sutton. He also showed him the Saddler colt, which he intended to run in the 1845 Derby.

• 7 June 1843: Ferguson took Goneaway back to Ireland. Goneaway died on the return trip.

• Approx. 14 June 1843: Goodman advised Carlin that Maccabeus (Goneaway) was dead – he died at Bedford.

• July 1843: Worley, Odell and Higgins discussed Goodman's entry for 1844 Derby.

• On or before 8 October 1843: James Manning (Weatherbys) entered Mr Goodman's Running Rein for the £50 Plate to be run at the Second October Meeting at Newmarket in 1843.

• October 1843: Running Rein (Maccabeus) was taken to Newmarket for the Sweepstakes and Clearwell Stakes and then returned to Sutton.

• On or before 29 October 1843: James Manning (Weatherbys), at the request of Mr Goodman, entered Goodman's bay colt Running Rein for a Sweepstakes of 50 sovereigns each, to be run at the Houghton Meeting at Newmarket in October 1843.

• After October 1843 and before May 1844: Worley told a number of people that Running Rein was the horse he had, known as Maccabeus.

• 27 November 1843: Running Rein (Maccabeus) returned to Smith's at Epsom.

• November 1843: The genuine Running Rein was taken away from Hallmead Farm.

• Early 1844: Higgins admitted to Worley that Running Rein was Maccabeus and apologised to him.

• January 1844: William Butt went into service with Smith and continued with him until 2 May 1844. As a witness he stated that he had been in his service previously, from September to November 1841; that he went again into his service on 1 May 1843 and remained until 2 July 1843; that he recollected two colts and a mare belonging to Goodman coming to Smith's in September or October 1841, a colt by Langar, a black colt by Voltaire and a brown filly, two years old; and that in the previous January a colt called Running Rein was in training at Smith's.

• 9 or 10 January 1844: Lumley of the Spread Eagle, Epsom, requested John Bartlett to inspect Running Rein (Maccabeus).

• 14 January 1844: Bartlett enquired of Smith why Mavor, the veterinary surgeon, had not been down to give a second opinion on Running Rein's teeth.

• 15 January 1844: Bartlett again examined Running Rein's teeth and wrote to Alexander Wood.

• 24 January 1844: Bartlett told Lumley that he would be writing to the Jockey Club unless Mr Wood made it known that the horse was a four-year-old.

• 24 January 1844: Bartlett wrote to the Jockey Club but received no reply.

• 4 February 1844: Mr Wood wrote to *Bell's Life* and Bartlett wrote to Weatherbys.

• 5 February 1844: Pearce, the groom who looked after Running Rein (Maccabeus), took the horse to Goodman's at Sutton and then on to London (possibly Haines's stables), returning on Thursday 8 February.

• 5 February 1844: Weatherbys responded to Mr Bartlett's letter.

• 7 February 1844: Higgins admitted to Worley that Maccabeus was the colt Worley had and that he was now dead.

• March 1844: Higgins asked Odell to intercede with Worley in order to keep him quiet.

• 23 April 1844: Mr Goodman came into Weatherbys office at Newmarket with a Mr Maugham, who paid Weatherbys £50 on the entry for the Tradesman's Cup at the Liverpool July Meeting 1843.

• 24 April 1844: Mr Goodman came into Weatherbys office at Newmarket with Mr Maugham, who paid £50 on the entry of Running Rein for the 2000 Guineas; a £25 forfeit on the entry of Running Rein for the £50 Sweepstakes at the 1843 Houghton Meeting at Newmarket; and a £5 forfeit on the entry of Maccabeus for the Tradesman's Cup at the Liverpool July 1843 Meeting.

• 20 May 1844: Higgins wrote to Odell regarding Worley's concern about the substitution.

• 20 May 1844: Letter sent from Lord Maidstone to The Jockey Club concerning the identity of Running Rein and Leander.

• 21 May 1844: Letter sent from Charles Cobb to Sir Gilbert Heathcote regarding the colour of the Saddler colt.

• 22 May 1844: Running Rein (Maccabeus) won the Derby.

• 22 May 1844: Someone, unknown to Robert King Smart of

Weatherbys, came into the Counting House and paid £125: £50 for the stakes of Running Rein in the Derby of 1844 and £75 for two forfeits of other horses' engagements.

• 22 May 1844: Letter sent from Baron de Tessier and Sir Gilbert Heathcote to Weatherbys requesting the stakes to be withheld.

• 25 May 1844: Mr Wood initiated a legal action against Weatherbys for the stakes.

• 30 May 1844: Letter sent from John Forth to *The Morning Post* regarding Leander.

• 4 June 1844: Mr Wood's case came before the Court of Common Pleas.

• 15 June 1844: Jockey Club meeting was held and a letter was read from Baron de Tessier. The meeting was postponed until 17 June.

• 17 June 1844: Jockey Club meeting held to discuss various points, including the age of the horses.

• 18 June 1844: Letter sent from Baron de Tessier to Weatherbys.

• 22 June 1844: Jockey Club meeting held to discuss the age of Leander.

• 24 June 1844: Colonel Peel made an application to the judge to inspect Running Rein, which was scheduled for Thursday 27 June.

• 1 and 2 July 1844: The trial was held at the Court of Exchequer.

• 14 July 1844: Letter sent from Mr Litchwald to *Bell's Life*.

• November 1844: Maccabeus was discovered in John Peck's stable at Beverley.

• June 1845: Maccabeus, renamed Zanoni, ran in the Ascot Gold Vase.

• 29 June 1845: Letter sent from William Sadler to Weatherbys, contributing to the cost of the trial.

• Approx. 1847: Zanoni was imported into Russia by Count Branicki.

• November 1854: Zanoni was reported in *The Sporting Magazine* to have died.

Chapter Notes

2 – Back to Denton and Malton

1.   R.G. Wilson, 'Merchants and Land: The Ibbetsons of Leeds and Denton, 1650-1850', *Northern History*, vol. 24, School of History, University of Leeds, pp. 85-86.
2.   *Ibid.*, p. 86.
3.   *Ibid.*, p. 92.
4.   *Ibid.*, p. 92.
5.   Pedigree, Sir Charles Henry Ibbetson.
6.   R.G. Wilson, *op. cit.*, p. 97.
7.   *Ibid.*.
8.   *Ibid.*.
9.   *Ibid.*.
10.   *Weatherbys Racing Calendar,* 1837.
11.   *General Stud Book*, vol. 5, p. 225.
12.   R.G. Wilson, *op. cit.*, p. 97.
13.   *Ibid.*, p. 97.
14.   *Ibid.*, p. 98.
15.   *Ibid.*, p. 98.
16.   *Ibid.*, p. 98.
17.   *Ibid.*, p. 99.
18.   *Ibid.*, p. 99.
19.   Queen Mary's complete profile can be found on www.bloodlines.net.
20.   Low Street, Malton, no longer exists. It was the last part of Castlegate just before it crosses the Derwent.
21.   Sutton House is now known as Sutton Farm. On old maps it is shown adjacent to and south of Sutton Grange.
22.   Evidence of Charles Cobb, Weatherby Case Notes.

3 – Abraham Levi Goodman and the Background to the Fraud

1.   Probably the Green Man.
2.   John Kent, *The Racing Life of Lord George Cavendish Bentinck M.P.*, Blackwood, 1892, p. 51.

3. Sylvanus, *The Bye-Lanes and Downs of England*, Richard Bentley, 1850, p. 179. Westminster Archives has no record of the location of the Little Nick.
4. *The Times*, 9 July 1828.
5. From old maps, Hallmead Farm would appear to have been located between Hallmead Road and Stayton Road, Sutton.
6. *Bell's Life*, 28 June 1840.
7. *The Sporting Review*, January 1841.
8. *The Sporting Review*, January 1840.
9. *Bell's Life*, 30 May 1841.

4 – The Fraud Begins

1. Evidence of Isaac Grey, Weatherby Case Notes.
2. Evidence of Edward Messenger, Weatherby Case Notes.
3. Watson was a pseudonym used by Ibbetson. This is proven in the *Racing Calendar* of 1841, as a horse by the name of The Black Knight is in the names of both Mr Watson and Sir Charles Henry Ibbetson.
4. This colt was named Botherem.
5. This filly was named Music.
6. Evidence of George Worley, Weatherby Case Notes.
7. The George Inn was Northampton's principal coaching inn, right in the centre of town, at the corner of George Row and Bridge Street. It was demolished in 1924 and Lloyds Bank now stands on the site.
8. The Odells owned The White Lion on Wood Hill in the centre of town, with stables behind in Dychurch Lane. The site is now occupied by the HSBC Bank.
9. Evidence of Charles Cobb, Weatherby Case Notes.
10. Grove House, on the Langton Road, is located just past the church. It has subsequently been converted into flats.
11. Evidence of John Watson, Weatherby Case Notes.
12. Elizabeth Crummack was the licensee of The Windmill Inn, Blossom Street, York. The Inn still stands to this day.
13. Evidence of John Watson, Weatherby Case Notes.
14. Evidence of Thomas Coleman, Weatherby Case Notes.
15. William Bean lived at Two Chimneys House, Finchley, adjacent to The Lodge, which was at the junction of Lodge Lane and Gainsborough Road. Today The Lodge is a block

of flats.

16. Evidence of Mrs Humphries, née Fanny Fage, Weatherby Case Notes.

17. Evidence of Edward Ing and William Bailey, Weatherby Case Notes.

18. John Morris Girling lived in Augustine Street, which has now disappeared under the inner ring road at St Peter's Way.

19. The George Inn was owned by the Higgins family. It was Northampton's principal coaching inn, right in the centre of town, at the corner of George Row and Bridge Street. It was demolished in 1924 and Lloyds Bank now stands on the site.

20. Vigo Cottage was on the Bedford Road in Northampton.

21. The Markhams were the town's most prominent solicitors. The practice no longer exists, but their office still stands at the top of Guildhall Road, on the corner of Derngate.

22. The Rose and Crown, which has since been demolished, was at 30 Gold Street, Northampton.

23. Benyon Drage lived at The Oaks Farm, to the east of the green, in Scaldwell.

24. Evidence of Richard Watson, Weatherby Case Notes.

5 – Gladiator, The Saddler, the Capsicum Mare and Mab

1. Edward Moorhouse, *The Romance of the Derby*, The Biographical Press, 1908, p. 219.

2. S.F. Touchstone, *Racehorses and Thoroughbred Stallions,* John Nimmo, 1890, p. 114.

3. *Ibid.*, p. 130.

4. Thomas Henry Taunton, *Portraits of Celebrated Racehorses*, Sampson Low, Marston, Searle & ivington, 1888, VolIV P.286.

6 – Enter Goneaway

1. Lord George Bentinck had visited Ferguson at Rossmore Lodge in 1841 and wrote to Sir William Gregory on 6 August, "With regard to the two-year-olds, both are fine animals – Fireaway bearing no resemblance to his half-brother Tearaway, but, on the contrary, with a beautiful head and fore-hand, and capital fore-legs. Goneaway is

bigger than Fireaway, but looks heavy and slow." Quoted by John Kent, *The Racing Life of Lord George Cavendish Bentinck M.P.* Blackwood, 1892.

2.   Evidence of Thomas Ferguson, Weatherby Case Notes.
3.   Thormanby, *Sporting Stories*, Mills & Boon, 2009.
4.   Evidence of Thomas Ferguson, Weatherby Case Notes.
5.   Now the premises of a number of retail outlets.
6.   Now the premises of Spanish high-class fashion company, Mango.
7.   Evidence of Thomas Ferguson, Weatherby Case Notes.
8.   Evidence of William Carlin, Weatherby Case Notes.
9.   'Physic' is an ancient remedy given as a drench, i.e., poured down a tube so that the horse cannot spit it out, and may have contained electrolytes (salt) and other minerals. It was also administered in the form of balls.
10.   Evidence of John Day, Weatherby Case Notes.
11.   Otherwise known as tusks or canine teeth, which do not appear in a male horse until generally four to five years of age.
12.   House of Commons Select Committee on Gaming, 1 July 1844, para. 861.
13.   *Ibid.*, para. 901.

7 – The Epsom Spring Meeting

1.   Evidence of George Odell, Weatherby Case Notes.
2.   Evidence of George Worley, Weatherby Case Notes.
3.   Evidence of Benyon Drage, Weatherby Case Notes.
4.   *Ibid.*.
5.   House of Commons Select Committee on Gaming, 1 July 1844 paras 1347 and 1352.
6.   *Bell's Life*, 10 April 1843.
7.   Evidence of Thomas Ferguson, Weatherby Case Notes.
8.   *Ibid.*.
9.   *Ibid.*.
10.   *Ibid.*.
11.   *Ibid.*.
12.   Evidence of Walter McGrath, master of the *Britannia* steamer, and James Taylor, Weatherby Case Notes.
13.   Evidence of Dominick Holland, Weatherby Case Notes.
14.   Evidence of George Worley, Weatherby Case Notes.

8 – Maccabeus Masquerades as Running Rein

1.   Evidence of James Manning, Weatherby Case Notes.
2.   Information provided by Surrey Archives.
3.   Evidence of William Webb, Weatherby Case Notes.
4.   Bean, Daniel White and George White maintained that the genuine Running Rein was removed from Bean's on 24 September 1842, but in fact it was later proved that he remained there until February 1843.
5.   Evidence of William Carlin, Weatherby Case Notes.
6.   Unknown to Carlin, in February 1843 he was in fact officially a two-year-old, although a couple of months short of his natural birthday.
7.   Evidence of William Carlin, Weatherby Case Notes.
8.   Evidence of George Odell, Weatherby case Notes.
9.   Sylvanus, *op. cit.*, p. 179.
10.   Evidence of Benyon Drage, Weatherby Case Notes.
11.   *The Sporting Magazine*, 1843, pp. 265-66.
12.   Evidence of Benyon Drage, Weatherby Case Notes.
13.   *Bell's Life*, 8th October 1843.
14.   *The Sporting Magazine*, 1843, p. 275.
15.   Evidence of William Webb, Weatherby Case Notes.
16.   Evidence of William Carlin, Weatherby Case Notes.
17.   Evidence of William Butt, Weatherby Case Notes.
18.   Evidence of John Bartlett, Weatherby Case Notes.
19.   *Ibid.*.
20.   *Bell's Life*, 4 February 1844.
21.   *Ibid.*, 11 February 1844.
22.   Evidence of John Bartlett, Weatherby Case Notes.
23.   *Ibid.*.
24.   *Bell's Life*, 18 February 1844.
25.   Evidence of William Carlin, Weatherby Case Notes.

9 – Ratan, The Ugly Buck, Orlando and Leander

1.   Henry Blyth, *Hell and Hazard*, Weidenfeld and Nicolson, 1969, p. 57.
2.   Quoted by Theo Taunton, *Famous Horses*, Sampson Low, Marston, Searle & Rivington, 1895, p.120.
3.   The Druid (Henry Hall Dixon), *Scott and Sebright*, p. 152.
4.   *The Sporting Magazine,* July 1843.
5.   *Ibid.*

6.   The Druid, *Post and Paddock*, p. 196.
7.   The Druid, *Scott and Sebright*, p. 160.
8.   *Ibid.*, p. 191.
9.   *The Morning Post*, 30 May 1844.

10 – The Derby
1.   Evidence of George Odell, Weatherby Case Notes.
2.   *Ibid.*.
3.   *Bell's Life*, 24 March 1844.
4.   Suffolk County Archives.
5.   *The Sporting Magazine*, 1844, vol. 1, p. 332.
6.   *Bell's Life*, 28 April 1844.
7.   *Ibid.*, 26 May 1844.
8.   Letter from Lord Maidstone to the Jockey Club, Weatherby Archives.
9.   Letter from Dr Charles Club to Sir Gilbert Heathcote, Weatherby Archives.
10. *Bell's Life*, 26 May 1844.
11. Sylvanus, *op. cit.*, pp. 181-82.
12. Evidence of George Odell, Weatherby Case Notes.
13. *Ibid.*
14. Evidence of William Carlin, Weatherby Case Notes.
15. *The Sporting Magazine*, 1844, p. 475.
16. Evidence of George Odell, Weatherby Case Notes.
17. Evidence of Henry Townsend Forth, House of Commons Select Committee on Gaming, 25 June 1844, para. 705.
18. *Ibid.*, para. 719.
19. Evidence of George Odell, Weatherby Case Notes.
20. Evidence of William Carlin, Weatherby Case Notes.
21. Evidence of John Watson, Weatherby Case Notes.
22. Evidence of George Worley, Weatherby Case Notes.
23. *Ibid.*.

11 – After the Derby
1.   Weatherby Archives.
2.   Mike Huggins, 'Lord Bentinck, the Jockey Club and Racing Morality in Mid-Nineteenth Century England: The 'Running Rein' Derby Revisited', International Journal of the History of Sport, vol. 13, issue 3, December 1996, pp. 432-44.

3.   *The Sporting Times*, 9 February 1895.
4.   Westminster Archives.
5.   *Ibid..*
6.   *Bell's Life*, 9 June 1844.
7.   *Ibid..*
8.   *The Sporting Magazine,* 1844, p. 488.
9.   *Ibid..*
10.   Letters between Mr Gill (Mr Wood's attorney) and Baron de Tessier and Sir Gilbert Heathcote, *The Morning Post,* 29 May 1844.
11.   *Ibid..*
12.   *The Morning Post,* 30 May 1844.
13.   W.C.A. Blew, *A History of Steeple-chasing,* John Nimmo, 1901, pp. 20-21.
14.   *Ibid..*

12 – The Litchwalds and the Exhumation of Leander

1.   *The Sportsman,* March 1841, p. 136.
2.   'Tom Paine' was the pseudonym of the thoroughbred Tybalt, who competed in races restricted to half-breds.
3.   Forth's son, Henry Townsend Forth, claimed that it was he who requested the certificate from Mr Wood; House of Commons Select Committee on Gaming, 25 June 1844, para. 791.
4.   *Ibid.,* para. 1249.
5.   *Ibid.,* para. 1255.
6.   *Bell's Life,* 26 May 1844.
7.   *The Morning Post,* 29 May 1844.
8.   *The Morning Post,* 30 June 1844.
9.   *Bell's Life,* 9 June 1844.
10.   Weatherby Archives.
11.   All statements taken from *Bell's Life,* 30 June 1844.
12.   *The Sporting Magazine,* July 1844, p. 68.
13.   *The Morning Post,* 28 June 1844.
14.   *The Morning Post,* and Bell's Life, 30 June 1844.
15.   *Bell's Life,* 14 July 1844.
16.   Sylvanus, *op. cit.,* p. 180.

13 – The Trial

1.   *Bell's Life,* 4 June 1844.

2. *Ibid*, 9 June 1844.
3. *Ibid.*
4. Evidence of William Carlin, Jockey Club Case Notes.
5. *Ibid.*
6. *Ibid.*
7. *Bell's Life*, 14 July 1844.
8. The horse had been taken to The Lord Nelson at Cheam, owned by the veterinary surgeon William Coleman; House of Commons Select Committee on Gaming.
9. Jaques was certainly not dead (he did not die until 1868), and was in fact a beneficiary of the Bentinck Fund to the sum of £10. It is possible that Jaques was the link in terms of Goodman hiring Ferguson's Goneaway. Jaques worked for Henry Higgins and also trained and rode some of Ferguson's horses. It is possible that Jaques was keeping a low profile, as he may well have known more about the fraud than was generally thought.
10. All dialogue and references to the main Trial are from *Bell's Life*, 7 July1844.

14 – After the Trial
1. *Bell's Life*, 7 July 1844.
2. Patrick R.Chalmers, *Racing England*, B.T.Batsford, 1939.
3. George Osbaldeston, *Squire Osbaldeston: His Autobiography*, ed. E.D. Cuming, John Lane, 1926, p. 153.
4. Jockey Club Case Notes.
5. *Ibid..*

15 – The Ratan Affair
1. *Bell's Life*, 7 July 1844.
2. *Ibid.*, 10 November 1844.
3. *The Sporting Magazine*, November 1844, p. 354.
4. Sylvanus, *op. cit.*, p. 70.
5. Thormanby, *op. cit.*, p. 22.
6. *Bell's Life*, 26 May 1844.
7. *The Sporting Magazine*, August 1844, p. 281.
8. *Ibid..*
9. *The Sporting Magazine*, November 1844, p. 355.
10. *Ibid.*
11. *Ibid.*, August 1844, p. 281.

12.	Sylvanus, *op. cit.*, p. 127.
13.	John Kent, *op. cit.* p. 162.

16 – Lord George
1.	*Bell's Life*, 14 July 1844.
2.	Bernard Darwin, *John Gully and his Times*, Cassell, 1935.
3.	Philip Whitwell Wilson, *The Greville Diary*, vol. 2, Heinemann, 1927, p. 196.
4.	William Day, *Reminiscences of the Turf*, Richard Bentley & Son, 1891, p. 78.
5.	Philip Whitwell Wilson, *op. cit.*, p. 198.
6.	*Ibid.*, p. 200.

17 – Zanoni
1.	Owen Henry Parry resided at 20 Albion Street, Reading.
2.	*Bell's Life*, 17 November 1844.
3.	*Ibid*, 16 March 1845
4.	*Ibid*, 13 April 1845.
5.	*Ibid.*, 20 April 1845.
6.	*Ibid*, 18 May 1845.
7.	*The Sporting Magazine*, vol. 2, 1845, p. 2.
8.	A bay colt out of a mare by Muley Moloch; and a grey filly out of a mare by Falcon; *General Stud Book*, vol. 7, 3rd edn.
9.	The Druid, *Silk and Scarlet*, Rogerson and Tuxford, 1859, p. 153.
10.	*Russian Racing Calendar*, 1863.

18 – Epilogue
1.	*Bell's Life*, 7 July 1844.
2.	Michael Seth-Smith, *Lord Paramount of the Turf, Lord George Bentinck, 1802-1848*, Faber & Faber 1972. p.111.
3.	Jockey Club Post Trial Case Notes.
4.	Sylvanus, *op. cit.*, p. 182.
5.	The Druid, *Silk and Scarlet*, Rogerson and Tuxford, 1859, p. 256.
6.	*Racing Calendar*, 1849, p .213.

Bibliography

Bird, T.H., *Admiral Rous and the English Turf 1795-1877*, Putnam, 1939.

Black, Robert, *Horse-racing in France*, Sampson Low, Marston, Searle & Rivington, 1886.

Blew, W.C.A., *A History of Steeple-chasing*, John Nimmo, 1901.

Blyth, Henry, *Hell and Hazard*, Weidenfeld & Nicolson, 1969.

Chalmers, Patrick R., *Racing England*, B.T. Batsford, 1939.

Darwin, Bernard, *John Gully and his Times*, Cassell, 1935.

Day, William, *Reminiscences of the Turf*, Richard Bentley & Son, 1891.

Huggins, Mike, 'Lord Bentinck, the Jockey Club and Racing Morality in Mid-Nineteenth Century England: The 'Running Rein' Derby Revisited', *The International Journal of the History of Sport*, vol. 13, no. 3, December 1996.

Jenkins, Eric, *Northamptonshire Practical Jokes and Hoaxes*, Cordelia, 2000.

Kent, John, *The Racing Life of Lord George Cavendish Bentinck M.P.*, Blackwood, 1892.

Moorhouse, Edward, *The Romance of the Derby*, The Biographical Press, 1908.

National Review Office, *Chapters from Turf History: Newmarket*, 1922.

Osbaldeston, George, *Squire Osbaldeston: His Autobiography*, ed. E.D. Cuming, John Lane, 1926.

Prior, C.M., *The History of the Racing Calendar and Stud-Book*, Sporting Life, 1926.

Robson, Pamela, *James Jaques (1792-1868)*, 2008.

Seth-Smith, Michael, *Lord Paramount of the Turf, Lord George Bentinck, 1802–1848*, Faber & Faber, 1971.

Slater, Don, *Sywell: The Parish and the People - A History*, Jema Publications, 2002.

Sylvanus, *The Bye-Lanes and Downs of England*, Richard Bentley, 1850.

Taunton, Theo, *Famous Horses*, Sampson Low, Marston, Searle & Rivington, 1895.

Taunton, Thomas Henry, *Portraits of Celebrated Racehorses*, Sampson Low, Marston, Searle & Rivington, 1888.

The Druid (Henry Hall Dixon), *Scott and Sebright*, Frederick Warne, 1862.

The Druid, *Post and Paddock*, Frederick Warne, 1856.

The Druid, *Silk and Scarlet*, Rogerson and Tuxford, 1859.

Thormanby, *Sporting Stories*, Mills & Boon, 2009.

Touchstone, S.F., *Racehorses and Thoroughbred Stallions*, John Nimmo, 1890.

Whitwell Wilson, Philip, *The Greville Diary*, vol. 2, Heinemann, 1927.

Wilson, R.G., 'Merchants and Land: The Ibbetsons of Leeds and Denton 1650–1850, *Northern History*, vol. 24, School of History, University of Leeds, 1988.

Index

Racing Welfare

The Running Rein fraud was solved solely by the judicious expediency of Lord George Bentinck. A subscription was raised to honour his efforts in solving the case, which he desired should be applied towards the establishment of a fund, with a view to secure in perpetuity, for children of deserving trainers and jockeys, support and education from infancy until they arrived at an age to seek their own living. This was established at the 'Bentinck Testimonial Fund.'

'Racing Welfare' is the natural successor, continuing the work of the 'Bentinck Testimonial Fund' and is a supporter of 'In Search of Running Rein – The Amazing Fraud of the 1844 Derby.'